DESIGNING THE MAINE LANDSCAPE

DESIGNING THE
MAINE LANDSCAPE

ENTRANCE TO EVERGREEN-CEMETERY.

THERESA MATTOR AND LUCIE TEEGARDEN

PREFACE BY EARLE G. SHETTLEWORTH, JR.

FOREWORD BY CHARLES E. BEVERIDGE

DOWN EAST BOOKS
AND THE MAINE OLMSTED ALLIANCE FOR PARKS & LANDSCAPES

PAGE 2: *The Ramp at River House is a major feature of this Colonial Revival landscape.*
RIGHT: *At Weatherend estate, rustic stone walls define the boundary between the natural and designed landscape.*
PAGE 6: *An original John Nolen sketch for Bates College shows a long, tree-lined walkway leading to a series of athletic buildings added in 1927 and 1928.*

Copyright © 2009 by Theresa Mattor and Lucie Teegarden
All rights reserved.

ISBN: 978-0-89272-729-2

Jacket photographs ©Greg Currier
Front: Asticou Azalea Garden
Back: View from Beech Nut
Front cover illustration:
Detail from the Olmsted Plan for the University of Maine
Design by Tom Morgan, Blue Design
(www.bluedes.com)

Printed in China

5   4   3   2   1

Published by Down East Books and the Maine Olmsted
Alliance for Parks & Landscapes
Additional funding provided by the Davis Family Foundation
and the Quimby Family Foundation

Library of Congress Cataloging-in-Publication Data

Mattor, Theresa.
 Designing the Maine landscape / by Theresa Mattor and
Lucie Teegarden ; preface by Earle G. Shettleworth, Jr. ;
foreword by Charles E. Beveridge. --
1st ed.
    p. cm.
 Includes bibliographical references and index.
 ISBN 978-0-89272-729-2 (trade hardcover : alk. paper)
 1. Historic sites--Maine. 2. Landscape--Maine--History.
3. Landscape design--Maine--History. 4. Landscape
architecture--Maine--History. 5. Landscape architects--
United States--Biography. 6. Landscape design--United
States--Biography. 7. Maine--History, Local. I. Teegarden,
Lucie. II.
Title.
 F20.M35 2009
 974.1--dc22
                        2008053662

Down East
BOOKS·MAGAZINE·ONLINE
w w w . d o w n e a s t . c o m
800-685-7962
Distributed to the trade by National Book Network

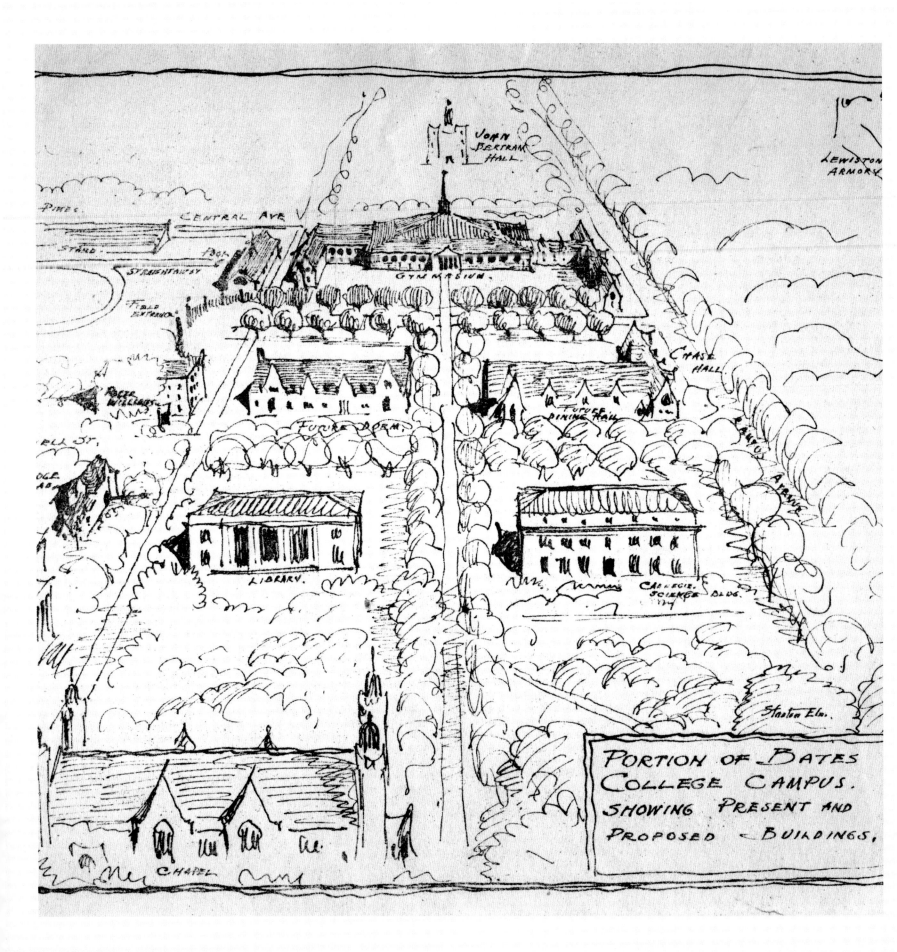

PORTION OF BATES
COLLEGE CAMPUS.
SHOWING PRESENT AND
PROPOSED BUILDINGS.

CONTENTS

PREFACE

In "The Gift Outright," the great psalmist of Northern New England life Robert Frost wrote: "we gave ourselves outright" to a land "still unstoried, artless, unenhanced, such as she was, such as she would become." Indeed, the primeval magnificence of Maine's rocky coasts, powerful rivers, dense forests, and mountainous terrain were natural forces that shaped the direction and pace of early English and French settlement. Only after the American Revolution did an increasing influx of population, the widespread impact of the Industrial Revolution, and the emergence of steam-driven transportation create an affluence and mobility that began to even the scales between man and nature.

The Age of Jackson ushered in highly visible public improvements to Maine's first two cities: the Eastern and Western Promenades in Portland and City Common and Mount Hope Cemetery in Bangor, as well as to its new capital city, Augusta, in the form of Capitol Park. The end of the Civil War brought the enhancement of private spaces as the state assumed the role of a summer refuge for the newly wealthy of the Gilded Age. The laying out of individual grounds for John D. Rockefeller, Jr., and Edsel Ford in Seal Harbor were the work of such nationally acclaimed landscape architects as Beatrix Farrand and Jens Jensen.

These significant trends and many more are addressed in *Designing the Maine Landscape* by Theresa Mattor and Lucie Teegarden. In 1976, *Maine Forms of American Architecture*, the first comprehensive survey of the state's architecture, devoted a chapter to the development of landscape design. Since then major strides in research have made possible an entire volume on the subject, and it is appropriate that as a highly effective educational organization, the Maine Olmsted Alliance for Parks and Landscapes has collaborated with Down East Books to make this fascinating material available to the public.

In 1991, the Maine Historic Preservation Commission partnered with the Alliance on a project to identify designed landscapes through documentary research and fieldwork, and to develop historic contexts in which to evaluate their significance. This comprehensive statewide survey, which was among the first of its type in the country, was supported with Federal funds from the National Park Service and administered by the Commission, whose staff also developed the survey methodology. It resulted in the identification of hundreds of landscapes, ranging from late eighteenth-century town commons to twentieth-century residential subdivisions. Although the designs for many of these landscapes were not executed, and many of those that were developed have been lost or are no longer recognizable, important examples of a variety of landscape types still remain. The information about the history of designed landscapes in Maine that was generated from the survey provides a basis on which to formulate strategies to protect them. Today, this effort is being advanced by the activities of the Alliance, and through the Commission's ongoing work to nominate designed landscapes to the National Register of Historic Places. This book will make a significant contribution in its own right to the growing awareness of the rich heritage of Maine's designed landscapes.

EARLE G. SHETTLEWORTH, JR.
Director
Maine Historic Preservation Commission

FOREWORD

Like many other Mainers, I was late in coming to appreciate the state's designed landscapes. Growing up on the shore and among the islands of Penobscot Bay, I was immersed from childhood in some of the most spectacular natural scenery in the state. Setting out from the North Haven farm of my great-grandfather, a fourth-generation islander, my parents and I explored many of the outer islands, discovering the special features and unique views offered by each. And even though the town of Camden, where we spent the winter months, possessed unexcelled examples of Maine's heritage of designed landscapes—the harborside park of the Olmsted firm and Fletcher Steele's superb amphitheater—I became fully aware of them only when I began in the 1980s to investigate the twentieth-century work of the Olmsted firm. Indeed, it was only a decade later, when I assisted in the restoration master plan for those two sites, that I came to appreciate their full value.

This was the principal way that landscape design came to Maine—preceded and strengthened by appreciation of the state's natural beauty. Much of what is most valuable in our designed landscapes stems from their setting and their relation to the natural scenery around them. This consideration is amply demonstrated by the remarkable range of locations, designers, and kinds of landscape designs that have been created in Maine over the past two centuries.

These landscapes have been the product of civic pride, as with the Portland parks or Berwick Academy, or state pride, as with the Capitol and Blaine House grounds in Augusta. At least as important has been the role of summer residents who dedicated both their energy and financial resources to creating municipal parks or to preserving and making accessible to the public areas of natural scenic beauty.

The variety of landscape architects with national reputations who designed in Maine is impressive: these include Beatrix Farrand, Jens Jensen, and some who made Maine their home, like Hans Heistad and Carl Rust Parker. Particularly interesting is the number of landscape architects who were members of the Olmsted firm or who had worked with and been influenced by them: Arthur Shurcliff, Carl Rust Parker, Warren Manning, and Joseph Curtis, among others.

Maine participated in the same stages of landscape design as the rest of the country, responding to trends begun elsewhere and providing unique versions of each category of design. In providing small urban parks, Portland took an early initiative, setting aside the Eastern and Western Proms in 1828. At the same time, the rural cemetery movement, which predated the park movement in this country, led to the founding in 1831 of Mount Auburn Cemetery near Boston. Just three years later, the city of Bangor chartered Mount Hope Cemetery, several years before Mount Auburn's more famous successors in Philadelphia and Brooklyn. Saco followed suit with Laurel Hill in 1844 and Portland with Evergreen Cemetery in 1852.

For the century following the Civil War, a major presence in landscape architecture in Maine, and one that reflects the changing issues of the profession, was the firm of Frederick Law Olmsted, Sr., and his sons. The first major urban park in this country, Central Park in New York, was designed by Olmsted, Sr., and Calvert Vaux in 1858 and set the example for park design for two decades after the Civil War, with emphasis on large parks of several hundred acres. By the 1890s the focus was on creation of park systems with several smaller parks and recreation grounds, often connected by parkways and boulevards. The Olmsted firm's work in Portland from 1895 to 1905 reflects this trend.

The firm's role in the parks of Portland and Camden reflected two particular aspects of its practice. One was the emphasis on areas with especially striking views, which found expression in the firm's 1905 plans for the Eastern and Western Proms in Portland and its 1928 plans for Harbor Park in Camden. The other was the creation of public open space by transforming areas of tidal mudflats into water basins surrounded by naturalistic settings with access by walks and drives. A prime example of this is the Back Bay Fens in Boston, planned by Olmsted, Sr., in the 1880s and repeated in the firm's later recommendations for Back Cove in Portland in the late 1890s.

In the realm of public buildings, too, the work of the Olmsted firm had its roots in the work of Olmsted, Sr. The firm's work on the Maine State House in the 1920s, in which the landscape was subordinated to the function and appearance of the building, was similar to the approach taken by Olmsted, Sr., in his plans in the 1870s for the Connecticut State House—also designed by Charles Bulfinch—as well as for the grounds of the U.S. Capitol in Washington. The elder Olmsted's proposals of 1867 for the land-grant Maine College of Agriculture and the Mechanic Arts marked the beginning of the firm's campus planning in the state. Although those proposals were not accepted, the Olmsted firm did return to Maine in later years for improvements to other campuses such as Berwick Academy and Colby College, and for extensive planning for the University of Maine at Orono.

Maine's summer residences have also provided rich opportunities for landscape architects to relate the designed landscape to the natural scenery. The building of such residences at Mount Desert Island and elsewhere in Maine represented the second wave of a movement begun during the late 1800s at Newport and other resorts less distant from metropolitan centers. Although at Newport formal landscape treatment was the norm, Olmsted, Sr., urged naturalistic treatment of the grounds he designed for shingle-style houses there. The residential work of Hans Heistad, Beatrix Farrand, Jens Jensen, and others show with what

skill and imagination those designers took advantage of the site of Maine's summer estates.

While the naturalistic treatment of summer residences drew from the region's natural landscape, the development of a Colonial Revival landscape treatment reflected the formality and elegance of the great mansions of Colonial and Federal periods, given impetus by the patriotism of the centennial observances of 1876. In Maine the movement inspired gardens for Federal mansions, as with Hamilton House and Spite House, or the grounds of Colonial Revival houses, as with River House.

The planning of residential communities has been another area of design activity in Maine. The proliferation of horse-car and streetcar suburbs that began with the surge of urbanization following the Civil War prompted development of numerous subdivisions in Maine, particularly in the greater Portland area. At the same time, industrial towns with residences for workers—a product of heavy industry in the 1890s—appeared in Maine with the 1891 company town planned and built by the Rumford Falls Power Company. Other privately developed suburban communities, represented by Sylvan Site in South Portland, reflected the great proliferation of subdivisions that attended the prosperity of the 1920s.

This book, *Designing the Maine Landscape*, provides a fascinating introduction to the range of designed landscapes in the State of Maine. It demonstrates the remarkable artistic skill and imagination that have been invested in our public and private landscapes by generations of landscape architects and their patrons.

Charles E. Beveridge, Series Editor
The Papers of Frederick Law Olmsted

INTRODUCTION

The story of Maine's natural landscape revolves around superlatives. The first sunrise in the United States occurs here, on Cadillac Mountain, followed two minutes later at sea level on West Quoddy Head in Lubec. Maine has the most islands of any state, with about 3,000 lying off the coast. Thanks to these islands and numerous long, narrow peninsulas, Maine also boasts the longest shoreline, more than 3,400 miles, of any place in the continental U.S. Maine is one of the most heavily wooded states in the nation; almost ninety percent of its total land area, nearly eighteen million acres, is covered in forests. For more than 125 years, Maine's remote lakes and rivers have attracted vacationers from around the country for fishing, hunting, and hiking. Mount Katahdin, Maine's highest peak, is the final destination along the arduous 2,200-mile Appalachian Trail, the nation's longest marked footpath.

The story of Maine's *designed* landscape is also exceptional, though less familiar. The practice of documenting historic architecture began in 1966 with the National Historic Preservation Act, which led to the formation of the National Register of Historic Places. The majority of early listings in the Register were of significant buildings; listings of ever-changing landscapes have traditionally lagged behind those of more permanent architecture. Interest in historic landscapes began to surface around 1972, with celebrations to honor the 150th anniversary of the birth of Frederick Law Olmsted, Sr. Also during the 1970s the Library of Congress began to consolidate its collection of Olmsted papers, and the National Park Service purchased Olmsted's home and office, "Fairsted," in Brookline, Massachusetts.

The National Association for Olmsted Parks, formed in 1980 in Buffalo, New York, was the first organization to call attention to the legacy of irreplaceable parks and landscapes and their role in enriching communities. Numerous similar organizations formed around the country, including the Maine Olmsted Alliance for Parks and Landscapes in 1990. Also in that year, the National Park Service published *Preserving Historic Landscapes*, which led to a dramatic increase in the study of historic landscapes and hands-on projects to preserve them. Now that the field of landscape preservation is firmly established, conferences, publications, academic degrees, and research opportunities are widely available throughout the country.

Maine's rich and complex landscape history remained largely untold until the Maine Olmsted Alliance began its program of advocacy, research, and public education; Maine's Survey of Designed Historic Landscapes grew out of this mission. Working with the Maine Historic Preservation Commission, researchers Shary Page Berg, Pamela Griffin, and I surveyed hundreds of historic Maine landscapes between 1991 and 2000; more than thirty volunteers assisted with research and site visits. The project, the first of its kind in the United States, was closely followed by landscape professionals, and I was honored to present the work on behalf of the Alliance at preservation conferences in Chicago and Cleveland.

Because of the large number of historic landscapes in Maine, the survey was divided into four phases, each of which is represented in this book. Our study of public landscapes took us to the heart of communities, to town greens and commons, to solemn war memorials, cemeteries, and spacious, well-loved parks. We selected about eighty-five public sites to document, visited town libraries and historical societies, and chatted with long-time residents who shared old photographs and family stories of these unique properties.

We next turned our attention to private homes and estates, where we were warmly received by homeowners who enjoyed sharing insights about their landscape's history. Of the roughly eighty homes visited, most were in coastal communities, from Kittery to Mount Desert Island, the favorite destinations of summer visitors for well over a century.

The third phase of the survey, called Community Planning, Subdivisions, and Suburban Designs, offered a real-world look at how Maine neighborhoods and communities have evolved over time. Our work brought us to historic suburbs, industrial towns, neighborhoods created for wartime housing, and summer communities, both on islands and on the mainland. Although coastal summer communities have many characteristics unique to Maine, they are not featured prominently here; their rich history and large numbers require a longer discussion than is possible in a single chapter.

The survey's final collection of historic landscapes had the rather generic title of Miscellaneous Landscapes, but the sites were anything but ordinary. We documented the landscape histories of schools and colleges, golf courses, public buildings and institutions, military forts, and churches. Not all of these categories are included here, following our decision to feature fewer landscapes in greater depth.

At the end of the survey, the Alliance had amassed a large collection of fascinating interviews, historic photographs, and drawings, along with a few hundred finished survey forms. In an effort to share newfound information with local communities, copies of completed survey forms were sent to various historical societies and libraries, but the question remained of how to reach a wider audience. In 2005 Charlton and Eleanor Ames met with Neale Sweet, at that time publisher of Down East Books, who enthusiastically supported the idea for *Designing the Maine Landscape*. The willingness of Down East to co-publish the book means that the story of Maine's designed landscapes and the importance of their preservation is now available to a national audience.

Designing the Maine Landscape shows the great diversity of the state's designed landscape heritage, presenting a mix of well-loved public places that readers may visit, along with lesser-known private ones of outstanding merit. All have an intriguing story to tell, whether about the personalities who created them, or about those responsible for embracing modern challenges. In a larger sense, they also tell the story of Maine: its distinctive and beautiful natural environment, the vision and energy of its people, and the sense of community that those of us lucky enough to live here deeply cherish. We invite you to enjoy some unexpected stories and memorable images of our landscape heritage.

THERESA MATTOR
Hollis, Maine
October, 2008

FOLLOWING PAGES: *Thuya Garden and the surrounding native landscape meet in this peaceful memorial to landscape designer Charles K. Savage.*

I. PUBLIC PLACES OF ENDURING BEAUTY

CHAPTER 1

THE PORTLAND PARK SYSTEM

The circuit of our public grounds, beginning with either Promenade and thence passing through our shaded streets and the Oaks to the other Promenade, affords a variety and natural beauty of scenery to be found in but few cities of the country.[1] — PORTLAND CITY AUDITOR'S REPORT, 1882

Portland is a vibrant oceanfront city built on a narrow peninsula bordered by the Fore River, the tidal Back Cove, and Portland Harbor. Thanks to its rich landscape history, Portland has five parks listed in the National Register of Historic Places: the Eastern and Western promenades, Lincoln Park, Deering Oaks, and Back Cove. The five parks comprise a total of 177 acres and are within two and one-half miles of each other. (In contrast, Boston's "Emerald Necklace" park system includes over 1,000 acres and stretches for five miles.)

Portland's parks are intriguing for their multiple historic layers and the fact that they were created by local designers, civic leaders, and patrons. Portland was also the focus of design efforts by the nationally known Frederick Law Olmsted, Sr., and his sons, but only portions of their work were actually installed.

The story of Portland's parks begins in 1828, when, following national trends to set aside public open space in cities, Portland civic leaders started buying land that eventually became the Eastern and Western promenades. The next seventy-five years saw the creation of Lincoln Park (1866), Deering Oaks (1879), and Back Cove (1904), many of which continued to be developed into the 1900s. Then, following periods of decline, the parks were again the focus of design

efforts in the 1990s, when local residents worked with the city and professional consultants to create master plans for restoration and rehabilitation. Renewed interest in the parks led to the designation of each park as a Portland Historic Landscape.

The local visionaries chiefly responsible for Portland's parks were Mayor James Phinney Baxter and civil engineers Charles Howe, Charles Goodell, and William Goodwin. (In the second half of the 1800s, civil engineers were frequently responsible for the design of public open spaces. The formal study of landscape architecture did not begin until 1900, when Harvard established the country's first four-year degree program in the field.) In Portland, Charles Howe created the first plan for Evergreen Cemetery in 1855 (pp. 131–135). Charles Goodell prepared plans for Phoenix Square (renamed Lincoln Park) in 1866 and Evergreen Cemetery in 1869.

The professional with perhaps the most impact on Portland's parks was William Goodwin, Portland's city civil engineer from 1872 to 1892. Goodwin valued public outdoor spaces as places for open-air exercise, social interaction, and "public cheerfulness." During his tenure he presented plans for improvements to the Eastern and Western promenades and Western Cemetery. He was also responsible for the design of

Deering Oaks, and proposed an integrated park system, though his name is often overshadowed by that of the Olmsteds, who provided consultation on Portland's park system in 1905.

The patron behind Portland's parks was James Phinney Baxter, who was mayor from 1893 to 1896 and 1904 to 1905. Baxter was a strong advocate of public open spaces and was well aware of the parks movement nationally; in 1905 he wrote, "Having seen the principal parks in this country and Europe, and realizing their great public importance, as well as the paucity of our own achievements in this regard, I resolved to do all in my power towards the creation of a park system in Portland."[2]

Baxter worked diligently to improve Portland's public grounds and to secure their future. He raised awareness about the need to purchase property, much of which the public assumed was already owned by the city. He appealed to reluctant land owners' sense of civic obligation; if that failed, he persuaded them to sell for future economic benefits. He repeatedly overcame opposition from the city council and enlarged existing parks by purchasing adjacent vacant land. He strove to remove unsightly buildings and incorporate these parcels into the public grounds. Finally, he wanted to connect the city's parks, most notably by creating a boulevard around Back Cove.

BELOW: *Views of Casco Bay from Fort Allen, as seen in this ca. 1913 postcard, have long been some of the best in the city. Note the numerous benches for visitors. Today the restored gazebo is a favorite destination.*

Portland, Me.
Fort Allen Park
Eastern Promenade.

66394

PORTLAND'S EASTERN AND WESTERN PROMENADES

...no city in this country can boast of two such prominent outlooks as our Eastern and Western Promenades, and it is hard to decide which is more beautiful. For a day view, Fort Allen Park, with its ever-changing scenery, is a drawing card to our summer visitors, but for a quiet hour late on a pleasant summer afternoon, say about sunset, the Western Promenade has charms known to only a few of the residents of Portland but is appreciated by the summer tourists, who flock there for the splendid view they get of the White Mountains and the gorgeous sunsets, which cannot be rivaled even by the blue skies of Italy.[3] — PORTLAND CITY AUDITOR'S REPORT, 1907

The first public lands to be acquired and improved in Portland were the Eastern and Western promenades (often referred to locally as "the Proms"), which bracket the peninsula and offer dramatic views over the Atlantic Ocean to the northeast and to the mountains to the west. The value of these overlooks was recognized as early as 1828, when city officials bought twelve acres on Mount Joy (Munjoy Hill), which eventually became the Eastern Promenade. The site was then mainly pasture land with rustic stone walls, a burial ground from the War of 1812, and some commercial uses along the waterfront. The city started buying land for the Western Promenade in 1836, and carriage roads and trees were installed there by the following year.

The views from these particular sites made them especially desirable as public open space. Munjoy Hill near the Eastern Promenade rises 160 feet above the water; the Western Promenade is even higher at 175 feet. In the 1830s, the Western Prom, known as Bramhall's Hill, offered "a pleasant and picturesque view of the country for miles around, with all the variety of hills and dales, of plains and waters, villages and farm houses, requisite to romantic scenery and a delightful landscape."[4] The Eastern Prom's location was said to surpass any other in New England, with its unrivaled water scenery, refreshing breezes from Casco Bay, and "retirement from the noise and dust of the city."

From 1851 throughout the 1880s the city regularly planted and cared for new trees at the Eastern Promenade; some years saw fifty to one hundred elms planted in one season. In fact, until about 1940, the city made yearly improvements of all kinds–purchasing land, grading the lawns, adding walkways and fencing, and planting thousands of trees and shrubs.[5]

Although the land for the promenades was acquired as early as 1828, formal designs were not prepared until almost fifty years later. In 1877 Mayor Moses Butler proposed hiring a "skilled and competent landscape engineer of the standing, for instance, of Olmstead [*sic*], in connection with our own city engineer, to furnish plans and designs for laying these promenades out...."[6] The following year, Calvert Vaux, who had designed New York's Central Park with Frederick Law Olmsted, Sr., visited Portland to suggest ways to improve public land there. Vaux spent two days with William Goodwin, but ultimately it was Goodwin who designed the Eastern and Western promenades.

At the Eastern Prom Goodwin laid out a new road between the existing trees and turned the old

road into a grass esplanade. A curving, tree-lined drive at the foot of Quebec Street offered a change from the straight rows of trees on the main street and provided a detour in the promenade. Goodwin also designed and installed the monument site at the terminus of Congress Street, in the foreground of the promenade's superb view. Here in 1883 the Parks Department installed a granite monument to George Cleeve and Richard Tucker, who established the first permanent English settlement on the peninsula in 1633. The Eastern Promenade is also home to Fort Allen, established in 1814. The site was named for William Henry Allen, a U.S. Navy officer killed in battle during the War of 1812.

INTEGRATING THE PARKS: THE OLMSTED INFLUENCE

James Baxter became mayor of Portland in 1893, a year after William Goodwin retired. Baxter expanded upon Goodwin's vision of creating an integrated park system in Portland and also sought to improve conditions in the polluted Back Cove. During his first term, he hired the nationally known landscape architecture firm of Olmsted, Olmsted and Eliot of Brookline, Massachusetts, to address Back Cove's sanitation issues and provide recreational opportunities for Portland residents. During his second term in 1905, he sought advice from the same firm, by then known as Olmsted Brothers, to design improvements to and a connection between the Eastern and Western promenades, as well as a connection between the Western Promenade and Deering Oaks.[7]

The Olmsted Brothers' simple and elegant *General Plan for Eastern Promenade* consists of gently

Eastern Promenade and Tukey's Bridge, Portland, Me.

P-67433

ABOVE: *Frederick Law Olmsted, Sr., photographed by James Notman for* The Century *magazine, October 1893. In 1895, Portland mayor James Baxter commissioned Olmsted, Olmsted & Eliot to address sanitation and recreational issues around Back Cove.*

LEFT: *This view of the Eastern Prom's Northern Concourse shows Tukey's Bridge across Back Cove. Baxter Boulevard has not yet been constructed in the foreground of these homes, which are located roughly near today's Front Street.*

OPPOSITE: *The Charles J. Loring, Jr., Veterans' Memorial Park is located on the Eastern Prom's Northern Concourse. Designed in 1999 by Anne Uppinton and Richardson & Associates, Landscape Architects, the memorial intentionally blurs the boundaries between sculpture and landscape.*

curving paths reflecting the natural topography, seats in convenient locations, large patches of open lawn, and trees "that would not too seriously block the view from the promenade." The Olmsteds recognized the significance of this view: "We believe that no intricacy of tree planting, for beauty in itself or for shade for another road, should seriously interfere with the free view from the present roadway."[8]

Their plan expanded on Goodwin's design and focused on plantings throughout the park. The north and south ends of the promenade were to be anchored by a circular concourse and Fort Allen Park, respectively. They also proposed a monument in the northern concourse "to form an architectural vista point" along the main road (where the Loring Memorial is located today). The Eastern Prom received active use by neighborhood residents, and as a consequence much of the Olmsted plan involved play areas for children of various ages: swings, a playfield with parallel and horizontal bars, swinging rings, places for running and jumping, and informal baseball diamonds, as well as a shelter and lawn areas. For older boys, they proposed to fill a shallow cove in order to build a baseball field.

Over the next several decades city staff implemented parts of the Olmsted plan, such as the connection to Washington Avenue and the circular overlook with extensive plantings at the northern tip. Into the 1920s they continued to buy additional land and make further landscape improvements, such as the Cutter Street parking area, walkways, and plantings. In the 1930s the city built softball and tennis courts on the promenade.

The Olmsteds prepared their *General Plan for Western Promenade* at the same time. The two plans are similar in that each shows a drive along the ridge lined formally with trees, curved walking paths to access the slope, open lawns, and a focal point at the end of a major city street. However,

BELOW· *The Olmsted Brothers' Eastern Promenade plan reinforced the formality of existing elms lining the promenade and added naturalistic paths to access the steep slope. Note the multiple railroad tracks along the shore, site of the Narrow Gauge Railroad and the Eastern Promenade Trail today.*

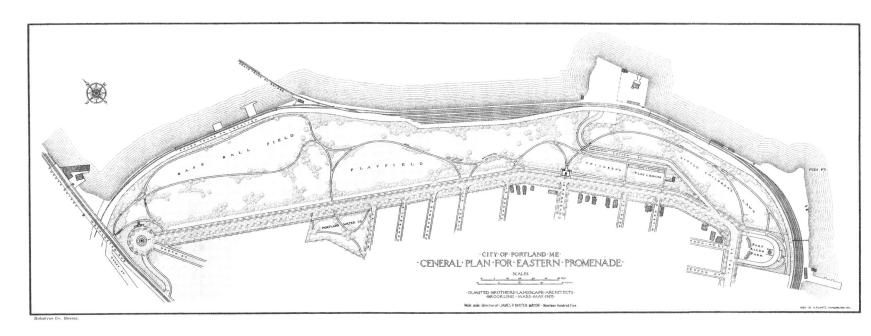

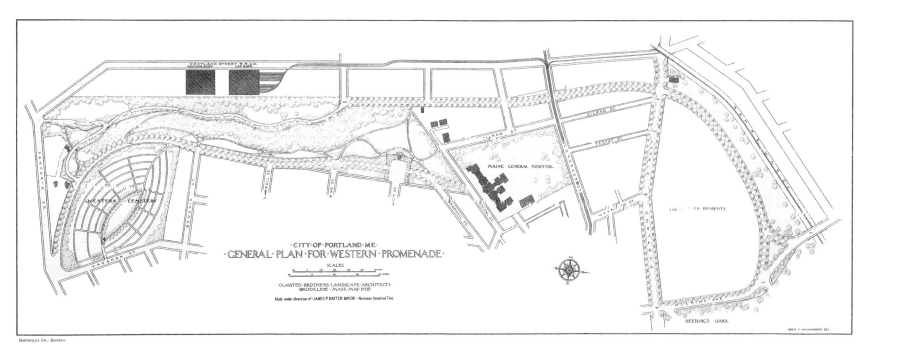

the Western Promenade, which bordered on a neighborhood of expansive homes, was designed as a place for walking and admiring the views, with no active play areas included. The Olmsteds also recommended a future memorial on the Western Promenade, noting that: "It is often the custom to construct in such places a monument as a memorial to some public spirited resident or benefactor of the City, or to erect a memorial to soldiers and sailors or something of that nature."[9] In 1910 the city erected a monument to Thomas Brackett Reed, a Portland native and 1860 graduate of Bowdoin College. In Reed's lengthy political career, he served as a member of Maine's House of Representatives and Senate and was elected to eleven terms in the U.S. House of Representatives.

As with the plan for the Eastern Promenade, only parts of the Olmsteds' design were carried out. A drive and adjacent walkway that were to provide access to the Western Promenade from Valley Street and the shelter and courtyard proposed at the end of West Street were not built, but the city did build a gazebo not far from where the Thomas Brackett Reed monument stands today. Finally, though no formal play areas were proposed by the Olmsteds, the Portland Recreation Department built a toboggan slide on the Western Promenade in 1919 and held a winter carnival there in the 1920s.

Few changes occurred at the promenades during the next several decades. In the 1960s the East End Beach was closed due to pollution, which eventually led to the construction of a sewage treatment plant in 1979 near the Olmsteds' proposed location for a baseball field.

ABOVE: *The Olmsteds' Western Promenade plan shows the Western Cemetery (left) and tree-lined streets leading to Deering Oaks (lower right). The two square buildings belonged to the Portland Street Railroad Company.*
BELOW: *Visitors on the Western Prom, overlooking the Fore River. The Portland International Jetport now occupies the land across the river.*

Portland, Me, View from the Western Promenade.

Visiting the Proms Today

The 1990s brought renewed interest in the condition of Portland's parks; a waterfront trail and a master plan for the Eastern Prom's renewal are two important recent developments. The Eastern Promenade Trail, a 2.2-mile recreational trail opened in 1996, is a popular destination for walking, biking, rollerblading, and enjoying scenic views of Casco Bay. Currently it stretches from India Street to the Back Cove Trail and continues to Payson Park and Evergreen Cemetery by way of city sidewalks. In the near future the Eastern Promenade Trail will connect to the Bayside Trail, which has been designed but not yet constructed. These trails are part of a greater network envisioned for the peninsula by Portland Trails, a nonprofit group founded in 1989.

In 2004 the Portland Parks and Recreation Department and Walker-Kluesing Design Group of Boston prepared the *Eastern Promenade Master Plan*,[10] which was recognized with a merit award from the Boston Society of Landscape Architects. The report reconfirms the historic character of the park while addressing modern needs such as recreational use, access to the water, safety of visitors, and the availability of traditional park elements (benches, picnic tables, fountains, etc.). The plan clearly illustrates the numerous contemporary issues that often compete with historic interests. The Parks and Recreation Department has been developing specific projects, such as landscape improvements surrounding the gazebo, based on the general themes described in the master plan.

Today the view from the Eastern Prom is unrivaled in Maine for its blend of urban activity and distant rural scenery. Commercial ships enter Portland Harbor here, and visitors can look across to South Portland's working waterfront as well as the nearby Bug Light (lighthouse). On a summer day, dozens of small sailboats dart across the water, while hundreds of others are moored in the bay. The best views may be from Fort Allen, where a spacious terrace entices visitors to stand safely at the edge of the steep slope. Here you can take in the numerous islands scattered in Casco Bay: Hog Island, on which Fort Gorges was built, Great Diamond, Little Diamond, Peaks, Cousins, Cushing, and Mackworth, among others, all staggered in such a way that land is visible as far as you look out into the bay.

Since its creation, the Western Promenade has seen fewer changes over the years than the Eastern. Today, the view from the Western Prom includes a great deal of commercial development and highways, but on a clear day you can still see the White Mountains. On the promenade itself, the scene is generally peaceful and quiet with visitors strolling the paths or enjoying a sunset view, backed by stately historic homes.

It may be hard to imagine the promenades as anything other than public parks, but they exist today only because of visionaries like William Goodwin and James Baxter. Together with other forward-thinking citizens they developed these unique open spaces for public recreation and relaxation. Today both promenades offer spectacular views of the harbor, islands, and the White Mountains, in keeping with the spirit of their original designs.

OPPOSITE TOP: *The scenery of Casco Bay from Fort Allen includes Mackworth Island to the left and a sandbar in the foreground of the view to Cousins Island.* OPPOSITE BOTTOM: *Historic homes overlook the Western Promenade.* BELOW: *The gazebo at Fort Allen was designed by Stevens and Cobbs Architects of Portland and was built in 1891. Restored in the 1990s, it is a landmark on the Eastern Prom.*

Lincoln Park: Memorial to an Honored Life

No greater homage could we to-day pay the memory of the great Lincoln than to dedicate anew, in his name, this enlarged park, wherein Portland's citizens and summer guests for ages to come, may find shade, rest and invigoration.[11] — PARK DEDICATION PROGRAM, 1909

Before William Goodwin designed the Eastern and Western promenades, in 1868 Charles Goodell, Portland's civil engineer, proposed a design for one of the city's most important public open spaces, Lincoln Park. Located at the intersection of Congress Street and the Franklin Arterial, this two- and one-half-acre park is somewhat overlooked today as the front yard of the Cumberland County Courthouse. In its early years, however, it was much visited and was the focus of a great deal of civic pride.

Lincoln Park was originally called Phoenix Square, a reference to the legendary bird that perished by fire and rose to live another 500 years. Planning for the new park began just four days after Portland's Great Fire of 1866, which destroyed more than 1,500 buildings and left more than 10,000 people homeless. The square was intended to "serve as a most effective check upon the spread of future fires that might break out in the business centre of the rebuilt city."[12] In addition, the park's creation followed a national trend of establishing public parks and breathing spaces within the business sections of crowded cities. The name Phoenix Square was short-lived; in 1867 the park was renamed in honor of Abraham Lincoln.

In his plan for Lincoln Park, Charles Goodell called for paths to divide the site into quadrangles and meet in a central circle, with clumps of trees within the quadrangles and a fence and sidewalk bordering the site. However, it appears that the city did not follow details of Goodwin's plan, but instead added diagonal paths and lined the edge of the park and paths with elm trees. The multi-tiered fountain that exists today was added in 1871. Although Lincoln Park lacked the dramatic scenery of the Eastern or Western Promenades, it served as a public promenade ground: "Every pleasant

day Lincoln Park is thronged with people, who, promenading its pleasant walks and enjoying its cooling shades and beautiful flowers, enjoy and appreciate this delightful breathing place."[13]

Fire struck the Lincoln Park neighborhood again in 1908, when City Hall was destroyed (Portland's current City Hall was built in its place). At about the same time, the Cumberland County Courthouse and Federal Courthouse were completed, and a Masonic Temple was proposed near Lincoln Park. A group of prominent citizens petitioned the city to acquire some unsightly commercial buildings located between the adjacent Pearl and Market streets to create a beautiful park annex to complement this dignified collection of government buildings. The land was acquired, the buildings were razed, and paths were added, but eventually the annexed site was turned over to the city fire department.

The name Lincoln Park had been formalized in 1867, but on February 12, 1909, hundreds of residents gathered to rededicate the park in honor of Abraham Lincoln's 100th birthday. In his address to the crowd, General Charles P. Mattocks shared this glowing tribute to Lincoln:

Immortal Lincoln! To your sacred memory we dedicate these grounds as an evidence of our devotion and gratitude. These sturdy trees typify the strong elements of your character. The beautiful flowers which will soon open their petals to the summer sun will remind us of the sweetness of your nature while the song birds shall in plaintive tones tell us of your trials, your sufferings, and your sorrows in behalf of your beloved people. Your memory shall remain as green and fresh as the grassy carpet which shall soon succeed to this covering of snow which now envelopes this beautiful spot, and reminds us of the purity of your honored life. [14]

Since its creation Lincoln Park has attracted public gatherings, ranging from a Civil War re-enactment in 1885, to Sunday visitors in the late nineteenth century, to farmers' markets in the early twentieth century. But like public parks across the country, Lincoln Park suffered a period of deterioration in the mid-1900s. The city stopped planting ornamental beds in the park, and the elm trees fell to Dutch elm disease in the 1960s and '70s; none remain today. One-quarter of the park's east end was taken to widen the Franklin Arterial around 1970, giving it its current asymmetrical appearance.

The city of Portland is interested in maintaining the park's historic character while considering contemporary needs and challenges. For example, to provide lighting within the park, new wiring would have to be installed underground without damaging historic paths or tree roots, and appropriate light posts would have to be selected for a park that historically never had lights. The Parks and Recreation Department notes that trees in the park are in good condition and receive regular maintenance. In 2005, as part of its conservation and maintenance program for public art and fountains, the city repaired and repainted the fountain and built a protective cover for the winter.

Although Lincoln Park receives few visitors except for those passing through on their way to the courthouses, it has recently been used for events associated with Merrill Auditorium. A local service club is considering a project for the park, perhaps making the ornamental iron gates functional again, and redevelopment of the nearby Bayside neighborhood may increase use by the public. In the meantime, Lincoln Park's historic formal design provides a contrast to the more naturalistic, Olmstedian designs found in Portland's other public landscapes throughout the city.

LINCOLN PARK, PORTLAND, MAINE. 215939

DEERING OAKS: NATURE IN THE CITY

The crowning glory of the Oaks will always be the "breezy dome" of the old woods, to which elms and beeches and birches, the maples and evergreens and shrubbery can never be much more than ornamental fringing.[15] —PORTLAND CITY AUDITOR'S REPORT, 1880

Deering Oaks is a fifty-five-acre naturalistic park known for mature stands of red and white oak, a formal rose garden, an ice-skating pond and historic warming hut, walking paths, play areas, and popular ball fields. In recent years, the city of Portland and the Friends of Deering Oaks have significantly improved one of the city's most treasured historic landscapes.

Some mistakenly attribute the design of Deering Oaks to the Olmsted Brothers, who included the Oaks in their 1905 *General Plan for the Portland Park System*. In fact, Deering Oaks was designed by civil engineer William Goodwin in 1879 and built largely according to his plan. Goodwin's

long-overlooked role is finally receiving attention as recent design efforts lean toward returning the park to his original vision.

In *Bold Vision: The Development of the Parks of Portland, Maine,* historian Herbert Adams recounts the history of the Oaks from the 1680s into the next centuries and introduces Nathaniel Deering. After settling in Portland in 1761, Deering accumulated about 260 acres around Back Cove. In 1804 his only son, James, built an elegant Federalist mansion on a hill overlooking the cove. Today, land once occupied by the Deering farm now encompasses part of the University of Southern Maine, several residential streets, and a portion of the interstate highway. Adams notes that all that remains of the Deering farm today is Deering Oaks.[16]

William Goodwin's philosophy followed the naturalistic approach to park design favored by Frederick Law Olmsted, Sr., and other nineteenth-century park designers. His goal was to preserve the site's natural beauty rather than superimpose a formal design on the landscape. He did so by creating a system of winding paths and roads that disturbed as few trees as possible while providing passages of scenery and connections to the city street system. He proposed connecting Deering Oaks to Portland's other parks via tree-lined roads.

Goodwin's naturalistic plan included the present-day Deering Oaks pond. According to historian Adams, in the early 1800s the pond was a large tidal flat that drained into Back Cove. The marshy area was transformed into a mill pond in 1806, thanks to tidal gates that were part of the construction of "Deering's Bridge" (today's Forest Avenue, near the post office). Over seventy years later, William Goodwin closed the tidal gates and created the four-acre Deering Oaks pond. (In 1912 the city installed a water line from Deering Avenue to the top of the ravine, as a permanent water source.) Goodwin's plan showed several coves and peninsulas along the pond's south side, the largest having a bridge wide enough for carriages. The effect of the peninsulas was to give the illusion that the pond was larger than it was.

Among Portland's historic parks, Deering Oaks is closest to its historic appearance. The pond's varying shoreline is quite similar to Goodwin's original design. A large grove of trees today echoes the largest patch of undisturbed native trees shown on his plan, and some of the park's roads still closely follow those laid out in 1879. Improvements made under Goodwin's direction in the 1880s included adding the spray fountain and ornamental duck house to the pond and preparing the area for winter skating. Elsewhere he added an attractive bandstand and wooden footbridges. He proposed a formal gateway at the State Street entrance in 1886, though nothing was built there until 1903.

Goodwin also designed an avenue across the park's northern boundary to connect Marginal Way with today's Deering Avenue. This formal park road, which was never built, was to have had a tree-lined esplanade and a rotary with a central fountain and would have been roughly where today's tennis courts are located. There were also no recreational facilities in Goodwin's plan. The playgrounds, courts, and fields in place today evolved from those built in 1902, when a growing public interest in playgrounds and organized sports prompted the development of more structured recreational areas.[17]

PORTLAND, ME. DEERING PARK AND POND.

Rustic Bridge, Deering Park.
Greetings from Portland, Maine.

Portland, Me. Gateway to Deering Oaks.

Portland, Maine., Easterly End, Deering Oaks.

ABOVE (CLOCKWISE FROM TOP LEFT): *Deering Oaks
historic postcards showing the Castle-in-the-Park, designed by
Frederick Tompson, with a swan boat in the foreground; the triple-
arched bridge (no longer existing); the pond as seen from Park
Avenue; and the Park Avenue entrance pillars, also designed by*

After Goodwin retired as city engineer in 1892, Mayor James P. Baxter continued to make improvements to the park. Baxter hired the Olmsted firm on two separate occasions, first in 1896 to prepare a plan for Back Cove and then in 1905 for a plan of the entire Portland park system. The design of Deering Oaks was well-established by the time the Olmsteds became involved. They proposed tree-lined roads to link Deering Oaks with the Western Promenade (via Park Avenue and a non-existent road along the railroad tracks near the baseball stadium) and to Back Cove Boulevard (via Deering Avenue and Bedford Street). They did not propose changes to Deering Oaks itself.

Deering Oaks continued to receive improvements throughout the 1900s. One of the highlights was the construction in 1911 of the arched bridge over the ravine, designed by Portland Parks Department engineer W. O. Tompson. Other improvements focused on extensive plantings of trees, shrubs, and flowers. The location of today's rose garden was the site of the Casco Tannery until the city acquired the land in 1922. Another Portland engineer, William Dougherty, designed the garden, hedges, and geometric paths in 1927.

Deering Oaks Today

Maintenance at Deering Oaks suffered during World War II and throughout the following years. Decades of heavy use and the addition of recreational areas took their toll before the park's historic significance was appreciated. In 1971, funding from the Federal Urban Beautification Program resulted in repairs to the 1911 footbridge and construction of a new playground, tennis and basketball courts, wading pool, fencing, and lighting. In the 1980s the city received additional funding from the Urban Park and Recreation Recovery Action Plan to upgrade courts and ball fields, improve roads and walks, address erosion and drainage issues, and improve the soil for the historic trees.[18]

Following the park's listing in the National Register of Historic Places, the city commissioned a master plan to guide future decisions in Deering Oaks. In their 1994 *Deering Oaks Master Plan*, the Halvorson Company of Boston addressed the park's vegetation, its pond and fountain, various recreational and quiet uses, roads and paths, and the balance of open spaces and wooded areas. The plan led to substantial improvements to Deering Oaks beginning in the 1990s.

The Deering Oaks ravine project created a beautiful space in a damp area that originally supplied water to the pond. Goodwin had planned a fountain, dam, and two waterfalls here, but limited water flow made this impractical. In 1997, friends and colleagues of Portland's urban designer Kay Wagenknecht-Harte chose the ravine project to honor her memory. The site was designed by Mohr & Seredin Landscape Architects of Portland, with a sculpted granite wading pool designed by artist Carol Hanson. In 2003 the ravine project received an honor award from Maine Preservation.

The next major project in Deering Oaks was the restoration of the 1894 Castle-in-the-Park, the historic warming hut and visitors' shelter designed by Portland architect Frederick Tompson. Tompson designed numerous commercial, civic, and residential buildings throughout the city, including at Evergreen Cemetery. His additional work in Deering Oaks included the twenty-three-foot granite pillars at the State Street entrance, installed in 1903. Tompson's Castle received several additions over the years that conflicted with its historic character. The Friends of Deering Oaks, the Department of Parks and Recreation, and the City of Portland removed the additions and restored the original stained-glass windows, fireplace, and varnished beadboard interior. In 2007 the Castle project, like the ravine, received an honor award from Maine Preservation.

Following the success of the Castle, in 2006 the Friends of Deering Oaks and the city replaced the fountain, which dated from the 1960s and was in poor condition. The new fountain has more than forty water spouts, sprays thirty feet into the air, and has decorative lighting for nighttime displays. In addition, the original duck house installed in 1887 has been repaired and is now back in the pond.

Today, there are an estimated 1,000 trees in Deering Oaks, including three trees on the State

OPPOSITE: *This concrete bridge near the Deering Oaks ravine was built in 1911 and replaced rustic, wooden versions built by William Goodwin around 1880.*
BELOW: *Frederick Tompson's warming hut, now known as Castle-in-the-Park, features stained-glass windows set in thick walls built of reused granite paving blocks. The restored castle is now open to the public as one of Portland's visitor centers.*

of Maine's "Big Tree" list, a pin oak, a Siberian elm, and a yellowwood. To protect and improve the health of all trees in the park and to respect Goodwin's original naturalistic design, the parks department now mows parts of the lawn only once or twice yearly. Grass clippings and leaves decompose and add nutrients to the soil, leading to a healthier, more natural woodland.

Two future projects in Deering Oaks include refurbishing and possibly enlarging the playgrounds and restoring the 1911 concrete bridge over the ravine. Since the park is designated a historic district, the projects will go before the city's Historic Preservation Board, whose challenge is to ensure that the work is consistent with Goodwin's original design.

BACK COVE, BAXTER BOULEVARD, AND THE BACK COVE TRAIL

With this park completed and connected with the promenades and Deering's Oaks, Portland and its suburbs will offer advantages for residence unequalled by any city in New England.[19]
— JAMES P. BAXTER, 1895

Portland's Back Cove has three components: Back Cove itself, Baxter Boulevard, and the relatively new Back Cove Trail. The first two are listed in the National Register of Historic Places, as is the Baxter Memorial, and are designated as a Historic Landscape District by the city of Portland. Back Cove is a 340-acre tidal basin that forms the northwestern boundary of the Portland peninsula. The cove is bordered by Baxter Boulevard and is surrounded mostly by residential neighborhoods, except for Interstate 295 to the east.

Although it is one of Portland's most popular recreation areas today, Back Cove in the 1800s was the final destination for the city's industrial waste and residential sewage. City engineer William Goodwin proposed a sewer system in 1884 to address the problem of the polluted mudflats, but his recommendations were not carried out. Eleven years later, Mayor James P. Baxter expanded upon Goodwin's ideas by commissioning Olmsted, Olmsted and Eliot to make recommendations for improving the cove's sanitation issues. The unsanitary situation in Portland paralleled that in Boston's Back Bay, for which Frederick Law Olmsted, Sr., prepared a treatment plan in the mid-1890s.

The Olmsteds proposed turning the cove into a saltwater pond, eliminating the tidal mudflats. They suggested building a dam or dike with a small inlet and outlet to Casco Bay, and dredging any remaining mudflats to below water level. The Olmsteds considered this, together with the city's efforts to build intercepting sewers, "a simple engineering solution of the problem of hiding the foul mud flats at Back Cove." Their ultimate goal was to "create a great public water park extremely agreeable to look at as well as immediately available for small pleasure boats."[20] However, as residents thought of the plan as "elitist," the dam and pleasure basin were never built.

For the highest residential value of the surrounding land, the Olmsteds suggested raising and widening the proposed dike to complete a circuit drive around the cove, envisioning a "beautiful shore drive and promenade" that would benefit all local citizens. They also identified sites around

ABOVE: *Joggers enjoy the Back Cove Trail lined on the left with historic linden trees.*
OPPOSITE: *The 1896 Preliminary Plan for the Improvement of Back Cove by Olmsted, Olmsted & Eliot shows the proposed pleasure basin with "salt water of nearly constant elevation" and a tree-lined circuit around the entire cove, an idea that took almost 100 years to materialize.*

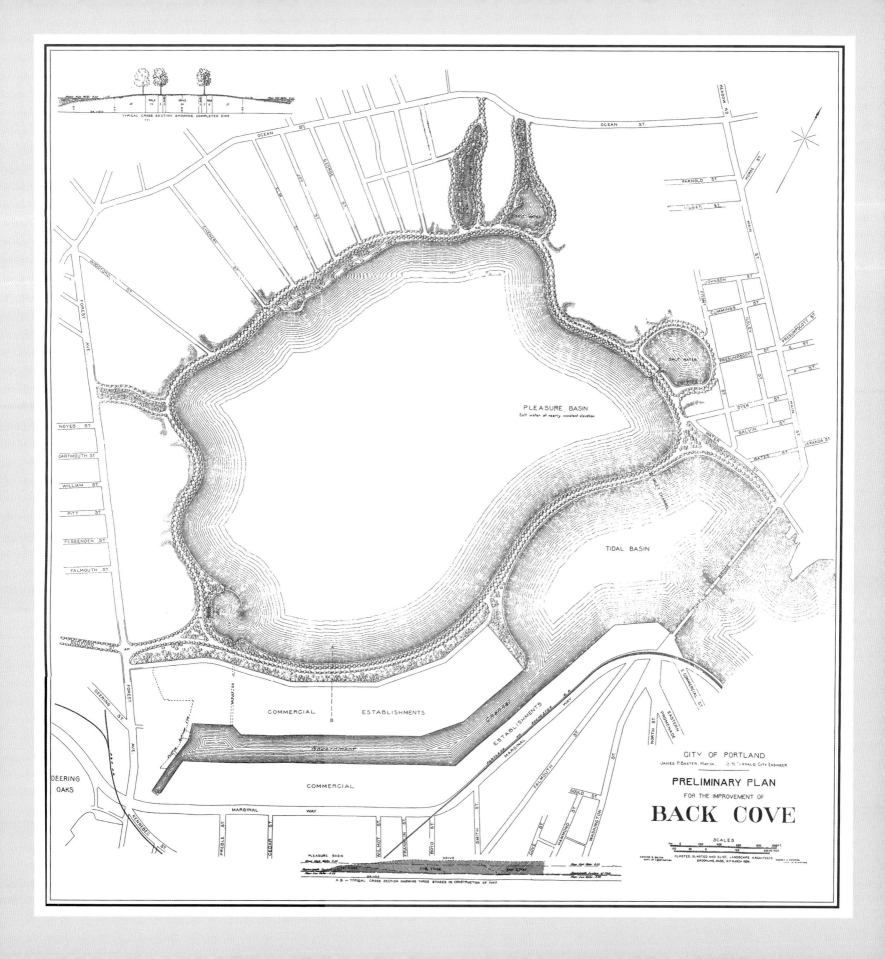

PLEASURE BASIN
Salt water at nearly constant elevation

TIDAL BASIN

COMMERCIAL ESTABLISHMENTS

COMMERCIAL

DEERING OAKS

MARGINAL WAY

CITY OF PORTLAND

JAMES P. BAXTER, MAYOR   G. N. FERNALD, CITY ENGINEER

PRELIMINARY PLAN

FOR THE IMPROVEMENT OF

BACK COVE

SCALES

OLMSTED, OLMSTED AND ELIOT, LANDSCAPE ARCHITECTS
BROOKLINE, MASS. 14TH MARCH 1896.

TYPICAL CROSS SECTION SHOWING COMPLETED DIKE

A.B — TYPICAL CROSS SECTION SHOWING THREE STAGES IN CONSTRUCTION OF DIKE

the cove best suited for house lots of varying sizes, from "large residence estates" to moderate and small house sites, and suggested that the land between Forest Avenue and Back Cove and between Bedford and Noyes streets be acquired for use as a public park. Instead of parkland, however, the area became the residential neighborhood known as Boulevard Park (pp. 190–191).

Mayor Baxter elaborated on the Olmsteds' report in his essay *The Story of Portland*. He envisioned transforming areas of "rank grass" into "paradise" by planting groups of evergreens, birches, willows, and other deciduous trees of light foliage, along with clumps of flowering shrubbery. Following the example of Boston's Franklin Park, designed by Frederick Law Olmsted, Sr., in 1885, Baxter imagined rustic shelters, a "broad corso" for carriages, and separate paths for pedestrians and horses.

Unfortunately, plans for Back Cove were put on hold when Baxter failed to be re-elected as mayor in 1897. However, following his re-election in 1903, he received approval from the City Council to lay out Back Cove Boulevard. The following year he commissioned the Olmsted Brothers to draw a plan of Portland's park system, linking the Eastern and Western promenades, Back Cove, and

OPPOSITE: *Linden trees line the newly completed Baxter Boulevard in this historic postcard.*

BELOW: *A 1933 view of Baxter Boulevard near Mackworth Street shows newly planted trees and yet-to-be-developed residential property overlooking Back Cove.*

Deering Oaks by a series of tree-lined parkways. This plan was shelved when, once again, Baxter was voted out of office in 1905. The new mayor, Nathan Clifford, chose instead to improve streets and sidewalks, "the wretched condition of which has caused the angry criticisms so constantly heard during the last year."[21]

Baxter's vision was expanded by the parks commissioners in 1911 when they recommended continuing construction of the boulevard. The Olmsted plan served as the basis for improvements, but, as at other Portland parks, the city's engineers oversaw the design details and construction of the boulevard. Over the next several years they brought in large amounts of fill, stabilized the cove's edges, graded the roads, and built bridges, sidewalks, and paths. City engineer Percy Richardson and Sanders Engineering Company designed two handsome brick and concrete bridges to cross Smith Creek and Fall Brook, the latter of which remains today. The boulevard was opened to the public in November 1917, with work continuing into the 1920s.

P-111   Baxter Boulevard, Portland, Maine

OB-H1676

Today the canopy created by the allée of linden trees along the boulevard is one of the site's most important historic features. The lindens were planted in the 1920s as a memorial to Portland men who died in World War I. In addition, during the 1920s and 1930s the city planted other trees such as maples and birches, along with ornamental shrubs such as barberry hedges, deutzia, hydrangea, forsythia, spirea, and privet. The boulevard was renamed in honor of James Baxter after his death in 1921, and the Baxter Memorial was erected in his honor in 1925. Located at the end of Vannah Avenue, the memorial's granite benches and bronze sundial overlook the boulevard, trail, and cove.

In a now-familiar story, the boulevard fell into a period of neglect beginning in the 1940s. The interceptor sewer system that Goodwin suggested in 1884 was not completed until the 1970s. In 1979 the city built a wastewater treatment plant on the Eastern Promenade, improving the condition of Back Cove and leading to increased use of the walking trail along the boulevard. Back Cove and Baxter Boulevard were listed in the National Register of Historic Places, with the unusual dual listing as both a park and historic roadway. The city also recognizes the cove and boulevard as a historic landscape.

By 1996 Back Cove and the boulevard had become the most intensely used park in Portland, prompting the city to commission the *Baxter Boulevard Improvement Plan*.[22] The plan proposed a separate multi-purpose path to accommodate joggers, bicyclists, rollerbladers, and pedestrians on this historic roadway. The improvement plan, which was seen by many as an intrusion into the historic landscape, was adopted by the city council as part of Portland's Comprehensive Plan, but no further work has taken place.

BACK COVE TRAIL

The Back Cove Trail is about three and one-half miles long and forms a complete loop around the cove, much as the Olmsteds envisioned in 1896. This is Portland's most popular recreation area; the city estimates that 250,000 walkers, joggers, and bicyclists use the trail each year. The path offers spectacular views of the water and Portland's skyline. The original walkway along the Boulevard was improved in the 1970s with a stone dust surface and the addition of a fitness course. The circuit around the cove was completed in 1989 with the reconstruction of Tukey's Bridge. The trail is part of a greater system developed by Portland Trails, which is developing a fifty-mile network of multi-use trails within the city, with Back Cove as its hub. The Back Cove Trail connects to the Eastern Promenade Trail near Tukey's Bridge.

In recent years the trail has suffered from serious erosion problems and maintenance issues due to its great popularity. In addition, a severe storm in April 2007 caused further damage to its unpaved surface. Engineers from Woodard and Curran recently developed a master plan to rehabilitate the trail, including stabilizing the surface, improving signs, creating handicapped accessible ramps, fortifying stone embankments, and adding plants to prevent erosion.

Like other historic parks in Portland, the Back Cove is a valuable natural and cultural resource. It is also unique among the city's public open spaces for its multiple roles: a scenic roadway with memorial trees approaching one hundred years of age; a linear park for runners, walkers, and bicyclists; an ecological filter for storm water pollutants that would otherwise enter Back Cove; a place to store storm water itself; habitat for wildlife in the marsh and mudflats; and a place to enjoy outstanding views of the city and saltwater bay. None of this would exist today without the dedication and foresight of benefactors, civic leaders, professional designers, and local residents who recognized the potential appeal of this attractive urban landscape.

ABOVE: *A bronze sundial is a focal point at the Baxter Memorial, dedicated in 1925.*

RIGHT: *The remaining historic bridge along Baxter Boulevard offers a scenic overlook of Back Cove and downtown Portland.*

OPPOSITE: *The memorial to James P. Baxter along Baxter Boulevard features granite seats that were set "separate with considerable space between them so that there will be no effect of crowding."*

CHAPTER 2

AUGUSTA: CAPITAL CITY ON THE KENNEBEC

Maine's capital city, Augusta, has a rich history that includes the earliest known, deliberately designed landscape in the state, Capitol Park. Augusta is also distinguished for the work of the best-known landscape architectural firm in the country, the Olmsted Brothers, represented by Carl Rust Parker. Parker's impressive career included all aspects of landscape design: residences, subdivisions, campuses, parks, memorials, cemeteries, and the grounds of major institutions. In the 1920s, he planned four Augusta sites simultaneously: Capitol Park, the State House grounds, the Blaine House, and Blaine Memorial Park. Over the years these have been altered, but today's visitor can still appreciate Parker's vision for some of Maine's most prominent public landscapes.

Capitol Park consists of roughly twenty acres in the foreground of the Maine State House, overlooking the Kennebec River. The Blaine House, also known as the governor's mansion, is directly opposite the State House. Blaine Memorial Park is located about a mile away at Green Street and Blaine Avenue.

In 1827, the Maine Legislature established Augusta as the state's permanent capital, due to its central location and the importance of the Kennebec River as a crossroads for trading and commerce. Local citizens donated thirty-four acres for the capitol building and its surrounding landscape overlooking the Kennebec. To ensure a dignified setting for the future State House and to provide a contrast to the surrounding agricultural landscape, several dozen elms were planted in Capitol Park in a formal allée between State Street and the river. Over the next decades additional plantings of trees reinforced this formal atmosphere.

Charles Bulfinch of Boston designed the Maine State House, which was built between 1829 and 1832, and prepared a landscape plan showing three terraced ovals surrounding the impressive granite building, with trees delineating the terraces' perimeter. Capitol Park and the State House grounds saw no major changes between the 1850s and 1920.

The early 1920s were a period of national prosperity. To celebrate the one-hundredth anniversary of Maine's separation from Massachusetts, a Centennial Exposition was held in 1920 in Portland's Deering Oaks (pp. 29–34) to showcase Maine-made goods, industrial and agricultural interests, and the state's natural resources. In Augusta, Governor Carl Milliken moved into the Blaine House, the elegant, remodeled mansion that had been donated for use as the governor's home the year before. He then set his sights on improving the landscape of that property as well as Capitol Park and the State House grounds. He commissioned the Olmsted firm to unite these landscapes into a single complex and to prepare plans for each site, as well as for the Blaine Memorial, a new site planned to honor James G. Blaine, a dominant figure in Maine and national politics following the Civil War. Despite the size and extent of the Augusta projects, the Olmsted firm's involvement was relatively brief. Parker first met with Milliken and visited the sites in May of 1920. Most of the design work was completed that year, although consultation and plan revisions occurred occasionally until about 1929.

CAPITOL PARK AND THE GROUNDS OF THE STATE HOUSE

While the various features of this park have been suggested either by the obvious need or by the beauty of the topographical features already existing, we believe that the scheme as it now stands is not only well organized and well related to the Capitol, which is, and should be, the dominant object in the neighborhood, but also unusually varied and unusually interesting in the separate units of which it is comprised.[1] – OLMSTED BROTHERS, 1920

In their designs for these prominent Augusta properties, Parker and the Olmsted firm faced a number of challenges. Capitol Park, the State House grounds, and the Blaine House all had extensive histories to consider, and funding for the projects was uncertain and subject to changing priorities of different administrations. The Blaine Memorial was a wholly new landscape project, but also one requiring sensitive management. Carl Rust Parker's plans for these areas recognized their circumstances and brought the Olmsted firm's expertise to bear on the state's flagship properties.

The allée of elm trees planted in the 1800s and aligned with the State House established Capitol Park as an extension of the capitol grounds. Parker's plan maintained this relationship with the added benefit of recreational areas and attractions, peaceful nooks, screening from busy roads, and paths designed around scenic views and connected to the neighborhood. Parker considered the park's existing four rows of elms its most important feature and proposed to emphasize them with wide gravel paths between the rows. Equally important was the site's connection to the State House; along the State Street border he proposed elegant steps and ramps leading to the park. He also suggested a garden with native trees and shrubs, large amounts of grassy open space, tennis courts, a grove for public speaking, and a bandstand.

At the State House, Parker proposed relatively minor landscape improvements while leaving Bulfinch's terraces intact. Parker prepared a planting plan, relocated the drives in front of the then-adjutant general's office, and suggested new paths to State Street.

Funding for these projects was a major concern, particularly after the change in Maine's administration in 1921. Milliken's successor,

MAINE STATE PARK —
AUGUSTA MAINE
Olmsted Brothers Landscape Architects
BROOKLINE, MASS

Frederic Parkhurst, died after just twenty-six days in office. He was succeeded by Percival Baxter (son of James Phinney Baxter), president of the Maine Senate, who did not share Milliken's vision. The legislature only partially funded new construction and maintenance for Capitol Park and the State House, resulting in a piecemeal approach to construction. Parker's designs relied heavily on plant material, much of which died the first winter due to neglect or ignorance.

The state did not hire the Olmsteds to oversee the Augusta work in 1921. Nevertheless, the Olmsteds wanted the work completed, partly so that it did not reflect poorly on them, and partly to protect the investment already made by the state. In a letter accompanying revisions to the State Street pedestrian entrance in 1929, Carl Rust Parker wrote that work in Capitol Park had been done "on very limited appropriations" from the legislature for the past few years and that the state should be congratulated for the amount of work accomplished with very limited funds. Few additions and changes occurred in the decades following the Olmsteds' work.

During the 1980s, Governor John McKernan sought to restore the Augusta landscapes to their original dignity. The elm trees in the Capitol Park allée had succumbed to Dutch elm disease and were replaced by red oaks, and the Maine Vietnam Veterans Memorial was installed in 1985. By the time the park was nominated to the National Register of Historic Places in 1989, the State Legislature had recognized the importance of preserving the open space by prohibiting construction within Capitol Park's boundaries.

In 1984 the legislature created the Blaine House Restoration Fund to restore the house and grounds of the governor's residence. Three years later, the State House and Capitol Park Commission was formed to create a plan to preserve and develop the aesthetic and historical integrity of these two landscapes.

Soon after the National Register recognition, the Commission hired Pressley Associates of Massachusetts to prepare a master plan for the State House grounds, Capitol Park, and the city's adjacent athletic facilities. The master plan addressed the site's pre-Olmsted history by calling for a formal re-creation of the allée that was established in 1827. Reminiscent of the Olmsteds, the plan also relied on new plantings of trees and shrubs to reinforce the structure of the park. Finally, the plan addressed modern issues such as improving the connection across busy State Street and establishing a path system to link historic and contemporary features. Based on the plan, in 1999 teams from the Maine Conservation Corps, with technical advice and equipment from the Maine Department of Transportation, helped build or reconstruct several of the stone dust paths in Capitol Park.

Major landscape restoration began at the State House in 1994 and included improving drainage around the building, replacing and refurbishing the iron fence based on original castings, and reconstructing the granite retaining wall. Architectural projects in 2000 included building an underground pedestrian walkway and a forty- by sixty-foot diorama room to connect the State House and State Office Building. The result above ground was a new plaza with skylight, walkways, lights, and plants between the two buildings. Following these projects, the Capitol Complex Historic District, which includes 400 acres and five buildings, was listed in the National Register of Historic Places in 2001.

Today the state is forward-thinking in its sensitive treatment of memorials in Capitol Park. In 2002 the Legislature passed a bill to "develop a Living Memorial in Capitol Park in Honor of the Victims and Heroes of the September 11, 2001 Tragedy." [2] In response, the memorial Shrub

Garden, designed by Pressley Associates and based on the Olmsteds' 1920 plan, was installed in 2006. To honor veterans in November 2007, local groups posted 2,500 American flags, starting at Capitol Park and flowing south along Interstate 95 to the New Hampshire border. These living memorials accomplish several notable goals: respecting the landscape's historic fabric by not adding new features, restoring part of the Olmsteds' 1920 design, and providing a space for memorials in a thoughtful manner.

Today, visitors to Capitol Park may notice that there are no recreation areas, no ball fields or playgrounds – just the opportunity to stroll among the trees, rest on shady lawns, or appreciate the park as it was originally intended, as a dignified setting for the Maine State House.

THE BLAINE HOUSE: A MAINE FAMILY'S LEGACY

It is my first and strongest desire, that this house, which has been a home for so many years and in which my son was born, shall be used and maintained as the official residence for the Governor of Maine…. [This] would meet the approval of my dear son who devotedly loved his home, Augusta, and his native state. I leave the fulfillment of this trust to the good faith of the State for whose honor my son with many others gave his life.[3] — HARRIET BLAINE BEALE, 1919

Such was Harriet Blaine Beale's loving tribute to her son, Walker Blaine Beale, who was killed in France during World War I. The home is Blaine House, which she donated as the Governor's Mansion in 1919. Her father, James G. Blaine, lived there from 1862 until his death in 1893, and Harriet Blaine Beale herself was born in the house and married there in 1894. James G. Blaine was a dominant figure in American politics following the Civil War. He was editor of the *Portland Advertiser* and the *Kennebec Journal* and had a lengthy career in state and national politics. Among other achievements, he was Secretary of State in the cabinets of presidents James Garfield and Chester Arthur in 1881, as well as Secretary of State under President Benjamin Harrison from 1889 to 1892.

Harriet Beale's donation followed a 1915 state law requiring the governor to have an official home in Augusta. The legislature resolved that the Blaine House be "improved, repaired, and suitably furnished as an executive mansion for the governor of the state while in office." Redesign and restoration of the Blaine House was entrusted to the state's most prominent architect, John Calvin Stevens. Stevens enlarged the main structure while maintaining room arrangements and architectural details wherever possible. A two-story gable-roofed ell had been added at the rear of the house by a previous owner. Stevens raised this ell to match other sections of the house and added a family dining room with a bay window on the first floor. He converted the veranda on the south side to an enclosed sunroom and built a two-story service wing on the northwest side, balancing the original ell.

The state purchased neighboring properties in order to enlarge the grounds. When Carl Rust Parker first visited in May 1920, the large crew already working there needed immediate guidance; Parker provided planting and access plans within the week. The final plan included a

service area, New England Garden, Shrub Garden, and improved connection to the State House through a new Governor's Gate.

Parker considered his proposal for the State Street entrance to be the most important part of the project. He wrote, "…[T]here is no one thing that can be done to give the property the dignity and the stately appearance…better than the treatment we have suggested."[4] He planned to replace a grassy bank and lilac hedge with a stone retaining wall, topped with a low Colonial fence to match others on the property. Wide granite steps would lead from State Street to a brick landing at the mansion's door. Off to each side, the entrance to the New England and shrub gardens would be under a "little hooded gate."

As with Capitol Park, the work received only partial funding, which covered flagstones for the New England Garden, the laundry yard fence, the path from the Governor's Gate to the mansion, preparation of planting areas, and partial fencing. Parker worked diligently to refine his concepts and reduce costs, but without sufficient funding, Governor Milliken chose not to build the wall or balustrade at the State Street entrance. Parker responded that he was "exceedingly sorry" that decision had been reached, but that he would "try and adjust matters to fit in with the decision."[5] The project was dropped for close to seventy years; Parker's design along State Street was finally unveiled in 1990, thanks to the efforts of Governor John McKernan, Senator Olympia Snowe, numerous volunteers, and large contributions from the community.

The idea of installing Parker's design began in 1984 with McKernan's creation of the Blaine House Restoration Fund, a non-profit corporation formed to restore the house and grounds. The grounds restoration committee researched the Olmsteds' plans, documented the existing landscape, and considered how to meet modern needs. They addressed major issues such as funding for installation and maintenance and use of the Blaine House as both a public space and private residence. Work from 1987 to 1993 including removing many overgrown trees and non-historic flower beds, restoring lawn panels, replacing shrubs, and adding handicapped access.

The restoration committee then sought to complete Parker's plan by building the State Street entrance. In 1989, based on an interpretation of Parker's plan by Reed & Barba Architects, contractors built nineteen-foot-wide granite steps, a curved retaining wall, a terraced landing, a pair of arbors, and brick paths leading to side gardens. Parker's vision was finally realized. The Blaine House Commission was established in 1994 to oversee all future work on the house and grounds and to ensure a continued commitment to their maintenance.

Governor John Baldacci and his family moved into the Blaine House in 2003. Karen Baldacci, an avid gardener, installed a cutting and herb garden and a vegetable garden and raised private funds to install a Victorian greenhouse. Most recently she continued McKernan's efforts by re-creating the New England Garden. This formal garden was designed by Parker and installed in the 1920s but had almost completely disappeared by the time of the 1980s restoration. Thanks to private donors, the garden was installed according to a plan by Pressley Associates, based on Parker's original design. Visitors today enjoy old-fashioned shrubs similar to those proposed by Parker, such as hydrangea, spirea, lilac, and viburnum. The garden also has native ferns, annuals, bulbs,

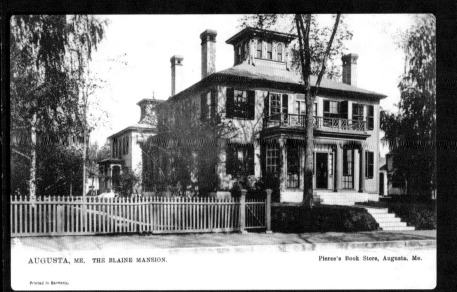

AUGUSTA, ME. THE BLAINE MANSION.

Pierce's Book Store, Augusta, Me.

Printed in Germany.

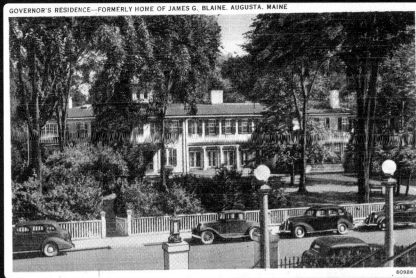

GOVERNOR'S RESIDENCE—FORMERLY HOME OF JAMES G. BLAINE. AUGUSTA. MAINE

60986

and dozens of perennials, many of which continue the old-fashioned theme: peony, phlox, aster, geranium, and iris, among others.

Maine residents today owe a debt of gratitude to those who created, and later restored, the Blaine House landscape: several governors, Carl Rust Parker and the Olmsteds, numerous volunteers, and members of the Blaine House Restoration Committee and the Friends of the Blaine House. Without these efforts since the 1920s, the governor's mansion would not stand today as Maine's most prominent state-owned landscape. A description from 1930 still applies today: "…no state is more fortunate than Maine in the combination of location, appointments, and historical interest which the home of its chief executive possesses."[6]

BELOW: *Carl Rust Parker's* Plan for the Blaine Memorial *offered a dignified setting in which to honor a beloved Maine statesman.*

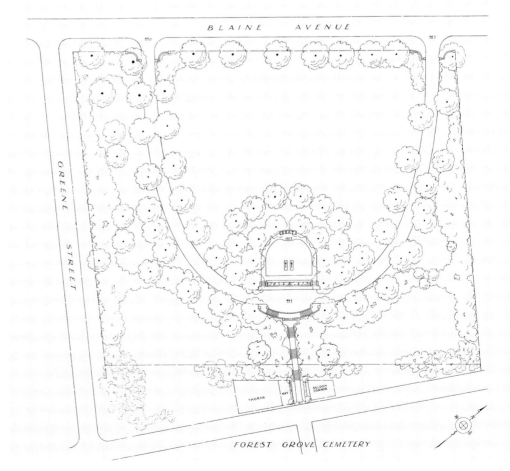

PLAN FOR THE BLAINE MEMORIAL
AUGUSTA MAINE
SCALE OF FEET
0   25   50   75   100   125   150   175   200
OLMSTED BROTHERS   LANDSCAPE ARCHITECTS
BROOKLINE MASS. OCTOBER 15, 1920

LEFT. *Carl Rust Parker's granite bench and horseshoe-shaped walkway surround the simple gravesites of James Gillespie Blaine and Harriet Stanwood Blaine.*

BLAINE MEMORIAL PARK

The lot to which the remains of Mr. and Mrs. Blaine were brought last June has remarkable beauty. Instead of the elaborate monument which some might have expected to see, the place itself has been made the Memorial, every part of which from the approaches to the very center has been made to express with dignified simplicity and perfect harmony this fundamental purpose.[7] – KENNEBEC JOURNAL, 1920

The State House, Capitol Park, and the Blaine House all had extensive histories when the Olmsteds came on board in 1920. The firm also designed a totally new landscape, Blaine Memorial Park, where James G. Blaine and his wife, Harriet Stanwood Blaine, are buried. This three-acre park, located at Green Street and Blaine Avenue, was donated by members of the Blaine family and designed in 1920 by Carl Rust Parker. Although many of the plantings have changed over time, the historic intent remains the same, and the serene park continues to honor the memory of James G. Blaine with dignified simplicity.

Blaine died in Washington, D.C., on January 27, 1893, and was buried there in Oak Hill Cemetery. Harriet Stanwood Blaine returned from her Washington, D.C., home to spend her final years at the Blaine House. When she died in Maine in 1903, she too was buried in Washington. In 1920, with approval from the Blaine family, the State of Maine received permission to re-inter them in the new park. The legislature authorized funds for improvements as "an expression of our gratitude for his services to us and of our deep respect for his memory."[8] Blaine had been dead for more than twenty-five years by the time that the Blaine Memorial was built, but he was so highly regarded that visitors paid their respects even during construction.

The park is located about a mile from Blaine's home and is said to have been one of his favorite strolling places.

> *The tract is located on the highest part of the cemetery overlooking practically the entire city of Augusta with vistas down the Kennebec River for two or three miles.... During Mr. Blaine's residence in Augusta there was an old house on the tract and he was accustomed to frequently visit this residence and to spend considerable time in meditation and study there. He was particularly fond of the views which could be had from this spot.* [9]

Parker's plan for the memorial featured three key areas: access from Blaine Avenue and Forest Grove Cemetery, plantings, and the gravesites of the Blaines. Visitors entered the park on a narrow, horseshoe-shaped lane that passed under a canopy of elms. They arrived at a small parking area near a stone terrace overlook where they could pay their respects while also appreciating "the State's choicest panorama."[10] A large set of stone stairs connected the memorial to Forest Grove Cemetery below. Opposite the terrace were the Blaines' gravesites, which were set in a semicircle, bordered by a granite walkway and backed by a curved granite bench and shrubs. Two slate tablets covered the graves; James G. Blaine's included a long epitaph, while Harriet Stanwood Blaine's showed only her name and her birth and death dates.

On this three-acre lot Parker proposed 2,787 plants, mostly trees and shrubs that lined the lane and defined the park's boundaries. There were 36 elms, 356 viburnums, 267 roses, and more than 100 each of Japanese barberry, mockorange, aromatic sumacs, and high-bush blueberries, among many other varieties and quantities of plants.[11]

The Olmsteds often worked with clients who contributed ideas about the development of their projects. Such was the case with Harriet Blaine Beale and her family; Parker wrote that they did not want "any costly mausoleum or some other form of monumental work." They preferred simple slate gravestones (laid flat, not upright), stone seats with a back and no inscription, and a stone terrace projecting out over a bank.[12] Mrs. Beale spent many hours on site with Parker; at one point he removed staging on the unfinished fieldstone wall so that she and her sister could fully understand its effect. Mrs. Beale seems to have had final say on many aspects of the project, from the wording of the grave markers, to the location and design of the stone seat, to the type of granite used for the bench, to viewing the rhododendrons before they were installed.

Parker also worked closely with Governor Milliken, who requested, for example, that granite for the seat come from Maine rather than Boston. Parker also advocated for key parts of the design that others failed to appreciate. He noted that some members of the "council" thought that the entrance from the cemetery was "entirely unnecessary and a needless expense."[13] Parker maintained that this approach was "absolutely essential to the development of the lot" and that Mrs. Beale would be highly disappointed if it were to be abandoned.

Much of Parker's design, specifically the horseshoe lane, stone terrace and steps, granite bench, and gravesites, was installed as planned, along with numerous plants. Overall, the park

ABOVE: *An engraved marker briefly tells of the Olmsteds' contribution at the Blaine Memorial.*

suffered when Governor Milliken left office at the end of 1920 and legislators temporarily refused to authorize further work. Construction stalled in the spring of 1921 but resumed in the summer. Despite repeated requests by the Olmsteds to oversee the work, they were not consulted. The result was disastrous for the plants, as many had not been properly installed and mulched for the winter or tended in the spring, leaving them as "merely sticks." Others were dead altogether. Fifty percent of the plants needed replacing less than a year after installation. The Olmsteds were told that replacements would be made in the fall, but not necessarily in keeping with their design. Writing to Mrs. Beale in August of 1921, the Olmsteds said they were "far from satisfied with present conditions, but are in no way to blame for them."[14]

According to a landscape assessment completed by Mohr & Seredin Landscape Architects in 1998, little is known about work at the memorial since the 1920s. What remained of the original plants has declined or died, and half of the horseshoe lane was removed for security reasons in the 1970s. The park is owned by the state but maintained by the City of Augusta; in 1998 the city and state's plan to improve the landscape mainly addressed the condition of trees and shrubs. Much of the ensuing work was intended to improve security (as in trimming lower branches of trees and removing shrub thickets), reduce maintenance, and remove "eyesores." The work also included a new black iron fence along Blaine Street. Only pedestrians are allowed inside the park today.

Today, Blaine Memorial Park remains a little-known historic landscape designed by the country's preeminent landscape architects in the 1920s. Despite the loss of plant material, the park continues to offer a quiet refuge in which to honor history, through the Blaine gravesites and through the Olmsteds' work, as well as to enjoy views of the greater Augusta landscape.

BELOW. *Carl Rust Parker advocated for this stairway connection between the Blaine Memorial and Forest Grove Cemetery.*

CHAPTER 3

Camden's Historic Gems: the Village Green, the Camden Amphitheatre, and Harbor Park

From Captain John Smith and Samuel de Champlain to Louise Dickinson Rich and more recent visitors, writers have long described Camden as a particularly beautiful coastal Maine town. Once "just another seaport and fishing town,"[1] Camden is now an especially attractive destination for visitors. In addition, nearby Camden Hills State Park (pp.161–163), one of the earliest state parks in the country, sees the largest day-use of any park in Maine.

Camden's notable selection of designed landscapes is to a great extent the legacy of several of the town's civic-minded summer residents, notably Mary Louise Bok Zimbalist, her father, Cyrus H.K. Curtis, and John Gribbel, all from Philadelphia, and Chauncey Keep of Chicago. Mary Louise Bok and her fellow donors had the vision and means to create a green town center worthy of the surrounding natural landscape. Mrs. Bok also had the foresight to bring to the small town of Camden two of the most important landscape architects of the twentieth century, Fletcher Steele and Frederick Law Olmsted, Jr.

Mary Louise Bok partially funded the Camden Village Green and donated the land and landscape improvements for the Camden Public Library and Harbor Park. During the Depression, she donated funds to remodel the Camden Opera House. She also sponsored numerous beautification projects in Camden and Rockport and generously supported the hospital, fire station, YMCA, and local road and waterfront improvements, providing jobs to many residents.

The Camden Village Green

Camden is a charming village. Many tourists motor through and with this little park developed to its prettiest, everyone passing through the town will, I hope, in the future remember it as a charming place.[2]
— Mary Louise Bok, 1927

Although many New England towns were built around central open spaces that served as pastures, gathering places, and town centers, this was not the case with Camden's village green. While the New Haven Green and Boston Common, for example, remain as historic centers of their cities, Camden, like many coastal Maine towns, was originally oriented toward the sea. The existence of a "restful spot of green in the heart of the town"[3] was due to the later efforts of the Camden benefactors named above.

ABOVE: *A corner of Harbor Park shows the Olmsteds' plantings and paths in this ca. 1934 postcard. The red roofs of Fletcher Steele's pavilions at the amphitheatre appear in the background.*

The Camden Village Green is located at the corner of Chestnut and Elm streets across from the historic Camden Opera House and adjacent to Chestnut Street Baptist Church. The green was the site of the Bay View House, a summer hotel with sweeping views of the harbor. It burned to the ground in 1917, leaving the last remaining open lot in downtown Camden. By May of 1927 Cyrus Curtis, Mary Louise Bok, John Gribbel, and Chauncey Keep had purchased the half-acre property. Mrs. Bok approached the Olmsted firm, hoping the job was not too insignificant for them, to design a small public park.

In turning to Frederick Law Olmsted, Jr., Mrs. Bok sought the advice of the firm best known nationally for its work on parks, both in major cities and in vast wilderness areas. By this time Olmsted had been a senior partner for thirty years, had planned the extension of the park system in Washington, D.C., and had designed the Boston metropolitan park system. As he began work in Camden, he was selecting the one hundred sites for the California state park system, was serving on the Secretary of the Interior's committee concerned with Yosemite National Park and the Niagara Reservation, and was participating in the planning of Acadia National Park and its scenic drives. Olmsted could draw on a remarkably wide range of experience in dealing with the design issues for all of the Camden sites.[4]

Landscape architect Leon H. Zach, a member of and later a partner in the Olmsted firm, served as site inspector for the Village Green project. At his first visit to the site in 1927, Zach described a bare lot with numerous elm trees and a boundary fence in poor condition. Zach concurred with Mrs. Bok's wish for "a place of simple quiet beauty, as much unadorned as possible."[5] He noted that "simplicity and ruggedness of plant types chosen are the key notes in my mind," as maintenance was a concern, and that plantings should screen out surrounding buildings. He thought that a simple war memorial could add a "sparkle of interest."

Following a site visit a month later, Olmsted, Jr., outlined his proposals to Mrs. Bok. He agreed with her wish for a simple design, much like an old New England common or village green, but wanted to correct two main "defects," a lack of trees and the poorly shaped landform. He suggested trees of different heights to screen the neighboring buildings: additional elms (transplanted from the surrounding countryside) for the upper story; shad or crabapples for the middle layer; and a single type of old-fashioned shrub, such as lilac, elderberry, or mockorange (which was ultimately planted) for the lowest level.

With detailed instructions about stockpiling topsoil, protecting elm roots, and reseeding the lawn, Olmsted proposed re-grading the site to create a longer sweep of lawn visible from downtown. He suggested improvements to the adjacent church service road and location of paths. He preferred no fence but noted that one was probably needed along Elm Street to protect the turf. He specified simple wooden rails set into rough-cut granite posts, "as was customary around New England commons in the last century."

ABOVE: *The Camden Village Green (clockwise from top left): the elms as seen from Chestnut Street, before the Olmsteds' involvement; the re-graded lawn following the Olmsteds' improvements; granite post and chain fencing next to the historic elms, 1930; the elms surrounded by concrete sidewalk.*

The installation at the green began in October 1927. As is often the case, the installation differed from the landscape architect's proposals. The wooden rail fence became one of smooth-cut granite posts and heavy iron chains, set farther from the existing elms than Olmsted intended, with a concrete sidewalk surrounding the elms. In a 1928 memo,[6] he outlined specific solutions for the green's aesthetic problems (including moving the fence and planting a continuous stretch of lawn between the elms, which did occur), but his planting suggestions apparently were never carried out; in visits in 1936 and 1949, he expressed disappointment at how the leggy shrubs failed to screen the neighboring buildings.

After World War II, the town erected a temporary honor roll listing the names of Camden residents who died in the war. In 1947 citizens wished to replace the honor roll with a permanent memorial. Although Mary Louise Bok Zimbalist objected to the concept, she hired the Olmsted

Brothers to design a new memorial. The town approved the memorial flagpole that exists today, which Mrs. Zimbalist presented to the town in June 1950.

As with many public landscapes following World War II, the green suffered a period of decline. The elms fell to Dutch elm disease, the lawn became threadbare, and townspeople avoided spending time there. In 1990 the Camden Garden Club received town approval to improve the neglected space as a way to commemorate the town's bicentennial the following year. The club proposed a new entrance and sitting area at the corner of Chestnut and Main streets, a memorial garden, and extensive beds to replace much of the lawn. The plan was publicized at the same time that the green was listed in the National Register of Historic Places as part of the Chestnut Street Historic District. Since the proposal was a major departure from Olmsted's original concept, groups such as the Chestnut Street Historic Society and the Maine Olmsted Alliance for Parks and Landscapes opposed it.

Armed with new knowledge regarding the historic significance of the green, the garden club and the town hired Heritage Landscapes, based in Vermont and Connecticut, to prepare a plan that favored a more historically sympathetic revitalization. Parts of this plan were installed and others were adjusted to address modern concerns, such as screening the neighboring driveway with evergreens. Work on the site began in 1997 with replanting the large bed along the driveway, improving the gravel path, and removing modern flower beds near the 1940s memorial.

The Veterans Honor Roll Monument was added in 2007, following a competition to commemorate post-World War II veterans. The winning entry was designed by Camden architect Christopher Glass, who proposed an elegantly simple, curving granite wall engraved with the names of Camden veterans. Glass aesthetically and functionally linked his proposal to Olmsted's design for the Village Green and the 1940s memorial. The profile of the new monument reflects the curve of the 1940s memorial, and the monument itself completes the visual screen intended by Olmsted. Glass proposed a buffer of shrubs so that a visitor could experience the memorial in its own "room" and so that it would not intrude on the green's historic design. Ultimately, this part of Glass's design was left out, so that the new memorial, at seven feet high and thirty feet long, is visible to drivers and pedestrians.

Today, with its small size and relatively simple design, the Camden Village Green is not as prominent as the town's other historic landscapes, and visitors driving into town, enjoying the views of downtown's brick architecture and the Camden Hills, may not even notice it. On a warm summer day, however, those in the know meet under a canopy of stately shade trees and continue to enjoy a restful spot of green in the heart of town, exactly as Mary Bok envisioned.

THE CAMDEN LIBRARY AMPHITHEATRE

I want all my places to seem the home of children and lovers. I want them to be comfortable and if possible slightly mysterious by day, with vistas and compositions appealing to the painter. I want them to be delirious in the moonlight.... [7] — FLETCHER STEELE, 1926

The Village Green was a prelude to two larger projects just one-quarter mile away, the library amphitheatre of Fletcher Steele and the harbor-side park of Frederick Law Olmsted, Jr. In 1927, work was underway on the Village Green, and the cornerstone had been laid for a new library on land donated in 1916 by Mary Bok. Following their work on the green, the Olmsted firm was the logical choice to serve as landscape architects of the library grounds. However, in Mrs. Bok's absence, the Library Committee had hired landscape architect Fletcher Steele instead. Steele had been recommended by his friend Charles J. Loring, one of the architects of the Camden library. For design of the adjoining Harbor Park, Mrs. Bok returned to Olmsted. The two landscape architects worked independently and with contrasting styles but maintained a reluctant collaboration throughout these projects, which many consider to be "a synthesis of genius."[8]

Fletcher Steele was considered one of the top landscape architects in the country when he began working in Camden. He had opened his Boston practice in 1913 and was known for his responsiveness to clients, appreciation for history and modern art, sense of proportion and balance, and his "ability to create a powerful volume of space that is both practicably usable and emotionally transporting."[9]

The design philosophy for the library grounds came from Mrs. Bok, who wanted the property to serve all activities suited to a town library, in the broadest way. Steele responded by designing an open theater and, radically, choosing not to align it on axis with the library itself. Instead he oriented the theater at a 45-degree angle to the library for a clear view of the harbor, which also meant that the theater would serve as the upper end of the view from the harbor. This arrangement broke sharply with long-established Beaux-Arts principles, one of which called for landscapes to be aligned on axis with architecture, in essence placing the landscape second in importance. By breaking tradition at the amphitheatre, Steele accomplished several objectives: the harbor scenery was secured, a powerful volume of space was created, and the garden became less subordinate to the building.[10]

Steele's planting plan straddled practical and modern concerns. At a time when plants were often gathered from the countryside, Steele used mainly those that grew within a twenty-mile radius of

BELOW: *The Camden Library Amphitheatre, ca. 1930, with construction nearly completed. Fletcher Steele's two brick pavilions are yet to be built, and circular pedestals await Steele's light posts.*

Camden: white spruce, American elm, maple, arborvitae, and hemlock. He also designed around existing elms and screened unpleasant views with hemlocks. Steele's biographer, Robin Karson, notes that his rather abstract use of trees was unprecedented in the history of American landscape design. In a modern style, he planted delicate white birch trees to "create a series of vertical punctuations across the sweep of broad terraces, varying and enlivening the curves."[11]

Another key component was the stonework that formed the horseshoe-shaped terraces, broad stairways, and planters, all created by Henry Rice, the rock expert at the Olmsted office. The stonework was a major undertaking during a time when materials were transported by horse-drawn carts.

Steele designed two pavilions that still serve important functions, whether viewed from inside or outside the amphitheatre. From inside, they punctuate the ends of the horseshoe and frame the harbor scenery, and from Harbor Park, they appear as gateways into the amphitheatre. The pavilions also create a sense of continuity between architecture and landscape, as the brick matches that of the library. Each pavilion is flanked by a wrought-iron arch set into brick piers and shaded by sprawling Camperdown elms.

In 1931 Mrs. Bok donated a bronze sculpture entitled *Two Little Fauns*, created by Benjamin Kurtz, a sculptor from Maryland known for his portraits. For *Two Little Fauns*, Steele designed a small garden with a naturalistic pool and low-growing evergreens at the base of the double staircase leading from the library to the amphitheatre.

In 1988 the library and amphitheatre were listed in the National Register of Historic Places as part of the High Street Historic District. In 2006 additional documentation was added regarding the amphitheatre, and it is now considered significant on a national level for its importance to modern landscape architecture.[12]

In 1997, prompted by a planned underground expansion of the library, the Board of Trustees hired Heritage Landscapes to prepare the *Historic Landscape Report and Preservation Treatment Plan*

OPPOSITE: *The newly-restored amphitheatre with Fletcher Steele's pavilions, lights, and horseshoe terraces, is a shady respite on a bright summer day.*
BELOW: *Fletcher Steele's brick pavilions frame the entrance to the Camden Library Amphitheatre, shortly after construction.*

for the Amphitheatre and Harbor Park.[13] Camden residents strongly rejected the plan and formed the independent Commission on the Library Grounds. The commission then turned to Heritage Landscapes to create a "consensus-building" plan in 2000. After much community input, Heritage Landscapes prepared the 2004 *Camden Amphitheater Restoration and Harbor Park Rehabilitation Plan*, which became the basis for recent restorations. This plan also led to the formation of the Conservancy for Camden Harbor Park and Amphitheatre, whose role was to ensure the proper restoration and ongoing stewardship of these two important landscapes.[14]

To restore the amphitheatre, workers pruned mature trees and removed others that had self-seeded. After re-grading the soil for better drainage, they planted new ferns, evergreens, and birch trees. They re-pointed the granite risers and steps, planted wild strawberries and sedums in the steps, and repaired Steele's unique lights. The community enthusiastically celebrated the amphitheatre's rededication at a ceremony in September 2004. Further restoration included repairs to the pavilions, one of which now serves as a public information kiosk and community event ticket office.

The next area to receive attention was the Fauns' Garden. In 2007 the Conservancy removed overgrown cedars and yews, replaced the plumbing and water pump, and restored the statue as a functioning fountain. Oddly, restoration revealed that the fountain was most likely designed to be installed in a pool, not freestanding, as it is at the library. The director of the Conservancy noted that the statue had four places from which water could spout, but three had been closed when the statue was originally installed at the library. In front of the Fauns' Garden are the newly restored Arabesque Gardens planted with low-growing evergreen shrubs, as shown on Steele's original drawing and in historic photographs.

Almost all of Steele's plan was originally installed as designed. An exception was his *Compass of the Winds*, an art piece designed with an antique millstone, cut granite, and bronze. The circular bronze sections were cast in the early 1930s but never installed; they were placed in storage for more than seventy years until the library acquired them as part of the restoration of the grounds. In an interesting turn of events, an old millstone found abandoned in Harbor Park matched the dimensions of Steele's bronze ring perfectly. In 2007 the *Compass of the Winds* was finally installed on the path leading from the Fauns' Garden to the amphitheatre.

With the complete restoration of the library grounds and amphitheatre, the next step is to designate the amphitheatre as a National Historic Landmark for its "exceptional value or quality in illustrating or interpreting the heritage of the United States."[15]

CAMDEN'S HARBOR PARK

The Camden Shore Front Park, as it was called in the Olmsted records, was to be a distinctive part of the town's public landscapes, connecting the active cultural center marked by the library and amphitheatre to Camden's historic harbor, which was both a working waterfront and a recreational setting.

While Steele was known for his brilliant manipulation of natural materials to create a work of art, as seen in the horseshoe terraces, boulders, and native plants in the amphitheatre, the Olmsteds intended their parks to look as though they had always been there, so that visitors were not aware of the art and engineering behind the project. At Harbor Park the attention of visitors was therefore focused on the view of the harbor, one of the Olmsteds' so-called "passages of scenery," rather than on an ornamental, obviously manipulated landscape. [16]

Traditionally, Frederick Law Olmsted, Sr., and his successors designed parks on a grand scale, with a preferred size of 300 acres. Harbor Park in Camden was smaller than two acres. The larger parks were intended to provide refuge from the rigors of urban life, a situation not necessary in Camden, where the park is a distinct part of the small village. Views to and from the harbor formed the basis of Olmsted, Jr.'s

1928 report and design for the park. He intended to open up the view from the library and amphitheatre towards the harbor, creating an attractive foreground to be seen from both the harbor and library.

As with any large landscape project, the first part of installation concerned earthwork. In Harbor Park that involved re-grading the slope between Atlantic Avenue and the water, rebuilding the seawall and retaining wall near the Megunticook River, and building a boat ramp. At Mrs. Bok's request, local labor was used to relieve the effects of the severe economic depression.

Olmsted's plan featured walking paths that curved gracefully from street level to the shore. Olmsted was adept at using plants to solve functional and aesthetic problems, such as to block out unsightly buildings beyond the park, provide privacy for seating areas, frame views, and stabilize steep slopes to prevent erosion.

In contrast to Steele's minimalist approach to planting the amphitheatre, Olmsted proposed large, organically shaped beds along the edges of the main roads and interior paths. These were filled with native and non-native varieties, in keeping with a tradition established by Frederick Law Olmsted, Sr., who based his landscape designs on native plants and enriched the palette and scenery with ornamentals. At Harbor Park the younger Olmsted proposed North American natives such as snowberry, American arborvitae, lowbush blueberry, common juniper, and laurel, among others. He complemented these with old-fashioned plants such as Japanese barberry, weigela, lilac, rose, and tree hydrangea. Historic photographs show that the park was built substantially as planned by the Olmsteds, and by 1935, many of the plants had flourished.

While no major intrusions or alterations had taken place since the park's construction in the 1930s, by the 1990s many plants had disappeared from the borders, and cars and buildings were visible from inside the park. The carefully structured views intended by Olmsted were lost. Paths and lawns were in poor condition, and the original benches had been replaced by others lacking historic character.

The 1997 *Historic Landscape Report and Preservation Treatment Plan for the Amphitheatre and Harbor Park* proved as controversial for the park as it was for the amphitheatre. In 2004 after resolving issues raised by citizens over cutting trees and re-grading the hillside, the library board of trustees moved forward with rehabilitating Harbor Park. Today the park recaptures the spirit of Olmsted's design with outstanding views of the harbor, mahogany benches fashioned after Olmsted models, sweeping lawns, and hundreds of trees, shrubs, and groundcovers.

Camden Harbor Park is not only a historic gem but a much-loved green space in the heart of downtown. Following the extensive rehabilitation of the amphitheatre and Harbor Park, Robin Karson noted that "not all historic landscapes can be conserved, but all historic landscapes that give so much pleasure to the people who use them and that figure so centrally in the history of American design certainly should be. That the people of Camden have found the energy, spirit, and funds to make sure that this happens deserves the highest praise."[17]

ABOVE: *At the Camden Library,* Two Little Fauns *by Benjamin Kurtz was recently restored as a functioning fountain.*
OPPOSITE: *The Camden Library and the sloping lawn of Harbor Park are seen at left in the foreground of Mount Battie. The Mount Battie tower is just visible on the hilltop.*

OPPOSITE: *This ca. 1935 view of the Asticou Terraces shows Joseph Curtis's naturalistic stone steps that lead to the First Lookout and eventually to Thuya Lodge.*

CHAPTER 4

NORTHEAST HARBOR: A LEGACY OF KINDRED SPIRITS

At Northeast Harbor on Mount Desert Island, three treasured gardens come to us from three designers of widely different backgrounds. At the center of this collaboration was Charles Savage, who was not trained as a landscape designer, but whose lifetime of care preserved and extended the work of Joseph Curtis and Beatrix Farrand. Joseph Curtis created Thuya Lodge as his summer home and personal creation, and the Asticou Terraces carried his style and creativity from his hilltop home to the shore below. Charles Savage used plants obtained when Beatrix Farrand dismantled her Reef Point estate (pp. 166–168) to create the Thuya Garden and the Asticou Azalea Garden. Savage served as designer and custodian of all three properties for many years, and all bear the mark of his particular creative skills and interest.

Mount Desert Island, called Pemetic, or "sloping land," by the Wabanaki Indians who camped and fished there, got its present-day name from Samuel de Champlain, who landed on the island on September 5, 1604, and named it "Ile des Monts Déserts" for its bare and rocky mountains. Later settlers developed farming, fishing, shipbuilding, and quarrying industries. Nineteenth-century artists, sportsmen, and writers—"rusticators"—made Mount Desert a destination for visitors, and by the 1880s, there were more than thirty hotels,

among them the Savage family's Asticou Inn, countless guest houses, and the first of numerous "cottage" estates of wealthy vacationers. By 1900, visitors to the area enjoyed an active social scene, with tennis matches, lawn parties, horse shows, and more. There was also great interest in experiencing nature on foot, which sparked a period of trail building by individuals and by Village Improvement Societies. In fact, visitors to Thuya Lodge arrived mainly on foot, coming up Asticou Hill on the Terraces Trail and picking up trails to Eliot Mountain, Jordan Pond, and Harbor Brook.

In 1901 George Dorr and other summer residents established the Hancock County Trustees of Public Reservations to permanently preserve land for public use, such as for hiking trails. By 1913 the Trustees had acquired 6,000 acres, which they offered to the federal government. President Woodrow Wilson accepted the offer and created the Sieur de Monts National Monument[1] within what is now Acadia National Park (pp. 169–172); by 1915, more than 200 miles of trails existed on the island.

The island today is characterized by its natural beauty and ocean views, and by its tourist facilities and attractions. It is the site of Somes Sound, the only fjord on the east coast of the United States; of Cadillac Mountain, the highest point

on the North Atlantic seaboard; and of Acadia National Park, visited annually by millions of people. The coastal areas of Northeast Harbor look across at neighboring Southwest Harbor or toward the distant Cranberry Isles. Here in the village of Asticou, Savage's grandfather, Augustus, built his inn in 1883, and Joseph Henry Curtis, a Boston landscape designer and civil engineer who had worked with Frederick Law Olmsted, Sr., constructed his Thuya Lodge between 1912 and 1916.

THE SAVAGE FAMILY AND JOSEPH CURTIS: A FRUITFUL FRIENDSHIP

In the late 1800s, prior to building the Asticou Inn, Augustus Savage and his wife, Emily, opened their private home to seasonal visitors, a common practice before hotels were constructed on Mount Desert Island. Their hospitality and the scenery of the island attracted many landscape painters, among them George Hollingsworth and Harrison Brown, along with Harvard President Charles Eliot and his friend, Joseph Curtis. The Eliot, Curtis, and Savage families became fast friends. Augustus Savage and his sons eventually built the Eliots' summer cottage, and Augustus sold Curtis the land on which he later built his Thuya Lodge.[2]

Curtis summered in Northeast Harbor from 1880 until his death in 1928. He built three summer homes at different times on his hillside property, sharing the last two with his wife, Amelie Lewandowska, and son, Henry. Thuya Lodge, a three-bedroom, one- and one-half-story rustic cottage, was their final retreat. Curtis's family life is a tragic story; Amelie died in 1913, just one year after construction began on Thuya Lodge, and Henry died five years later.

With its wooden clapboards, wooden roof shingles, and numerous windows overlooking the native woods and two small fields, the cottage was well suited to its site. Curtis named the property Thuya Lodge for Mount Desert Island's numerous stands of northern white cedar, *Thuja occidentalis*,[3] and specifically for the grove surrounding the cottage. He also designed the Asticou Terraces, a series of trails, granite steps, and rustic shelters that connected the house with the shore below.

Charles Savage was an eighteen-year-old student at boarding school in Boston when his innkeeper father died in 1922. Abandoning his plan to study architecture at the Massachusetts Institute of Technology, he returned to Northeast Harbor to help his mother run the Asticou Inn. With his family, he devoted his considerable energies to it for the rest of his life. Savage "developed a talent for landscape design by reading widely in the field and becoming knowledgeable in all its aspects."[4] He was also a talented innkeeper and accomplished woodcarver. His carvings and signs are still displayed throughout the island at inns, in private homes, at the Northeast Harbor Library, and at Thuya Garden.

Savage's return to Northeast Harbor brought him in closer contact with Joseph Curtis at nearby Thuya Lodge. The two were years apart in age and had different careers but were united in their devotion to this beautiful section of the coast. Together, between 1922 and 1928, they developed a plan to protect Curtis's beloved land and lodge in the permanent Asticou Terraces Trust. Savage became the first trustee after Curtis's death and served in that capacity for thirty-seven years.

THE ASTICOU TERRACES: A MOUNTAINSIDE TREASURE

People who take the time and trouble to walk over the reservation find features here which they do not often discover in other places, and many have stated that the element of pleased surprise, with desire to return, is perhaps the chief reward.[5] —CHARLES K. SAVAGE, 1954–55

The Asticou Terraces are part of a 140-acre preserve located on Peabody Drive (Route 3) overlooking the harbor. The Terraces are open to the public, thanks to Joseph Curtis's public-spirited nature. His first donation came in 1909, when he allowed residents of the town of Mount Desert access to the harbor dock, known as Asticou Terraces Landing. He also opened the hillside paths to public use in 1912 and established the Asticou Terraces Trust in 1928, donating about twenty acres in trust to townspeople. Curtis felt that: "[T]he Asticou Terraces Trust has an important function in the entire region of the upper end of Northeast Harbor. Over a limited area it can provide a place of visitation embracing walks, shelters, shore, trees, shrubs, books, with an enduring assurance of meticulous care, which is so important for aesthetic enjoyment."[6]

The trail that exists today is due to the combined efforts of Joseph Curtis and Charles Savage. In addition to creating the stone steps and paths that crisscross the steep slope, Curtis built two lookouts and a shelter along the path, all of which exist today. In the decade following Curtis's death, Savage resurfaced some of the paths, added fencing, and created additional lookouts based on Curtis's model. These feature weathered cedar posts and railings, rustic benches, and shingled roofs painted red, like those in the Thuya Garden's pavilions. The largest of the shelters is the Stone Lookout added in 1933, located immediately above the Curtis Memorial.

The Joseph Henry Curtis Memorial was designed by Savage, in consultation with sculptor Robert Tait McKenzie, and was dedicated in 1933. This spot was said to be a favorite of Curtis's, and he had improved it with coping stones and boulders to create an area for open-air performances. This large, level, inviting terrace is backed by a high granite ledge; a low granite wall lined with native blueberry bushes forms the outside edge. The ground is paved with irregular granite stones, and native groundcovers fill the gaps between the stones.

Today, from the parking area on Peabody Drive, you can still climb the quarter-mile trail to the overlooks, lodge, and gardens, just as Curtis intended. Visitors may also drive to the lodge but parking is limited, following Curtis's original wish to discourage "the excursion element," or sightseers who arrived by car.[7] The parking area also leads to the Asticou Terraces Landing, a boat landing designed by Charles Savage's brother, George, in the 1930s, as Curtis had suggested in his will. In addition to a float and pier structure, the area included a pavilion, bench shelter, rock garden and other plantings, lighting, and a flagpole. In the 1980s the landing was rebuilt in a joint effort between the town of Mount Desert and the Asticou Terraces Trust. Today visitors can dock their boats and follow the terrace trails to the lodge.

An ongoing issue at historic sites open to the public is how to meet modern needs, such as parking and increased numbers of visitors, while protecting historic character. The Mount Desert Land

and Garden Preserve has begun to assess the landscape and architecture of Asticou Terraces and Landing, Thuya Lodge and Garden, and the Azalea Garden. In 2007 the Preserve hired Tuckerbrook Conservation of Lincolnville, Maine, to prepare a conservation report on Thuya Lodge. At the same time, Richardson & Associates, landscape architects from Saco, Maine, prepared a cultural landscape assessment for the Thuya Garden and Asticou Terraces. Both consultants identified key historic features and established a framework for making informed management and maintenance decisions in the future. The Preserve has already implemented some recommendations, such as addressing climate control in the lodge and restoring the garden's reflecting pond to its original dimensions.

THE ASTICOU AZALEA GARDEN: AN ARTFUL MELDING OF EAST AND WEST

[The garden] would permit all passersby to witness a display of color the brilliance of which would be doubled by the reflections in the pools. No other situation so easily permitting such an arrangement and display exists on the south side of Mount Desert.[8]
—CHARLES K. SAVAGE, 1956

Initially, just setting up the trusteeship and seeing to the care and maintenance of Curtis's properties must have been a major undertaking for Savage, especially coupled with the responsibilities of running the Asticou Inn. He and his wife, Katherine, devoted themselves to what was then "the acknowledged center of social activity on the south side of Mount Desert Island."[9]

Savage was one of the directors of the Reef Point Gardens, established by Beatrix Farrand as a teaching and horticultural institution in Bar Harbor. In 1955 Farrand made the difficult decision to dismantle her gardens and donate the library, drawings, and herbarium specimens to the landscape architecture department at the University of California at Berkeley. She sold Reef Point to a long-time friend, architect Robert Patterson, who then sold the plant collection to Charles Savage. With financial assistance from many summer residents, especially John D. Rockefeller, Jr., Savage located two sites for Farrand's plants: the fields of Thuya Lodge and an alder swamp across from the Asticou Inn. Savage designed the latter as the Asticou Azalea Garden.

According to landscape architect Patrick Chassé, Savage insisted that his main intent for the Asticou Azalea Garden "was not to create a traditional Japanese space, but primarily to provide a sympathetic setting for the magnificent azaleas...."[10] The exotic azaleas, combined with the site's abundant water, resulted in Savage's Japanese-inspired design of wet and dry pools, weathered Maine granite, contemplative rooms, and secluded paths. Savage also used native plants extensively– Canadian hemlock, pitch pine, lowbush blueberry, bunchberry, and haircap moss.

An extensive crew assisted Savage with the construction of the garden. His daughter Mary Ann made colored pencil swatches to match the colors of various azalea blooms. Arthur "Mike" Coombs and his laborers made daily trips to Reef Point to dig by hand all of the shrubs and perennials. Local

excavating contractors and quarrymen rounded out the construction crew and even helped locate native plants to add to the garden.

Construction began with the excavation of the reflecting pond, and Savage formed additional ideas as the pond took shape. He studied books and illustrations of Japanese gardens and visited those in Boston and New York for inspiration. From the native landscape he gathered local beach stones and aged boulders; from demolished estates he acquired salvaged granite and roof tiles, all incorporated into the new garden. To create the Sand Garden, which was inspired by Ryoan-ji in Kyoto, Japan, and is perhaps the site's best-known and most authentically Japanese feature, Savage had crews fill the wetland and clear the alders. He then arranged weathered Maine granite "islands" in a "sea" of raked white sand from West Virginia.

Savage continued to maintain the Asticou Azalea Garden until 1966, when he donated it to the town of Mount Desert, just as Joseph Curtis had donated Thuya Lodge. Following a request by town officials, the Asticou Terraces Trust then took over care of the garden. (Savage lived nearby and continued to offer advice until his death in 1979.) The town was unable to provide as much attention and funding as the garden deserved, prompting summer residents to action. In 1971 David and Peggy Rockefeller had formed the nonprofit Island Foundation (now known as the Mount Desert Land and Garden Preserve) as a future repository for some of their Maine property; the Asticou Azalea Garden was added to this collection with the agreement that it would remain open to the public.

In the 1980s the Island Foundation had limited funds for maintaining the garden, but another benefactor, Mary Clark Rockefeller, generously provided financial assistance. The Foundation formed an all-volunteer garden committee whose members recognized the need for renovation and modern adaptations in the garden and commissioned a master plan by Landscape Design Associates of Bar Harbor, Maine. They also hired horticultural experts such as Fred Galle, the country's foremost authority on azaleas and rhododendrons at the time. During the 1980s, visitor access was improved with construction of a Japanese-inspired entrance gate near a new parking area and additional garden paths. Plants that had self-seeded were removed to favor the Farrand collection, and overgrown trees and shrubs were pruned to restore lost vistas. The two ponds were dredged and mugo pines were added along Route 3 to create a more secluded garden atmosphere.

The Asticou Azalea Garden is a fairly small garden with a wealth of detail at every turn. Visitors appreciate the varied textures of azaleas, smokebushes, rhododendrons, and ferns, among other plants, that line the narrow garden paths. Even the paths themselves are beautiful, as they are made of pink crushed granite, and garden workers carefully rake away footprints before the next day's visitors arrive. Paths wind past a heath garden set among native boulders, a stone bridge reflected in Great Pond, stone Japanese lanterns tucked into shady nooks, and magnificent specimen trees such as a flowering cherry and weeping hemlock.

Over the past several decades the garden's trustees, stewards, and

gardeners have continued Charles Savage's vision while recognizing the inevitable changes that occur with plants, ponds, and even increased automobile traffic. In recent years the Mount Desert Land and Garden Preserve purchased adjacent property and razed a small house in order to expand the garden and add another roadside buffer of evergreens, azaleas, and weathered granite boulders.

THUYA GARDEN: A HILLTOP SANCTUARY

The design was made to fit the site – not the other way around.[11] —CHARLES SAVAGE, 1964

W hen Joseph Curtis summered at Thuya Lodge, he maintained a small vegetable garden and an apple orchard and devoted his attention to the native landscape, specifically the hillside Asticou Terraces. As trustee of the Asticou Terraces after Curtis's death, Charles Savage opened Thuya Lodge, located at the top of the Terrace trail, to the public in 1931. He also began collecting botanical and horticultural books with the intention of creating a research library, which he opened there in the 1950s. The Lodge now houses a reception room and reading rooms on the first floor and the library upstairs. Thuya Garden as we know it today was built between 1956 and 1962, some twenty-eight years after Curtis's death.

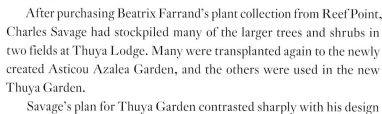

After purchasing Beatrix Farrand's plant collection from Reef Point, Charles Savage had stockpiled many of the larger trees and shrubs in two fields at Thuya Lodge. Many were transplanted again to the newly created Asticou Azalea Garden, and the others were used in the new Thuya Garden.

Savage's plan for Thuya Garden contrasted sharply with his design at the azalea garden. Whereas the latter featured curving paths, Thuya Garden was modeled after formal gardens with axes and perpendicular cross-axes punctuated by focal points. Savage created a "long vista" that was terminated by a pavilion at the upper elevation and a naturalistic pool at the lower end. To offset the "sheer rigidity," he cleverly created a diagonal cross axis between a second pavilion and the spring house.[12]

Savage was most likely influenced by Farrand's goals of landscape education and plant trials, as he referred to Thuya Garden, the Lodge, and the Asticou Terraces as "a philanthropic, botanical-landscape institution." Savage hoped that Thuya Garden would serve as a place for experimenting with plants, similar to Reef Point. His intent was to complement the existing native plants with "suitable introductions, many of which are well displayed in this wild setting."[13]

Recent research by Richardson & Associates revealed that it is not possible to identify what specific plants from Reef Point were actually installed at Thuya Garden or survive there today. Charles Savage wrote vaguely that "the finest and most outstanding specimens from Reef Point came to the Thuya Garden," and these are generally thought to include rhododendrons, azaleas,

OPPOSITE: *The formality of Thuya Garden's herbaceous borders contrasts with the surrounding native woods. Charles Savage's upper and lower pavilions are also visible in this 1990 view.*

BELOW: *Workers ready a dwarf Alberta spruce, moved from Reef Point, for its new home at Thuya Garden, as photographed by Charles Savage, ca. 1957.*

mountain laurels, and perennials such as globe thistle and *Helianthus*. Two documented plants from Reef Point are the dwarf Alberta spruces at the garden's main entrance.[14] In addition, the lead urn now found at the Upper Pavilion originally came from Reef Point, after moving with Farrand to Garland Farm (pp. 172–175). The large garden urn near the Reflecting Pool and the urn near the Lower Pavilion also were part of Farrand's collection. These were designed by Gouldsboro potter Eric Soderholtz in the early 1900s.

The biggest changes to Thuya Garden since Savage's time have been in the plants, which, by the 1980s, had become overgrown and out of proportion. Landscape architect Patrick Chassé recommended that one of the most important projects was to restore the perennial borders. Basing his work on historic photographs, he created a planting plan suggestive of Farrand's work at Reef Point and Savage's original plans for Thuya Garden; the result was a subtle color palette that flowed seamlessly from warm to cool and exaggerated the distance to the Upper Pavilion. (Today the planting scheme continues to evolve from year to year.) Chassé especially noted the skill with which Savage originally created the double-sided English borders, allowing visitors to stroll along both sides, an effect that Chassé re-created. He also designed the Evergreen Border adjacent to the dwarf Alberta spruces, where visitors can enjoy a variety of textures and colors among the labeled evergreens.

In addition to its exquisite plant collections, Thuya Garden is well known for its fine woodworking, much of which was designed by Savage. The large cedar entrance gates have multiple panels with carved scenes of birds, small animals, lady's slippers, cattails, ferns, and other natural scenes. The gates were designed by Savage, who also carved the lettered panels. The remainder was carved by Augustus Phillips, who also built the handsome cedar fence, including hand-hewn posts, lintels, and rails, to enclose the garden and deter deer.

Maintaining historic landscapes such as Thuya Garden, Asticou Terraces and Landing, and Asticou Azalea Garden and planning for their future require an enormous commitment of resources. The Island Foundation, now the Mount Desert Land and Garden Preserve, assumed ownership of the Asticou Azalea Garden in 1973 and the Thuya properties in 2000 and established a multi-million-dollar endowment fund for their care. The famed Abby Aldrich Rockefeller Garden designed by Beatrix Farrand will also eventually be turned over to the Preserve, thanks to the extraordinary generosity of the Rockefeller family.

In 2008 the Preserve celebrated the fiftieth anniversary of the opening of Asticou Azalea Garden and Thuya Garden with programs and exhibits of Charles Savage's landscape designs, illustrations, drawings, wood carvings, photographs, and handmade books. In addition, the Preserve commemorated the gardens' histories with a pair of well-illustrated and informative books by Letitia Baldwin, entitled *Two Island Gardens*.

When we visit and enjoy these extraordinary landscapes today, we can be grateful for the foresight and imagination of Curtis, Savage, and many others who for nearly one hundred years have enhanced and preserved these beautiful examples of the designed Maine landscape.

OPPOSITE: *Thuya Garden's cedar entrance gates, designed by Charles Savage, were carved by Savage and Augustus D. Phillips in the 1950s.*
BELOW: *A page from Charles Savage's ca. 1958 sketchbook illustrates the Upper Pavilion.*
FOLLOWING PAGES: *Kebo Valley Golf Course abuts the natural landscape of Acadia National Park.*

II. EDUCATION, RECREATION, AND REPOSE

CHAPTER 5

EDUCATIONAL ADVANCEMENTS: MAINE'S HISTORIC DESIGNED CAMPUSES

When Thomas Jefferson designed the campus of the University of Virginia in 1817, he planned what he called "an academical village," following a new American ideal that saw colleges "as communities in themselves–in effect as cities in microcosm."[1] In his 1984 landmark book *Campus: An American Planning Tradition*, Paul Venable Turner compared American schools and universities with their European counterparts and described the educational philosophy and goals that influenced campus planning and design in this country.

Many of America's early educators had studied in England at Oxford and Cambridge universities, which were organized as a group of collegiate halls or houses. These halls were built around quadrangles and were usually surrounded by walls to shelter young scholars from city distractions. Students slept, ate, and studied in their colleges, which had much in common with monasteries of earlier times. Some of the Scottish universities and Trinity College in Dublin also offered successful examples of small, largely residential centers of learning.[2] In continental Europe, on the other hand, at such places as the University of Bologna (founded in 1088) and the University of Paris ("the Sorbonne," dating to 1253), students lived on their own in the cities and, dressed in academic gowns, made their way to the rooms of their teaching masters. The city surrounded the university, and the college was part of the urban setting.

The founders of this nation's first schools thought the British model better suited their goals of providing educated clergy and leaders for a new society. The New England colonies led the way in setting up colleges and schools of this type, with Harvard College founded in 1636, Yale in 1701, and such academies as New Haven's Hopkins Grammar School dating to 1660.

For much of the eighteenth century, Maine was still frontier territory, despite its long history of exploration and settlement. Harvard and Dartmouth "satisfied the small demand on the part of those rich or ambitious enough to educate their sons as gentlemen."[3] But as the population of the area nearly doubled between 1784 and 1790, local leaders began looking for opportunities to locate "academical villages" in their own territory–institutions suited to the task, as set forth in the 1794 Bowdoin College charter, of "effectually promot[ing] Virtue and Piety, and the Knowledge of such of the Languages, and of the useful and liberal Arts and Sciences, as shall hereafter be directed...."[4]

The schools and colleges of Maine, like the public and private landscapes, owe much of their character to Maine's natural environment and to the imagination and insight of

those who oversaw their development. In chronological order of their founding, Berwick Academy, Bowdoin College, Colby College, Bates College, and the University of Maine at Orono all offer illustrations of the ideas that shaped American campus planning. In addition, these schools and colleges reflect to some extent the work of well-known landscape designers and campus planning firms, many of them also involved in the other private and public commissions that make up Maine's enduring landscape.

BERWICK ACADEMY: AN ENTERPRISING VILLAGE SCHOOL

I am afraid that when I went to Berwick Academy, I really cared more for the outside of the school than the inside. I remember a good deal more about the great view toward the mountains, or down river, and the boys and girls themselves, or even the ground sparrows and little field strawberries that grew in the thin grass, than I do about learning my lessons.[5]
— SARAH ORNE JEWETT, 1887

Berwick Academy was established in South Berwick in 1791, only two years after an act of the Massachusetts legislature required the citizens of Maine to provide publicly available education. The law, which had governed towns in Massachusetts since 1647, now called for District of Maine towns of more than one hundred householders to establish a "grammar school" or academy to prepare youths for university study. Such schools were not always free, but the towns had to provide some support (originally forty cents per student per year), and fees were to be kept modest and competitive. Attempts to provide state funding for education in Maine did not begin until 1828.[6]

By 1800, only seven towns in Maine had upper-level academies. York had set up its academy in 1701, and Wells in 1715, and for a time those schools served both younger children and the few in those areas whose families could manage further education. But in 1791, citizens of Berwick and nearby New Hampshire towns founded a separate secondary school, Berwick Academy, now the oldest continuing academy in Maine. Others that still exist followed in quick succession—Fryeburg Academy in 1792, Lincoln Academy in 1801, Hebron Academy in 1814—but by 1820 there were still only twenty-five schools in the state that provided what we now think of as secondary education.

Berwick Academy originally enrolled only boys and offered courses in languages, liberal arts, and sciences, in addition to the expected instruction in moral character and Christian doctrine. The board decided to admit girls in 1797 but rescinded their admission in 1813; only forty students could be accommodated, and preference would be given to boys as enrollment grew. In 1828 the board decided to answer the market demand to educate girls as well. They sold and moved the original school building, built a bigger school, and founded the South Berwick Female Seminary under the same roof as the boys' school. (The original 1791 building was reacquired in the 1960s, moved back to the campus, and restored for use as the admissions and alumni offices.)

Berwick Academy served as the comprehensive high school for the town of South Berwick until the 1950s, when it reverted to private status. For a time, it was a boarding school for boys and a day school for girls, until a middle school and lower school were added in the 1970s. The academy now enrolls about 600 day students in kindergarten through grade 12. The campus covers seventy-two acres and includes buildings for the lower, middle, and upper schools, with special facilities for arts, athletics, the sciences, and a library. The campus was first listed in the National Register of Historic Places

OPPOSITE: *Recent buildings, such as the Jeppesen Science Center (facing) and the Whipple Arts Center (right) surround a central quad at Berwick Academy.* **BELOW:** *This image of Berwick Academy's 1853 building, designed by Richard Upjohn of New York, appeared in* Ballou's Pictorial Drawing-Room Companion, *a popular nineteenth-century magazine. This building replaced an earlier structure destroyed by arson.*

ACADEMY AT SOUTH BERWICK, MAINE

in 1978. As of 1996, it is part of the expanded Berwick Academy Historic District, significant for its architecture, landscape architecture, and role in education.

One of the academy's best-known graduates was Sarah Orne Jewett, a member of the class of 1865. In her 1894 essay "The Old Town of Berwick," Jewett included notes on the school's history in a glowing account of the town, which she described as "an enterprising village."[7] Prominent among the school's founders was Colonel Jonathan Hamilton, whose Hamilton House (pp. 141–144) is an example of a historic designed landscape in the Colonial Revival style.

Jewett spoke fondly about Old Berwick's setting—the tidal river, with its gundalows, boats modeled after Egyptian scows, and the great forests and open fields surrounding the village. The original academy was housed in "a small and modest building… which cost about five-hundred pounds New England currency, built on the ten acre lot which Judge Chadbourne gave…." A second building was added around 1830. According to Jewett, "It had a high white belfry and fine rows of Lombardy poplars led up to it from the street. The old oaks were already decaying, but nobody thought to put young ones in their places. This was burnt in 1851, and the new building seems to have poorly replaced it…."[8]

Jewett's reference to the burnt building skipped over a tumultuous period in the history of Berwick. Between 1845 and 1855, "rum, murder, and arson"[9] kept the town in an uproar. A new cotton textile mill had brought in hundreds of transient millhands, many from rural Maine farms. The laborers' harsh working conditions, crowded tenements, and heavy drinking led to alarming outbreaks of violence. Local support was strong for the evangelical temperance movement that resulted in Maine's 1851 prohibition law, the first in the United States. With the exception of alcohol used in "medicinal" preparations such as Berwick's Dr. Trafton's Buckthorn Syrup, sales of alcoholic beverages were to be strictly controlled by a state agency. Meanwhile, the ready availability of rum and whiskey just over the river in New Hampshire kept the problems alive and local distributors enraged. Over three years, arsonists struck a number of buildings, with the climax coming in August 1851, when homes, a powder house, a mill storehouse, and, finally, the Berwick Academy building were destroyed.

A new schoolhouse, completed in 1853, was designed by Richard Upjohn of New York, in a style very similar to that of First Parish Church in Brunswick, also by Upjohn; Jewett was dismayed that the architect "should have shown so little imagination." This building was the school's main structure until the Fogg Memorial Building was constructed in 1894. The Upjohn building was then moved behind the new one, where it served as a gymnasium for some years; it was dismantled by 1903.

Fogg Memorial Building was designed in the Romanesque Revival style by Boston architect George A. Clough, a Maine native. The building, which had the important enhancement of electricity, served as the library for the town of South Berwick as well as for the academy, and also housed the school's science laboratories. Funding for the building came from the estate and family of William Hayes Fogg, a Berwick native and highly successful merchant in the shipping trade with China. Fogg and his wife, Elizabeth Perkins, had been world travelers and art collectors whose taste called for a new style of building.

The Fogg Building, a massive granite structure with large, Palladian-style windows and a bell tower, was a dramatic departure from the New England domestic style of the school's earlier

ABOVE: *Sarah Orne Jewett, beloved author of* Country of the Pointed Firs, *was a member of the Berwick Academy Class of 1865.*

South Berwick, Me. Fogg Memorial Berwick Academy, Founded 1791.

buildings. To provide a dignified setting for this center of learning, the Fogg family turned to the firm of Olmsted, Olmsted & Eliot for a landscape plan for the entrance and circulation surrounding the building. The Olmsteds planned a stone retaining wall, sweeping lawn, pedestrian paths and steps, and a horseshoe-shaped driveway for carriages. This 1894 plan is significant as one of the few designed in Maine while Olmsted, Sr., was part of the firm (the majority were designed after his sons succeeded him). The plan was implemented, though it was adapted over time through widening of the road and deterioration of some features. In the 1990s, parts of the plan were restored, including the Fogg Building's stone entrance path and steps. The stone retaining wall remains, and paths that the Olmsteds designed are in use or discernible in the landscape.

The Fogg family also turned to Sarah Orne Jewett, who asked her friend, Boston artist Sarah Wyman Whitman, to design fifty-two of the library's one hundred stained-glass windows, including a Civil War memorial stained-glass window on the second floor.[10] Whitman had an extensive career as a painter, designer of book covers and stained glass, interior decorator, author, poet, and teacher. She also served as the interior designer of the building and added frescoes and busts for the inspiration and education of students.[11]

Over time the windows at Berwick Academy fell into disrepair with faded paint, cracks, and sagging glass. Recognizing the building's historic significance, the academy hired a stained-glass professional to repair all of the Fogg Building windows in the 1990s. The academy also subsequently restored the Fogg Building's bell tower, marble mosaic flooring, and bas-relief sculpture placed by Sarah Whitman. In recognition of this work, Berwick Academy received a statewide historic preservation honor award from Maine Preservation in 2000.

Bowdoin College: A Dedication to the Common Good

The Colleges are...three in number, forming three sides of a square... [on] the east side of the twelve rod road; a neat fence encloses them with about six acres of land. A row of flourishing balm of gilead trees beautifully borders the square. To the south east, you enter a growth of pitch pine.... This is preserved with scrupulous care, and may be truly called an academic grove, affording a charming walk for the students. It is...carpeted with blueberry bushes, a few inches high, which yield in great abundance. I have seen a bunch of gathering them in a time....[12]
—A Gentleman from South Carolina, 1820

The same impetus that led to the founding of Berwick Academy prompted a group of clergymen, landowners, and lawyers from Portland, York, Falmouth, and Gorham to petition the state of Massachusetts for a college charter. Their concentrated efforts resulted in the 1794 charter for Bowdoin College. The college was to be funded from the sale of unsettled lands in the District of Maine as well as with support from the town that would house it. Although Portland, Freeport, Augusta, and other towns had their proponents, the final decision favored Brunswick, which offered "the degree of rural retreat, of isolation from urban temptations, that Americans were beginning to expect of colleges and academies."[13]

The name Bowdoin was chosen to honor James Bowdoin II, a former governor of Massachusetts and father of James Bowdoin III. At the time, the younger Bowdoin was a member of the governing body of Harvard and also a member of the Massachusetts Senate. His promised support of the new institution took the form of $1,000 in cash and 1,000 acres of saleable land in the town of Bowdoin, and in return the college took on his family name. He later donated collections of art, books, and scientific equipment and samples.

In 1802 the college opened. Eight students joined their president and professor, Rev. Joseph McKeen, in Massachusetts Hall, a two-story brick building that has served many purposes — including science laboratory (for the internationally renowned geologist Parker Cleaveland) and "cabinet of curiosities" (a museum housing James Bowdoin's scientific collection). By 1808, a brick student residence, Maine Hall, was added, along with two wood buildings, a chapel and a house for President McKeen. The four structures established the quadrangle format that is still a prominent feature of the central Bowdoin College campus.

Three more residence halls were built between 1808 and 1822; these were arranged in a brick row similar to the Yale campus of the time, where a row of five buildings faced the New Haven Green. Bowdoin's Romanesque stone chapel, designed by Richard Upjohn and constructed between 1844 and 1855, was set in the middle of the brick row, completing the eastern edge of the quadrangle. Early depictions show the buildings along the east and north sides facing a spacious, well-kept green surrounded by a rail fence.

Construction of buildings for specific academic purposes began with Adams Hall, added in 1861 to house the expanding Medical School of Maine (1821–1921). By 1900, a gymnasium and

ABOVE: *In his inaugural address, Bowdoin's first president, Joseph McKeen, famously stated that "literary institutions are founded and endowed for the common good and not for the private advantage of those who resort to them for education."*

OPPOSITE: *Massachusetts Hall, built in 1802, still centers one end of Bowdoin's historic quadrangle. Originally the building provided housing and classrooms for President McKeen and the first groups of students.*

theater, a science building, a large library, and a special building to house Bowdoin's art collection had been added; many of these were designed by well-known architects, notably Henry Vaughan and McKim, Mead and White. (Charles Follen McKim designed the Museum of Art's Walker Art Building, and the firm continued to design a number of neo-Georgian buildings around the central quad through the 1950s.) These buildings faced the quadrangle and were spaced apart, setting an approach that still distinguishes the Bowdoin campus: a variety of architectural styles, unified in their use of brick and stone, around an open green, set apart yet open to the surrounding community. Tall elms originally shaded parts of the quadrangle. Today, tall, old maples, oaks, and one surviving elm tree line the main north-south path. The legendary Bowdoin Pines, a thirty-three-acre stand of cathedral white pines believed to be one of Maine's few remaining old-growth forests, are in evidence on the north and east edges of the campus.

Throughout Bowdoin's periods of growth, administrators and planners continued to preserve and enhance the central quadrangle as a primary feature. The buildings around it served all the essential purposes of a college—instruction, research, worship and ceremony, housing, and athletic activity—and that mixed-use principle continues as an important component of Bowdoin's planning efforts today. As the college grew, buildings were added around the perimeter of the campus, with spaces for the sciences, student activities, and athletics concentrated on the east side; library and administration buildings and student housing to the south; and art and music facilities along the west edge of the campus. Fraternity houses, now college housing, were added along Maine Street and to the south of the quadrangle.

Between 1902 and 1940, seven memorial gateways were constructed to mark entrances to certain areas of the campus. The first of these was the Class of 1875 Gate, designed by McKim, Mead and White and built in 1902 in the center of the Maine Street side of the campus. This gate, which stood opposite the Chapel, featured "a pair of large Maine granite Doric columns, twenty feet high, with flanking urns, similar in effect to but smaller than the columns … used to frame the Grand Army Plaza entrance to Prospect Park in Brooklyn."[14] Today the Class of 1875 Gate leads to the Visual Arts Center, a modern addition by Edward Larrabee Barnes (1975), but provides a view of the Chapel through a wide archway designed for that purpose.

In 1929, following a period of construction, Bowdoin's Governing Boards voted "to consider the matter of a comprehension [*sic*] survey and plans for the rearrangement and construction of walks and paths and the planting of shrubs, etc., on the College campus…."[15] The college approached a lengthy list of well-known landscape architects, including the Olmsted firm, John Nolen, Arthur Shurtleff [Shurcliff], Fletcher Steele, and Mabel Keyes Babcock, and received estimates varying from $25 per day to a fee of $4,000 from the Olmsteds. A total budget of $3,000 was set, but in fact no appropriation was made, and the matter was postponed until 1938 and then turned over to McKim, Mead and White, who were serving as campus architects.[16] Their 1938 campus plan "indicated buildings, paths, and plantings, [and] also outlined ideal future development."[17]

Subsequent plans by Sasaki Associates helped to develop athletic facilities on

Gates of '75, Bowdoin College

the perimeter of the campus. A 1996 plan by Carol R. Johnson Associates gave particular attention to the quality of the campus landscape, providing many recommendations about plantings, care of the tree canopy, sightlines and approaches, and parking.[18] A notable effect of the Johnson plan was to simplify vegetation around Bowdoin's unusual collection of buildings so as to highlight their architectural diversity. The Johnson firm returned in 2008 to provide landscape design for a section of the central campus surrounding a new Fitness, Health, and Wellness Center.

In 2004 Bowdoin commissioned the Chicago office of Skidmore, Owings, and Merrill to create a master plan to help guide future development of the campus. The SOM plan continues to place a high priority on a mixed-use, walkable campus, with an emphasis on the main quadrangle and smaller auxiliary quadrangles and on sightlines and approaches that keep the campus visually and physically connected. Bowdoin has recently added a landscape master planner to its staff to help oversee ongoing work. A particular emphasis today is on "building green" and on adhering to a set of sustainable design guidelines for new construction and renovation. Several recent Bowdoin projects have earned LEED (Leadership in Energy and Environmental Design) certification, using building techniques such as geothermal wells and conserving energy, water, and other natural resources.

In anticipation of the 2011 closing of the adjacent Brunswick Naval Air Station, the U.S. Department of Education has given preliminary approval for Bowdoin to acquire approximately 175 acres of this property, contingent on remediation of any environmental contaminants found at the site. Plans call for using part of the site for maintenance and technical operations, while other portions may be developed as athletic fields and ancillary parking. In addition, a classroom/laboratory building to support wetlands restoration and environmental studies is under consideration.

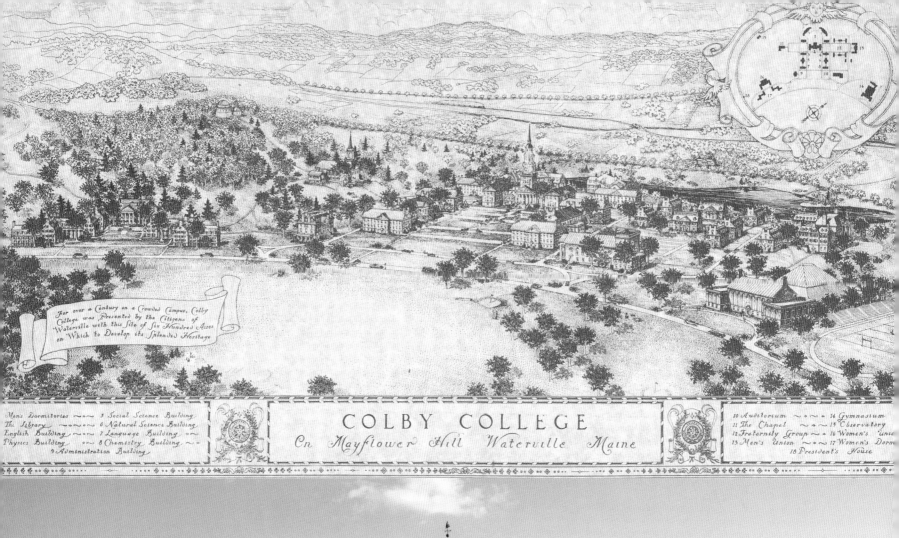

Mens Dormitories ～～ 5 Social Science Building
The Library ～～～ 6 Natural Science Building
English Building ～～ 7 Language Building
Physics Building ～ 8 Chemistry Building ～
9 Administration Building

10 Auditorium ～～ 14 Gymnasium
11 The Chapel ～～ 15 Observatory
12 Fraternity Group ～ 16 Women's Union
13 Men's Union ～～ 17 Women's Dorm
18 President's House

COLBY COLLEGE
On Mayflower Hill Waterville Maine

For over a Century on a Crowded Campus, Colby
College was Presented by the Citizens of
Waterville with this Site of Six Hundred Acres
on Which to Develop its Splendid Heritage

Colby College: The Mayflower Hill Story

Standing in the field below where the chapel would go, the group gaped at the vast expanse: acres and acres to far horizons, …mainly old pastureland with an occasional small woodlot, and an orchard on the steep facing slope near a place called Beefsteak Grove, where critters once fed among the trees. The fields were crisscrossed with half-fallen fences that had divided farms; here and there could be seen the ubiquitous ledge, soon to confound the construction. Growing along the edges of the woods were expanses of trailing arbutus [mayflower], the fragrant flower that gave the place its name. [19] —Earl H. Smith, 2006

Colby College began in Waterville in 1813 as the Maine Literary and Theological Institution, founded by Baptists to train their own independent, free-thinking clergy. Since the first professor, Jeremiah Chaplin, "agreed to teach religion, nothing more,"[20] the school was in fact a theological seminary when the first seven divinity students began classes in 1818. In 1820, the Maine State Legislature gave the institution the right to grant degrees and approved a new charter, which was carefully framed to prevent a sectarian focus. Professor Chaplin then became president, and the institution was renamed Waterville College.

The original thirty-acre campus was located along the Kennebec River. North and South Colleges flanked Recitation Hall, a substantial building with a three-stage bell tower holding a Revere Bell. An early campus view shows a bucolic scene with three elegant brick buildings overlooking a serene river.

Forty years later, enrollment had grown to 120 students, but the Civil War created a severe drain on students and finances, and the young college was threatened with closing. Gardner Colby, a Boston textile magnate who had grown up in Waterville, stepped forward with a $50,000 endowment gift that saved the day. The college was promptly renamed in his honor —initially as Colby University, changed in 1899 to Colby College. In the period after the Civil War, President James Champlin added a science program, opened the college to women in 1871, and established relationships with Maine "fitting schools"— today's prep schools—to bolster enrollments.

The arrival of train service in Waterville and construction of a dam and water power facility on the Kennebec changed the college's setting dramatically. Charles Hathaway's shirt company was soon followed by manufacturers of cotton cloth, furnishings, tools, boots, and more. An influx of workers had begun in 1827 and continued in waves following the Civil War. Waterville began to crowd in upon the college, with the city and its industry encroaching on the landward side and the river restricting growth on the other.

By the dawn of the twentieth century, the College found itself on an island: a growing business district to the south; a trolley line and railroad with its belching coal-fired steam engines to the west; ironworks and a locomotive shop and its clanging roundhouse switch to the north; and, looming across the river in the east, a wonderful new paper mill, stinking of sulfur. [21]

ABOVE: *Memorial (Recitation) Hall, constructed in 1867, provided space for classrooms, the chapel, and a library wing. The building was demolished in 1966, but its Revere Bell and two-ton statue of the Lion of Lucerne were moved to the Mayflower Hill campus.*

OPPOSITE TOP: *Jens (Fred) Larson's highly decorative 1931 plan for Colby's new campus shows his vision of a complete academic community. Construction began in 1937, but the move to the new campus from downtown Waterville was not completed until 1952.*

OPPOSITE BELOW: *Johnson Pond reflects the spire of Miller Library.*

Under the persistent leadership of Franklin Winslow Johnson, a Colby trustee who was chosen as president in 1929, the college's trustees voted to move to a new site, but effecting the move took much effort and many years. Newspaper magnate William Gannett offered a site in Augusta, with seed money to make such a move possible. Waterville's leaders were aghast, concerned about the economic impact of such a move on the town. Support grew for keeping the college in Waterville, and the decision to move the campus to Mayflower Hill was made in November 1930. The Depression-era timing was unfortunate, but eventually, President Johnson and the trustees raised enough of the $3 million goal to begin work, and 13,000 contributors helped to make it possible.[22]

President Johnson had sought the advice of several architects on the choice of a site. These included Jens Frederick Larson and two Boston firms, Shepley, Bulfinch and Abbott, and Coolidge and Carlson. Carl Rust Parker of the Olmsted firm was also in contact with Johnson.[23] Responsibility for designing the campus was given to Larson, but the Olmsted firm was also engaged as landscape architects in 1932, and they continued in that capacity until the 1950s. Their numerous plans included general planting, improvements to the Lorimer Chapel area, and grading and parking near fraternities.

Jens ("Fred") Larson had begun his career as a designer of college campuses in 1919 as architect in residence at Dartmouth. He went on to design master plans and buildings for many institutions and became official architect of the Association of American Colleges. His 1933 book, *Architectural Planning for the American College,* was one of the first on the subject and continued to influence campus design for many years. Larson went on to design buildings and master plans for more than thirty colleges, universities, and schools in his long career.[24]

When Colby made its decision to move, Larson was ready with ideas and a philosophy that matched Johnson's ideas. He had already prepared a plan for the proposed flat Augusta site in 1930; when he was hired in 1931, he quickly revised that plan for the "rolling Waterville hillside."[25]

Planning and building a whole new campus for a historic college was an unusual opportunity and an equal challenge. Colby College could now become the ideal "academical village," and its campus plan could anticipate the wider needs of a twentieth-century institution. Larson's site plan featured the library at the head of an open green. Academic buildings faced the green on both sides, and separate quadrangles contained the chapel on the south side and college housing for men on the north. Along the curving main drive, Larson proposed a cluster of buildings for women's housing to the left of the main quadrangle and an area for athletics to the right. The College Pond, later named Johnson Pond, provided a naturalistic background for the central campus. In his 1931 plan, Larson included an "Open-Air Theatre" flanking the pond, with an "Observatory Park" to the left and a proposed "faculty village" to the right, beyond the athletic fields. These were not built, but much of the campus plan was constructed over time, following Larson's design.

Larson chose Georgian Revival forms for the buildings to provide instant tradition and nineteenth-century character. In his 1933 book on college planning, he stated: "If there is any institution in modern life which cannot cast off the past, which must

BELOW: *A 1959 aerial view shows the Colby campus soon after the move to Mayflower Hill was completed.*

ABOVE (CLOCKWISE FROM TOP LEFT): *An 1834 view of the early campus shows North and South Colleges ("The Bricks") flanking the newly completed Recitation Hall. The Colby campus*

be built upon the treasures of its rich inheritance, it is the college…. [The architect should] envisage the contemporary problem and clothe it in traditional architecture."[26] Work on Lorimer Chapel began in 1937 (though the building was not complete until 1948), and the groundbreaking for Roberts Union took place in 1938. The library was begun after George Averill, a Waterville business owner and investor, came to the rescue, not only providing funds to complete Miller Library and build some dormitories, but also purchasing the old Colby campus for use by the local Boys' Club.

It would be almost fifteen years before the transition to Mayflower Hill was completed in 1952. Works Progress Administration workers had begun the process of site preparation in 1935, digging sewers, laying out access roads, and building a bridge and railroad overpass. The campus was only about half built when World War II intervened, but work could proceed on installing the landscape. Johnson Pond was created and the sloping terraces around Miller Library were laid out; these were later redesigned by the Olmsted firm as a gift from Mary Louise Curtis Bok. As the campus took shape, more than 1,000 trees were planted, lawns and terraces were installed, and donations of tulips brightened the scene.

The area surrounding the campus remained agrarian and largely undeveloped as late as 1960. Former orchards and fields were becoming more heavily wooded, but views of Messalonskee Stream and the surrounding countryside still formed the backdrop. In 2002, when the firm of Shepley Bulfinch Richardson and Abbott was brought in to provide an updated campus plan, they found that "the image of the campus today is one of a clearing in the Maine woods."[27] College buildings and playing fields occupied more of the 600-acre site, but the woods had grown even faster. Key goals of the campus plan were to enhance the neo-Georgian architectural fabric of the campus; celebrate the architectural diversity of post-Larson buildings; capitalize on the informal, picturesque style of newer campus buildings and landscaping; and allow for "transformative stylistic expression" as facilities are added.[28]

The planning firm's recommendations are most notable in the new Colby Green, a fourteen-and one-half-acre area across Mayflower Hill Drive that faces the central core of Larson's original campus design. The actual Colby Green is a two-acre elliptical lawn intended to complement Miller Lawn. The form echoes Larson's curving roadways that flanked the geometric central campus, with a succession of arcing slopes that follow the contours of the land. Completed buildings include the admissions office, an alumni center designed by Ann Beha Associates, and an academic building for the social sciences and interdisciplinary studies. A science building is scheduled for completion in 2010. As at other campuses, "green" construction is an important goal, and geothermal wells contribute to reduced energy costs.

Reed Hilderbrand Associates, Inc., from Watertown, Mass., developed the schematic plans for the Colby Green and for landscape improvements. Mohr & Seredin Landscape Architects of Portland have translated master plan concepts into tangible projects. Their recent work has included site planning for many new buildings, detailed plans for replanting the mall, changes for handicapped accessibility, and restoring the landscape at the chapel's main entrance.

BATES COLLEGE: INSPIRED BY PRINCIPLE

Bates College in Lewiston began as a seminary, or private high school, and, like Colby and Bowdoin, was named for an early benefactor whose gifts provided critical support for a young institution. But unlike the earlier Maine colleges, Bates was very much the inspiration and vision of one man who dedicated his life to making it a reality.

The Reverend Oren B. Cheney was a Freewill Baptist minister who left his Augusta pastorate after an inspiring dream of a new school on the night of September 22, 1854. Cheney, a Dartmouth graduate, had attended, taught at, and been principal of Parsonsfield Seminary in southwestern Maine. When that school burned to the ground under suspicious circumstances, Cheney was inspired "not merely to build a replacement, but to establish a different school, as he later described it, one of 'a high order or grade somewhere between a College and an Academy,' and to do so in a conveniently central location in Maine."[29] The Maine State Legislature chartered Cheney's school on March 16, 1855, and provided an initial sum of $15,000 for the Maine State Seminary, as it was called. Cheney added a "collegiate department" in 1862 and received a new college charter in January 1864. The expanded school was renamed Bates College in honor of benefactor Benjamin E. Bates, a Boston and Lewiston industrialist.

Oren Cheney's personal convictions and his belief in the doctrines of the Freewill Baptists had a strong impact on the character of the college. Like many prominent New Englanders of his time, he was "an ardent abolitionist and temperance man." An incident recounted in a biography written by

ABOVE: *The Reverend Oren B. Cheney founded a new school based on his personal ideals and zeal for education.*

LEFT: *Parker and Hathorn Halls, shown soon after 1857, with Lewiston farms in the background.*

Emeline Burlingame-Cheney tells that "even on his deathbed he refused a sip of watered-down brandy," and that as a youth in New Hampshire he "had befriended runaway slaves and as a Dartmouth undergraduate had helped conduct special school sessions for Native Americans."[30]

The Freewill Baptists, or "Free Baptists," as they came to be called, rejected the Calvinist doctrines of predestination and election for salvation and embraced a group of freedoms that gave the denomination its name: "free salvation, free grace, free will, and free communion."[31] Taking its inspiration from these principles, the school operated from its earliest days with an unusual degree of academic freedom for the period. The seminary enrolled men and women and offered a non-college ("English") program and a normal school, or teacher training program, in addition to the pre-college program. By the 1880s, the college program was well established. Coeducation was "a solidly established feature of the Bates scene in practice as well as in law and ideal," and Bates "led most of its peers in achieving early racial integration," with nine black students having attended by 1874.[32]

The Maine State Seminary's first major buildings, Parker and Hathorn, were completed in 1857 and are still at the core of the college campus. Parker Hall was simple and unadorned in style. Many windows and a forest of chimneys seen in an early photograph indicate a large residence hall, heated by individual fireplaces or stoves in student rooms. Hathorn, with its pedimented elevations and crowning cupola, was clearly the center of educational and administrative functions. The two substantial brick buildings were set in a broad lawn, surrounded by a rural landscape of farms and fields in what is today a busy residential section of Lewiston.

The "Yankee frugality" that had characterized Bates from the beginning seems to have guided development of the campus during its first half-century. By 1914, President Cheney's successor, George Colby Chase, had added eleven buildings to accommodate an enrollment of 500 students and a faculty of thirty-eight professors. A chapel was under construction and would serve a firmly egalitarian institution,[33] and the Coram Library had been built in 1902, in an unusual collaboration between a pair of Paris-trained New York architects; leading members of New York's Jewish community; a Lowell industrialist, Joseph Coram; and visionary administrators at the college.

The new library was to be devoted to "individual learning and student interaction outside the classroom."[34] To design this center of learning, the college chose Henry B. Herts and Hugh Tallant, two young architects who had studied at the École des Beaux-Arts in Paris. Coram Library is similar in design to the Brooklyn Academy of Music, where Herts and Tallant used the Beaux-Arts style and their own gift for ornamentation with great success.[35] Herts and Tallant had also worked closely with clients Isaac and Julia Rice in New York, designing their home on Riverside Drive and the Harmonie Club, the leading Jewish philanthropic organization in Manhattan. (It was probably through the architects that the Rices' philanthropy came to benefit Bates as well, with additional funding for the library and its collections.)

ABOVE: *Lake Andrews is bordered by a lakeside memorial walk that offers scenic views of the campus.*
OPPOSITE: *Coram Library was designed in the Beaux-Arts style by New York architects Henry B. Herts and Hugh Tallant and constructed in 1902.*

By this time, the area around the college had changed dramatically, thanks to the post-Civil War emergence of Lewiston as an important textile city. The former rural Maine State Seminary was now in an urban setting. Bates's response to that setting provides an illustration of two competing styles of American colleges, as Paul Turner has described them—Thomas Jefferson's "academical village" and the "City Beautiful" of newer nineteenth-century campuses.

The City Beautiful movement was launched with the 1893 World's Columbian Exposition in Chicago. The exposition's Beaux-Arts White City sought to bring the glamour of old European cities to the American heartland. Even before the advent of the City Beautiful, American colleges and universities began to be influenced by the German university model of a collection of departmental faculties with an emphasis on research and scholarship as well as on teaching. New universities like Johns Hopkins in Baltimore and Clark University in Worcester followed this model, as did many larger colleges located in urban areas. The City Beautiful style offered an ideal setting for these ambitious cultural and intellectual centers. However, as Paul Turner notes, "the [American] collegiate model was too strong to be replaced by it, and ultimately the two systems merged and compromised with each other."[36]

Bates was still a small college and would remain one, but it had always had the aspects of openness to all and varied approaches to education that characterized more urban campuses. The building of Coram Library, with its influences of New York and Paris, also indicated a "more cosmopolitan, liberal, and sophisticated institution than some … may have realized."[37] It was in this environment that President Chase turned in 1914 to landscape architect and city planner John Nolen for the first Bates campus plan, though he had also been in correspondence with the Olmsteds, and perhaps others. Nolen's extensive plan guided the gradual development of the campus for many years; his final suggested building was constructed some ninety years later.

Originally from Philadelphia, John Nolen had received a degree in landscape architecture from Harvard in 1905 and had opened an office in Cambridge, Massachusetts. When he began work on the Bates campus, he had surveyed park sites for the state of Wisconsin and had completed the first of several plans for the city of San Diego. He became nationally known for his pioneering work as a city planner. His work at Bates, in the first decade of his professional career, seems to have been his only commission specifically for a college.

Nolen's plan for the campus survives, as does a sketch of new buildings adjoining those that existed in 1914. His accompanying "note" illustrates the approach of a city planner to a college campus. Any reconstruction and future development at Bates, Nolen stated, should provide "as compact and economic a utilization as possible of all College property" and "as complete as possible a closing in of the campus by new buildings, so as to give a sense of academic seclusion."[38] He recommended separation between academic and residential and recreational areas of the campus and sought to preserve Hathorn Hall as the "dominating center of interest" of the campus. City streets on the boundary and roads through the campus created an axial layout, which Nolen reinforced in his design of campus quadrangles. Vistas

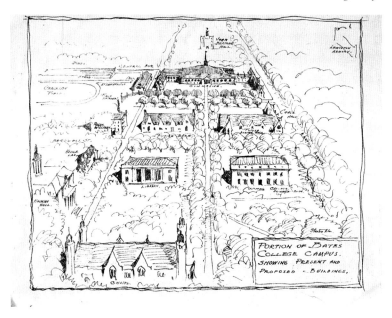

PORTION OF BATES COLLEGE CAMPUS. SHOWING PRESENT AND PROPOSED BUILDINGS.

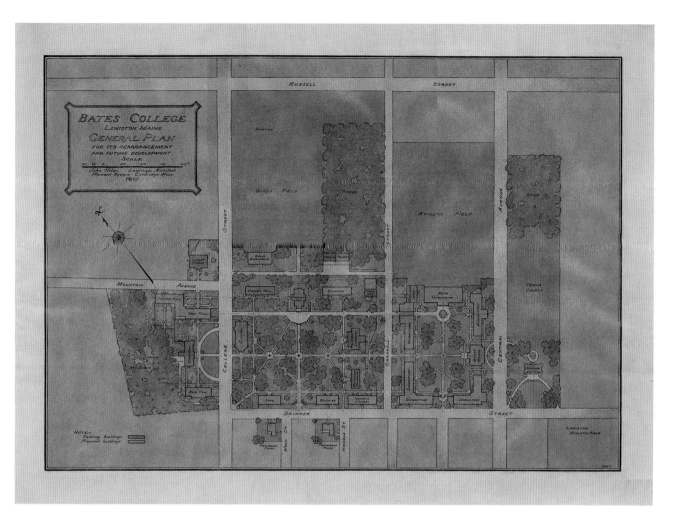

and views were a concern, but only within the campus, and the plan provided for lawns, trees, and areas for recreation within the college property.

After President Clifton Daggett Gray took office in 1919, Nolen wrote to suggest that Bates retain his services as a consulting landscape architect. He would plan and supervise planting of the grounds and would make recommendations for the siting of new buildings and their landscape designs as required. His proposal emphasized economy and order, as well as attractiveness, and added the further inducement that such a plan would be useful in attracting support from donors.[39] Bates presidents may have sought Nolen's advice from time to time, but college records do not show continued involvement on his part. President Gray's attention turned to sustaining the college through the Depression and the years leading to World War II. An athletic building and gymnasium were designed by the firm of Coolidge and Carlson, who also provided a plan for their placement.

Under presidents Phillips and Reynolds, further development of the campus continued gradually from the 1940s through the 1980s, with an emphasis on thrift and conservative financial planning. President Hedley Reynolds also turned to architects Sasaki, Dawson, and DeMay, who provided a 1967 plan intended to cover a twenty-year period.

In 1990, Bates chose Richard Dober of the firm Dober, Lidsky, Craig and Associates to review the growth and development of the campus and to create a new campus plan. Dober characterized

Bates as "a paradigm New England campus, the college on the hill,"[40] and noted Nolen's axial design of a central quadrangle and two east-west quadrangles. Dober's plan called for a fourth quad to be developed along a "spine" formed by Andrews Road. He proposed moving some athletic facilities to an outlying area of the campus, expanding the library and adding new academic buildings and residence spaces.

In 2004, under President Elaine Tuttle Hansen, Bates returned to Sasaki Associates for a new comprehensive master plan. As at Bowdoin and Colby, emphasis today is placed on "green" construction, notably in the newly completed dining Commons. Adding greenery in the traditional sense, a landscaped Alumni Walk now provides a two- and one-half-acre verdant corridor through the middle of the campus. The walk replaces the former Andrews Road with walking paths, benches, lighting, birch trees, and 140,000 blue scilla bulbs to bloom during Maine's famous mud season.

The walk adjoins Lake Andrews, which was originally transformed in the 1940s from a boggy area into a real pond. In 1998, with funding from alumnus Jack Keigwin and his wife, Beverly Keigwin, the college once again restored the pond, dredging tons of silt and repairing the edge with massive amounts of river rock, and created a naturalistic planting of hundreds of trees, shrubs, grasses, and perennials, many native to Maine. The pond is bordered by a lakeside memorial walk that offers scenic views of the school's handsome brick buildings. On the northeast edge, the Florence Keigwin Amphitheater overlooks the pond and serves as a popular public gathering space.

The University of Maine at Orono: A Land-Grant College for Maine

The site of the college is an attractive one. The farm on which it is located borders on the Stillwater River, one mile from the pleasant village of Orono and nine miles from the thriving city of Bangor. It embraces 376 acres of land, affording a variety of soil for experimental purposes.[41] —President M. C. Fernald, 1887

The Land-Grant College Act (the First Morrill Act), which was sponsored in 1859 by Senator Justin Morrill of Vermont and signed into law by Abraham Lincoln in 1862, provided a note of hope and optimism in the early years of the Civil War. The act provided land grants of 30,000 acres per member of Congress, with a maximum of one million acres for any state. Some of these lands were used as college sites, but most were sold to create endowments for this new form of public education. Maine's share came to 210,000 acres, of which all but about 16,200 acres were sold in 1866 at the low price of fifty-three cents per acre, resulting in an initial endowment of about $130,000.[42]

The land-grant colleges were a deliberate change from institutions that were prevalent at the time. Some agricultural and manual labor colleges had been founded in the 1840s and '50s, and a handful of engineering and scientific schools offered specialized training, but the land-grant colleges were established to provide a practical education, with an emphasis on "agriculture and

ABOVE: *Stevens Hall on the Orono campus faces the University Mall, a central green area designed by Carl Rust Parker for the Olmsted Brothers firm.*
OPPOSITE: *Fogler Library stands at the head of the Orono campus mall. Oak trees line the mall, replacing the original elms lost to Dutch elm disease.*

the mechanic arts,"[43] open to all social classes, that gave students the freedom to choose their own course of study.

The idea of a university geared to practical learning had great appeal for Frederick Law Olmsted, Sr., who had "only a passing exposure to higher education."[44] His early education was received from a succession of minister tutors, with whom he boarded. He then joined his younger brother John for a year at Yale, but ill health and his restless nature kept him from finishing his studies there. Instead, he engaged in farming, extensive travel, and writing and publishing until he found his calling as a landscape architect.

Olmsted began immediately to lay out his ideas for the kind of setting that would best suit the new land-grant colleges. He was already engaged in designing the private College of California campus on its new site in Berkeley, where he planned a community in a naturalistic park setting, with "meandering roads and parkland," separate areas for athletics, and a "cottage system" of residential villages for students.[45] He was also asked to design the grounds of a federal land-grant college at the University of Massachusetts at Amherst. Again he proposed a comprehensive design, but the Massachusetts trustees had asked only for a landscape plan for the area surrounding a large central building, and they rejected his plan.

In the fall of 1866, the Maine State College's board of trustees invited Olmsted to visit Orono and to make a plan for the new College of Agriculture and Mechanic Arts. The site consisted of two farms on Marsh Island, which is formed by the Penobscot and Stillwater rivers.[46]

Olmsted's role as executive secretary of the national Sanitary Commission, which provided medical care for Civil War combatants, had given him strong convictions about the need for military training and improvements in sanitation. He also insisted on the benefit of residential communities for students and the importance of training knowledgeable workers for agriculture and industry. These values were also espoused by the Maine college trustees, who had specified that the college "would be situated on a working farm; students would be required to engage in physical labor at the school; students would live in a household situation in order to receive the moral benefits of family life; and military strategy and tactics would be part of the curriculum."[47]

Olmsted's 1867 plan placed experimental farm fields on a flat, cleared eastern section already occupied by the two working farms. Near the Stillwater River, he proposed a parade ground for military training and an arboretum. Between the two, he located academic buildings—a library, classroom building, laboratory, and museum, with lodging houses clustered near a boarding house that would offer a place for meals and various administrative functions. He "advised that the campus function as a small village with the buildings surrounding a proposed parade ground that would serve as the 'village green.'"[48]

While Olmsted was preparing his plans, the founding board of trustees was replaced with a new board, and the state legislature provided only enough funding for two buildings, whereas Olmsted had called for three buildings for every forty students. The trustees rejected Olmsted's plan, but they did adopt several aspects of it as development of the site went forward.

The campus that housed the first twelve students in September 1868 consisted of the existing farm buildings and White Hall, which provided classroom and dormitory spaces. A chemical

ABOVE: *Merritt C. Fernald was hired in 1868 as the Maine State College's first professor (of mathematics) and second president. His wife Mary, a professor of languages, joined the faculty by 1871.*

OPPOSITE: *Frederick Law Olmsted, Sr., titled his plan for the Maine College of Agriculture and Mechanical Arts a "Plan for an Industrial Village." A parade ground abuts the river, with the farm buildings and fields across the road. A curving road passes between orchards and botanic gardens, with academic buildings located along the road.*

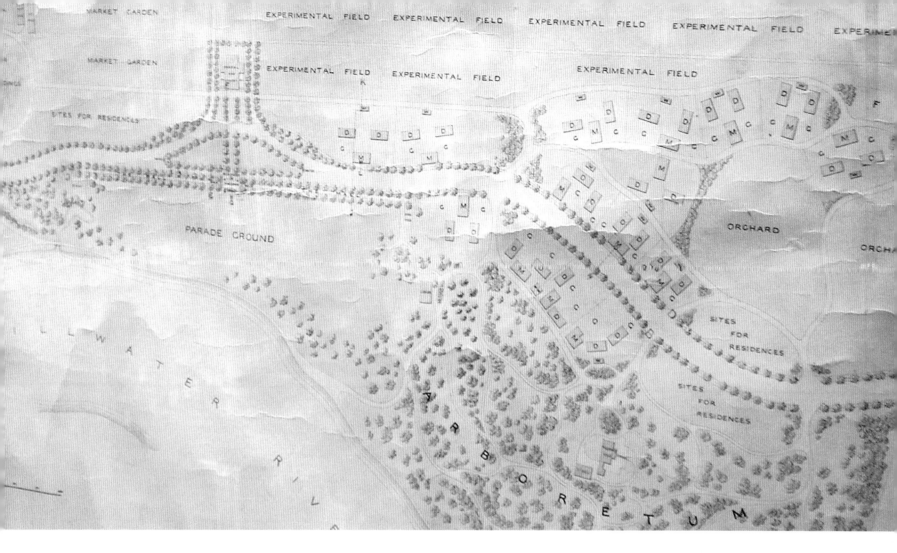

laboratory and a forty-eight-room dormitory were added in 1870 and 1871. By 1883, a shop for the mechanical department, houses for the president and three professors, and a group of farm buildings completed the campus. Many of these buildings faced the Stillwater River, as Olmsted had suggested. Throughout the college's first period of growth, buildings were sited either on the hill facing the river or along the road and facing the campus. Utilitarian buildings were placed where it was most convenient, a practice that probably led to numerous later proposals to move, demolish, and otherwise rearrange existing facilities. The land between the road and the river and the central area facing the road remained undeveloped.

The college grew quickly in the late nineteenth century. The admission of women, beginning in 1872, led to increased demand for liberal arts programs, and the country's industrialization strengthened engineering programs. New programs were added in law and pharmacy in the 1890s, and President Abram Harris succeeded in having the college renamed the University of Maine in recognition of its range of programs. However, the college's founding emphasis on agriculture had tenacious supporters in the deans of that program, and strong competition for space and resources presented a challenge to campus planners brought in to address these needs.

The first such campus plan was prepared in 1893 by a professor of horticulture, Welton M. Munson. His plan preserved campus green spaces along the river and in front of existing buildings and added a roadway for access to buildings to be placed east of the original campus. Munson's plan also helped to "define the southeast portion of the campus as the focus of agricultural activity."[49]

Continuing growth in the early 1900s led President Clarence Cook Little to turn to his brother's firm, Little and Russell of Boston, for a plan to accommodate new construction and to address changes along College Avenue, where ten fraternity houses and three faculty houses stood between the main road and the river. In their 1923 plan, Little and Russell preserved Munson's green space, which became the campus mall, recommended placement of proposed buildings, and suggested a second mall at the south end of the campus.

Although the university adopted some aspects of the Little and Russell plan, the proposals ran into particular opposition from Leon Merrill, dean of the School of Agriculture. Declining enrollments in the agricultural program on campus had been somewhat offset by federal funding for agricultural research provided by the Smith-Lever Act of 1917, and the School of Agriculture had acquired land in Monmouth and Presque Isle for research on fruit and potato crops, but its "footprint" on the campus had been reduced dramatically.

This was the context in which the Olmsted firm returned to the Maine campus in April 1932, sixty-five years after Olmsted, Sr., prepared his first plan for the University of Maine. Carl Rust Parker, who was assigned to the project on behalf of Olmsted Brothers, had been closely involved in other projects for the state in the 1920s, notably in Augusta (pp. 40–51). Now his challenge was to create a campus plan for a university that had 1,600 students and hoped to expand enrollments to 3,000, while addressing the needs of growing departments and avoiding strong opposition from the School of Agriculture.

Parker's recommendations and challenges were fairly dramatic. He proposed eight to ten new buildings, suggested removing or relocating several others, and wanted to cut down numerous trees to create a vista toward the river. Prefiguring a common campus concern today, he sought to provide parking "for six hundred cars per day (with expansion for 2,000 to 2,700 at sporting events)."[50] He also had to site two Civil War cannons from the U.S.S. *Constitution* that had been donated to the university.

After extensive negotiations and revisions, Parker and the Olmsteds arrived at a plan that received approval in October 1932. In contrast to the senior Olmsted's orientation toward the river, Parker and the younger Olmsteds chose to orient the campus along a formal, north-south axis that had no relationship to the river. They proposed a rectangular mall lined with a formal allée of trees and flanked with symmetrical buildings. In contrast to this formality, they also proposed a small naturalistic lake surrounded by landscaped paths; the library was to overlook the lake. The plan also included a list of buildings to be torn down, recommendations on parking regulations, and a proposal to move the athletic fields to the periphery of the campus.

Initially, because of financial constraints, only the landscape for the mall was installed. World War II further intervened, and the major buildings Parker had proposed were not completed until the late 1940s. The Olmsteds and Parker created a revised plan in 1948. The later version shows an extension to the mall, the library in its current location, and three future buildings surrounding a green to replace the proposed lake.

Part of the campus was listed in the National Register of Historic Places in 1978, a period before landscapes were recognized as historically significant. The National Register listing recognizes several historic buildings south of the library but not the Olmsted mall, for example. Nevertheless, the tree-lined mall is probably the most significant piece of the younger Olmsteds' plan remaining today. The original trees were elms, but when these died they were replaced with oaks. An area shown as "The Bowl" on the 1932 and 1948 plans also remains today and is included in the National Register listing.

Today's 600-acre campus, with more than 200 buildings on the main campus, is more densely developed than Olmsted or his sons and Carl Rust Parker might have envisioned. Some student residence halls are clustered in "villages," as Olmsted, Sr., had suggested, though the buildings are considerably larger than cottages. Along the river, Olmsted, Sr.'s, planned parade ground and arboretum are devoted to a riverside recreation area with a dock and boat launch, a large parking area, and several fraternity houses. Athletic fields and parking areas mark the outer edges of the campus, and the university farms, research facilities, and Demeritt Forest occupy about 6,500 contiguous acres.

Among the special agricultural and mechanical facilities of the campus are the Littlefield Ornamental Trial Garden and rose gardens; the Page Farm and Home Museum; aquaculture, small animal, and poultry research facilities; a USDA plant, soil, and water laboratory; an observatory; and research facilities for wood composites and advanced manufacturing. Arts and culture spaces include the Maine Center for the Arts, the Museum of Art, and the Hudson anthropology museum.

Soon after his selection as president in 2005, Robert A. Kennedy, a botanist, arranged to have the entire campus established as an arboretum. Kennedy was raised on a farm in Minnesota and has a strong personal and professional interest in the campus's natural resources. He has also noted that he is "a product of land-grants" and has been "affiliated with six different land-grant universities as either a student or a faculty member."[51]

In 2008, senior landscape horticulture students prepared a management plan for the campus. Student teams developed how-to manuals on managing large landscapes from an environmentally friendly perspective, incorporating guidelines on proper plant care and pest management techniques. The students' best recommendations form part of the university's landscape management plan.

In addition to its land-grant designation, which provides federal support for numerous programs, the University of Maine was named a sea-grant college, first in 1980 in conjunction with the University of New Hampshire, and independently for its own program in 2004.

Planning and design for the University of Maine campus today is based on its *Historic Preservation Plan* of 2007, which was funded by a $175,000 grant from the Getty Grant Program's Campus Heritage Initiative. A campus plan by Sasaki Associates seeks to preserve and restore historic buildings and landscapes, enhance the mall's status as the symbolic center of the campus, and provide clarity and coherence for overall campus planning and future growth.

CHAPTER 6

HISTORIC GOLF COURSES: PURE AIR AND INSPIRING SCENERY

The competitive sport of golf may seem an unusual subject in a book about historic landscapes. Unlike parks, for example, golf courses are extremely specialized and regulated for conditioning and public safety. But they require as much planning and manipulation of the land as any of the parks, cemeteries, and private estates featured in *Designing the Maine Landscape*. By hand or with horsepower, at these historic courses, landscape crews moved massive amounts of soil and boulders, filled large areas of wetland (in the pre-regulatory era), and cleared numerous acres of trees and stumps. They converted stony pastures into smooth, grassy tracts on which to play the new game of golf. And just as ocean views, cool mountain air, and accessibility prompted development of other landscapes, they also ensured that golf as a sport would come to Maine early in its history in the United States.

Poland Spring and Kebo Valley, both public courses, and Megunticook, a private golf club, were some of the earliest courses in Maine, indeed in the country, and were planned by nationally known golf course designers and landscape architects. They represent a significant era in Maine's history, when out-of-state families spent entire summers at resorts on Mount Desert Island, in mid-coast Maine, and in the forested interior.

Scotland is universally recognized as the home of the game of golf; the oldest club with documentary proof of its origin is in Muirfield in East Lothian, Scotland. "As early as the 15th century, golfers at St. Andrews established a customary route through the undulating terrain, playing to holes whose locations were dictated by topography."[1]

Golf arrived in the United States in 1888, when the country's first permanent golf club was formed at St. Andrews in Hastings-on-Hudson, New York. Maine was in the forefront in the development of golf in this country, with the opening of Kebo Valley in 1892, Poland Spring in 1896, and Megunticook in 1902. Each was sited to take advantage of stunning views of the surrounding landscape, from the mountains of Acadia National Park, to New Hampshire's White Mountains, to Penobscot Bay.

Poland Spring Resort and Golf Course: Leisure in the Genteel Tradition

"...on no course can it be said that the wonders of golf are worked in purer air, more inspiring vision, or under pleasanter influences than on the hillside links at this resort." [2]
– The Hill-Top Magazine, July 15, 1916

The Poland Spring golf course, in the town of Poland, was the first course built at a resort in the United States. The original six-hole course was designed in 1896 by Arthur Fenn, who is considered the country's first native-born professional golfer. Today, the site is an eighteen-hole public course located in the rolling foothills of western Maine. Situated near the top of Ricker Hill, 200 feet above Middle Pond and Lower Range Pond, the course offers commanding views of the White Mountains to the west.

In *Poland Spring–A Tale of the Gilded Age, 1860–1900*, historian David Richards provides an extensive history of the resort. The Ricker family began selling its spring waters in 1845 and operated the Mansion House, a popular inn for guests seeking the curative qualities of the spring water. Business was so successful that in 1876 the new Poland Spring House opened with 120 guest rooms. This inn was enlarged and remodeled over the next few decades, including by architects John Calvin Stevens and Albert Winslow Cobb in 1889. The final remodeling was in 1903 by architect Harry G. Wilkinson, who provided the designs for the inn's signature features, the elaborate corner and entrance towers. At this time the Poland Spring House, complete with its extensive piazzas, dining rooms, fine Victorian furnishings, and six-story tower capped by a French mansard roof, held 400 rooms. [3]

Over the decades the resort expanded to include the Music Hall (1884), Casino (1887), Photo Studio (1894), the Maine State Building from the Columbian Exposition (1895), a state-of-the-art spring house and bottling facility (1904), and the All Souls Chapel (1912), among other improvements. In line with popular trends, guests enjoyed all types of outdoor recreation: fishing, boating, bicycling, carriage driving, horseback riding, baseball, tennis, croquet, and golf.

According to Richards, Poland Spring Resort offered "relief from the modern morass…. Remote from rails and highways and cut off from newspapers, letters, and telegrams, guests could drink pure water, breathe clean air, eat fine food, converse with congenial companions, walk along shaded avenues, exercise with the golf club… and be as happy as it was possible to be. Venturing into the 'wilds of Maine' …would make a visitor feel as if a tremendous weight had been removed." [4]

Following golf's increased popularity in the 1890s, the Rickers invited Arthur Fenn, one of the country's leading golfers, to lay out the

POLAND SPRING HOUSE FROM GOLF LINKS, POLAND, MAINE.

course at Poland Spring. Fenn spent summers at Poland Spring for thirty years as the resident golf professional and course supervisor. He also flourished as a self-taught golf course designer at a time when Scotsmen dominated the field in this country.

Richards describes Fenn's design intentions for the course as a combination of scientific outlook, careful study, and emphasis on variety. To achieve the latter, he varied the length of fairways within a range of 125 to 550 yards, gave thoughtful consideration to placement of hazards and bunkers, and observed his guiding rules that "a good stroke should never be punished" and the course should be "neither too hard nor too easy."[5]

> *[Fenn's] annual tinkering with his masterpiece lengthened the course from 2,465 yards with a par of thirty-eight in 1897 to 2,875 yards with a par of forty-one in 1900. All the while, work continued to improve the greens and bunkers. Three years of laying new sod and dumping tons of wood ash, along with careful nursing by human hands, constant tending with horse-drawn lawnmowers, and sporadic unleashing of the groundskeeper's secret weapon, sheep, finally produced the perfect course—one virtually free of poor lies. Everyone who played the course agreed that no other resort could rival, let alone surpass, the "best hotel links in the country."[6]*

Fenn's work won acclaim from a popular magazine, *Outings Monthly Review of Amateur Sports and Pastimes*. "When they first opened two years ago they received little attention, but gradually they claimed favor, till last season they fairly won and held first place. They are a nine-hole links and require delicacy of play rather than strength."[7]

Throughout the country golf course designers regularly revised the layouts of courses installed by others, especially as the players' skills increased, as golf equipment evolved, and as maintenance practices improved.[8] This trend began early in the game's history, as shown in this article from 1898:

> One of the most noticeable features at this early state of the golf season is the large number of
> clubs that are making extensive improvements in their courses. In some cases the outlay of
> expense runs up into the thousands of dollars.... In the vicinity of New York there are few clubs
> that have not made some changes, for there is probably not a course in the United States that
> is not capable of being somewhat improved.... The mania for eighteen-hole courses has been,
> perhaps, the most characteristic feature of the present season.[9]

Such was the case at Poland Spring, where Scotsman Donald Ross redesigned Fenn's nine-hole course and added nine more holes in 1913. In his career, Donald Ross designed or revised more than 400 golf courses in the United States and Canada, including eleven in Maine. Among his nationally known courses are Pinehurst No. 2 in North Carolina, Seminole in Florida, and Oakland Hills outside of Detroit.

Poland Spring differs from Kebo Valley and Megunticook in that originally there was no separate clubhouse. However, not long after Ross's redesign of the course, the resort added modern accommodations for golfers, such as reading and lounging rooms, lockers, bath facilities, and a room for repairing equipment.

In the early 1900s Poland Spring enjoyed a reputation as one of the largest resorts in the world. Results of its golf tournaments were published regularly in the *New York Times*, and *The American Golfer* regularly included the course in its pages. The same period also saw a surge in automobile travel, which changed the nature of vacationing in Maine. Increased mobility meant that fewer families chose to stay in one location for their entire vacation. Tourism declined at Poland Spring Resort, and the Depression ended any significant business. Nevertheless, the golf course continued to thrive, as shown in this 1934 description: "It would be difficult to find a more thoroughly enjoyable and attractive setting than one finds at Poland Spring.... Today its course is a real delight to those who demand the best there is in the way of turf conditions, both on the putting greens and through the fairways."[10]

A few years later, the Ricker family sold the resort to out-of-state investors who sold it again in the 1960s. Out of the hands of the Rickers, the resort continued to decline. Disastrous fires struck in the 1970s and destroyed the historic Poland Spring House and the Mansion House. The surviving Maine State Building was listed in the National Register of Historic Places in 1974, and All Souls Chapel was listed in 1977. The Poland Spring Preservation Society was formed in 1975 to oversee the preservation and restoration of these two historic buildings.

Today the Poland Spring Resort continues to thrive as a popular seasonal destination, with three inns, eleven cottages, and 800 acres accessible by numerous trails. Within walking distance is Preservation Park, home of the Poland Spring Museum and Spring House. These historic buildings underwent a three-year restoration by their owner, Nestlé Waters North America, and are listed in the National Register of Historic Places. They are open to the public, as are the Maine State House and All Souls Chapel. But the greatest attraction at Poland Spring remains the historic golf course, with its spectacular views of the White Mountains, velvet greens, and beautiful fairways, ponds, and tees.

OPPOSITE: *The view from Hole No. 8 at Poland Spring looks north over Lower Range Pond.*
BELOW: *A vintage postcard shows without a hint of the modern mirage at Poland Spring's bottling, packing, and store houses. Today several of these buildings make up Preservation Park, an informative museum open to the public.*

7981. NEW BOTTLING, PACKING AND STORE HOUSES AT POLAND SPRING.   DETROIT PUBLISHING CO.

Kebo Valley Golf Club: The Social Center of Bar Harbor

"Bar Harbor is balancing on the verge of its annual plunge into a Summer's gayeties....[The] streets are filled with faces, some strange, some familiar; excursion parties arrive semi-weekly, and tourists daily, and the Kebo Valley links are filled with golfers. Everywhere are evident the signs of a season approaching which promises to be freighted with unusual success in a social way."[11] – New York Times, July 8, 1900

Kebo Valley Golf Club is an eighteen-hole classic link and parkland course located just one and one-half miles south of Bar Harbor. Nestled between Cadillac and Dorr mountains, the public club shares a border with Acadia National Park. For well over one hundred years, Kebo has served as a major social center for golfers and vacationers in Bar Harbor.

The Kebo Valley Club was incorporated in 1888 under the Acadia Park Company to promote "the cultivation of athletic sports and furnishing innocent amusement for the public for reasonable compensation."[12] Landscape engineer Joseph H. Curtis (pp. 66–77) prepared a well-laid out plan of thirty house lots, four tennis courts, a casino, theater, "Base Ball Ground, Concourse," and a half-mile horse-racing track.[13] The house lots were never developed, but the other recreational facilities, especially the race track, became a major attraction at Kebo. It is not surprising that Curtis's plan did not include a golf course, since the first permanent course in America was built that same year.[14]

The Kebo club hired Philadelphia architect Wilson Eyre to design the gatehouse and a separate clubhouse, which opened in 1889. The Shingle-style clubhouse was massive at 230 feet by 50 feet and was one of the largest structures built in Bar Harbor up to that time. It included a theater (that doubled as a ballroom) that could accommodate 500 to 600 people, as well as reading and dining rooms. Despite its large size the clubhouse had a "homelike scale," with fireplaces, cozy nooks, exposed ceiling beams, and warm paint colors.[15]

As was true at Poland Spring, it did not take long for golf to arrive at Kebo after it gained popularity in the United States. The first six holes were designed in 1892 by Herbert Corey Leeds, a talented all-around sportsman, golfer, and course designer, who went on to design Myopia Hunt Club in South Hamilton, Massachusetts. In 1915 Kebo board members voted to enlarge the course to eighteen holes, but their efforts were sidetracked by World War I. The enlarged course was finally built in the early 1920s.

The Liscomb family also played a key role in the history of Kebo Valley golf. Andrew Liscomb served as superintendent of the grounds from 1893 until the early 1930s. He was succeeded by his son, Shirley Liscomb, who held the job until 1955. Member Waldron Bates, Shirley Liscomb, and famed course designer Donald Ross redesigned parts of Kebo at different times, but the eighteen-hole course that remains today is largely due to Leeds, who continued to make adjustments over the years.

Kebo Valley's stately clubhouse burned to the ground on opening day of the 1899 season; the cause was never determined. Golfers were undeterred, however; just one week later, the *New York*

*Time*s reported the results of the first weekly tournament at Kebo Valley. The club immediately made plans for a second, less elaborate clubhouse. "The new clubhouse will be simply a headquarters for golf players. There will be no huge dining room for dinners, for table d'hôtes; no large ballroom for the big dances...."[16] The new building was designed by local architect and club member Fred Savage. Opened in 1900, it featured a main reception room, two small dining rooms, and verandas above and below for views of the links. In addition, Wilson Eyre's original gatehouse, which survived the fire, was moved and incorporated into the new clubhouse.[17]

Even with the smaller clubhouse, Kebo maintained its position as the center of Bar Harbor's social life, as described in 1901: "The season was formally opened here to-night with a dinner and ball at the Kebo Valley Club. There had been no previous entertaining whatever, for the custom is always to wait for the word from Kebo as to when the Summer frivolity shall begin."[18]

Frivolity was temporarily halted in 1947 when the second clubhouse was destroyed, this time by the fires that claimed over 17,000 acres on Mount Desert Island. Local architect Ambrose Higgins designed the new clubhouse, and architect and club member Robert VanSummern redesigned it for the club's centennial in 1988.[19] Prior to the 1947 fire, membership was limited to summer residents only; tourists were not welcomed and local residents could play for a modest fee only after 4:00 p.m. Ironically, this was considered by the Greens Committee of 1903 as the best time of day to play, when "...the later afternoon light with its falling shadows, makes the scenery more beautiful than it is at any other time of day."[20] Following the fire, when very few summer estates were rebuilt and membership plummeted, local residents were encouraged to join, and day-players were welcomed, as is still true today.

The Kebo Valley Golf Club consistently ranks among the country's best public courses for its challenging game and stunningly beautiful landscape. Gently rolling hills contrast with the rugged natural scenery of Mount Desert Island, and before the leaves emerge in spring, Frenchman's Bay is visible from the clubhouse. The granite-exposed mountains of Cadillac, Champlain, Dorr, and Kebo provide a splendid backdrop to another of Maine's enduring landscapes.

MEGUNTICOOK GOLF CLUB: RUSTIC BEAUTY ON PENOBSCOT BAY

"The location of the links is one of great natural beauty, with views of the ocean or mountains from every part of it…. On the wide covered verandas at all times of the day may be found members and their guests, who, while not entering actively into golf or tennis, use the club house as a general meeting place, greatly promoting that informal social life and intercourse which the club aims to foster."[21] — SCENIC GEMS OF MAINE, 1898

Megunticook Golf Club is a nine-hole course on sixty-six acres in Rockport, nestled against the shore of Penobscot Bay. The club is among the oldest surviving private golf clubs in Maine, first organized in 1899, incorporated in 1901, and opened in 1902, and its clubhouse is the oldest golf club building in Maine.[22] Today, about 80,000 properties are listed in the National Register of Historic Places; Megunticook is a rarity as one of only twenty-four golf courses or golf club houses

included in this listing. [23] Megunticook is also unusual for its conservation easement with Maine Coast Heritage Trust. The easement prevents this valuable open space from ever being developed for residential or commercial use.

ABOVE: *The Megunticook Golf Clubhouse's low profile, rubble stone foundation, and rustic shingles make it well-suited to its naturalistic site.*

OPPOSITE: *The first and third fairways overlook Penobscot Bay at Megunticook Golf Club.*

Unlike Poland Spring and Kebo Valley, Megunticook Golf Club was started specifically for golf. The game was introduced in Camden in 1898 by summer visitors who laid out a six-hole course on nearby Ogier's Hill, where "[the] situation is one of great natural beauty and wide and various views of mountain and sea to be had from Ogier's hill cannot fail to charm the visitor."[24]

This first course did not satisfy the golfers for long, as they were unhappy with the property itself as well as with the owner's terms of use. Summer resident Charles Wolcott Henry of Philadelphia then donated land for the current course on Beauchamp Point. Groundskeeper Thomas Grant is credited with laying out the new course, with installation by local landscape contractor George Ingraham. The transformation of the former pasture and swampy woodland began in September 1901.[25]

The rustic clubhouse at Megunticook perfectly suits both the natural landscape and summertime atmosphere. The clubhouse was designed ca. 1901 by Boston architect Charles Brigham, who also designed the Lewiston City Hall (1890), the rear wing of the Maine State House in Augusta (1891), and the First Church of Christ Scientist in Portland (1915), among other Maine buildings.[26] The beauty of the Megunticook clubhouse lies in its dramatically low profile and the views from its sixteen-foot-wide veranda, which completely surrounds the building. From this shady overlook, club members may follow the progress of golfers or tennis players or enjoy the sight of sailboats passing in the bay. Inside, the clubhouse remains largely unchanged from its original design, with a large main club room and a parlor, each with a stone fireplace, chimney, and rustic interior finish.

The beauty of the Megunticook landscape lies in its combination of natural and manmade features. Parts of the course are left naturally steep, with high points from which to see the bay. The native landscape contrasts dramatically with the manicured greens, some of which are hidden by ledge and stands of native trees. Two of the holes are reached through woodland trails, a feature not found at Poland Spring or Kebo.

Unlike Poland Spring and Kebo Valley, Megunticook saw improvements by nationally known landscape architects who were well-versed in all aspects of design, rather than by golf specialists. In 1912 landscape architect Warren Manning prepared an elaborate plan of the Megunticook course. Manning worked for the famed Olmsted firm specializing in horticulture and planting design from 1888 to 1896 before starting his own practice in Cambridge, Massachusetts. He was one of eleven founding members of the American Society of Landscape Architects, and his client list contains more than 1,700 jobs, with about forty commissions in Maine. Manning and his associate, Albert Taylor, were well-known among Camden summer residents, and three of their projects abutted Megunticook Golf Course.[27] It is possible that Manning and Taylor were introduced to the club through these residential contacts.

Unfortunately, there is little information documenting Manning's work at Megunticook. It is unclear if his 1912 plan shows existing conditions or his new design ideas. The Warren Manning Papers at Iowa State University list only a "general map of property" (1913) and a "record plan of drainage" (1914).[28]

In 1914 Albert Taylor opened his own practice in Cleveland but continued to work in Camden, including at the Megunticook Golf Club. According to the National Register form, the original northern part of the course was congested and players were often hit with golf balls. In response, neighbor A. H. Chatfield donated twelve and one-half acres to expand the course, a job designated to Taylor. Today, the size and design of the northern part of the course reflects Taylor's intent.

The Megunticook Golf Club recognized the value of this historic landscape in 1988 when Mohr & Seredin, Landscape Architects, prepared a historic landscape report with recommendations for restoration of some original features of the course and guidelines for ongoing maintenance.[29] The golf club was listed in the National Register of Historic Places in 1993, significant both for its historic architecture and for the integrity of its early 1900s landscape.

CHAPTER 7

RURAL CEMETERIES: LANDSCAPES FOR THE LIVING AND THE DEAD

Maine is home to some of the earliest rural cemeteries in the country. Mount Hope in Bangor was established in 1834, just three years after the first American example, Mount Auburn Cemetery in Cambridge, Massachusetts. Laurel Hill Cemetery (1844) in Saco and Evergreen Cemetery (1852) in Portland also provide excellent examples of the national rural cemetery movement, which lasted roughly from 1830 to 1870. These rural cemeteries were intended to be not only burial grounds, but also beautiful landscapes for the enjoyment of the living, and these in turn influenced the design philosophy for public parks.

The rural cemetery movement was a dramatic departure from earlier modes of burial in churchyards or municipal graveyards that prevailed in Europe and America. The custom of churchyard burial, and the practice of burying the dead either within the church itself, or as close to it as possible, goes back at least to the seventh century in Europe. It was tied to fears of death and damnation and reflected the hope that being buried in a sanctified space would improve one's chances of salvation. Elaborate burial protocols developed to determine how the advantages the deceased had enjoyed in life would be preserved for all to see in their funeral processions and monuments.[1] In the New World these burial practices lost many of their ceremonial aspects and took the simpler form we associate today with New England's oldest cemeteries, many of which still exist along our roadsides and near country churches.

As cities grew, both here and in Europe, municipal burial lots supplemented churchyard grounds. But these city plots were soon considered unhealthy places, especially in times of epidemics and war, and the movement to find alternatives was spurred on in part by civic unrest and widespread protests. Furthermore, as urban areas were claimed for business or housing, the human remains in many of these graveyards were often dug up and relocated to outlying areas. This 1830s diary entry from New Yorker George Templeton Strong, quoted in Jeffrey Richman's fascinating history of Green-Wood Cemetery, makes the case for a new solution:

> *"...for in this city of all cities some place is needed where a man may lay down to his last nap without the anticipation of being turned out of his bed in the course of a year or so to make way for a street or a big store or something of that kind."* [2]

Notions of life after death were changing as well. The idea of death as eternal rest had begun to gain ground, influenced by the writings of philosopher Jean Jacques Rousseau and other

119

Age of Enlightenment thinkers. To rest in peace, in union with Nature, in a setting that reflected the kindliness of a Creator, became the new ideal. A new word was even adopted to signify this new reality: "cemetery" was derived from the Greek and early Christian "koimeterion," meaning "sleeping place."[3] Rural, park-like cemeteries began to replace the city churchyards and crowded urban burial grounds.

The first of these garden cemeteries was Père Lachaise Cemetery in Paris, established in 1804 by Napoleon and developed according to an 1815 plan by the architect Brongniart.[4] Burial conditions were particularly horrendous within and near the city of Paris, and a solution was urgently needed. To ensure that Parisians would purchase gravesites in the new cemetery, which was purposely located at a distance from the city center, authorities arranged to move there the bodies of Molière and LaFontaine, as well as Héloïse and Abélard, with attendant publicity. Père Lachaise developed quickly, and with its landscaped grounds and monuments of the famous, it became a destination for the living as well as the dead. (Today the cemetery, with its 70,000 graves—and 300 to 400 resident cats—attracts close to two million visitors annually.)[5]

It did not take long for the example of Père Lachaise to reach other places struggling with the same challenges. The movement, which was inspired by "romantic perceptions of nature, art, national identity, and the melancholy theme of death,"[6] found an immediate response in England and America. The first rural cemetery in the United States, Mount Auburn, was built in 1831 on a hilly site on the outskirts of Cambridge. It quickly became the model for others around the country: Mount Hope in Bangor, 1834; Laurel Hill in Philadelphia, 1836; and in 1838, Mount Hope in Rochester, New York, Green-Wood in Brooklyn, and Green Mount in Baltimore; and ultimately many others.

These rural cemeteries were developed as "romantic pastoral landscapes of the picturesque type. Planned as serene and spacious grounds where the combination of nature and monuments would be spiritually uplifting, they came to be looked on as public parks, places of respite and recreation acclaimed for their beauty and usefulness to society." Sites chosen for cemeteries were often hilly and wooded and offered possibilities for picturesque treatment. A substantial gateway was usually added to "establish separation from the workaday world, and a winding drive of gradual ascent slowed progress to a stately pace. Such settings stirred an appreciation of nature and a sense of the continuity of life."[7]

One of the key concepts of rural cemeteries, established in part to help sell gravesites, was to offer family burial plots, rather than individual sites. These plots were often enclosed by decorative iron fencing and had a central monument with the family's name, with smaller, individual markers for specific family members. Other characteristics of rural cemeteries were winding roads, extensive plantings, and elaborate, hand-carved monuments. As expansive parks within or near city limits, these cemeteries provided a destination for visitors, who came to enjoy the scenic drives, fresh air, and landscaped grounds with their ponds and picturesque buildings. Green-Wood Cemetery, for example, drew hordes of visitors before Central Park and Prospect Park offered alternatives. By the 1850s, "the yearly total [of visitors] was up to 500,000…and America's rural cemeteries rivaled Niagara Falls as the country's greatest tourist attraction."[8]

The tradition of providing attractions for visitors continues today at many of the rural cemeteries,

ABOVE: *The granite and bronze Webber Waiting Room at Mount Hope Cemetery, designed by George Mansur and donated in 1928, sheltered visitors waiting for the electric trolley car.*

partly for their historic interest and natural beauty, and partly because programming for visitors helps to support maintenance. Mount Auburn in Cambridge offers nature tours, bird-watching, and a book club featuring works by authors buried at the cemetery. Woodlawn Cemetery in the Bronx offers concerts commemorating the jazz greats buried there—Duke Ellington, Miles Davis, Lionel Hampton, and others. Green-Wood Cemetery provides tours and lectures, battle reenactments, parades, and an immensely popular Halloween tour.

Maine's rural cemeteries may be quieter places, but they still provide a serene garden setting open to the public and are excellent early examples of the rural cemetery movement.

MOUNT HOPE CEMETERY, BANGOR

A spot situated like this, with the beauties of nature scattered on every hand, is calculated to give a chastened and holy calm to the mind and lead the thought to study nature in her works and to God as her great author.[9] —BANGOR MAYOR EDWARD KENT, 1836

Incorporated in 1834, the same year as the city of Bangor, Mount Hope Cemetery is distinguished as the oldest rural cemetery in Maine and the second-oldest in the United States. It is also home to the oldest Civil War memorial in the country, the Soldier's Monument, dedicated in 1864. The nonsectarian cemetery, which today contains approximately 264 acres, was consecrated in 1836. It is listed in the National Register of Historic Places.

Bangor's strategic location at the head of the navigable Penobscot River, near the vast northern

ABOVE: *This imitation fort at the Grand Army of the Republic (GAR) Lot at Mount Hope Cemetery remains today, along with the flagpole and historic cannons.*
LEFT: *The GAR Lot was set aside for those who died in the Civil War.*

Soldier's Monument, Mt. Hope, Bangor, Me.

forests, made lumbering and sawmills important industries, while the river made trade and ship-building profitable. With a population of about 8,000, Bangor in the mid-1830s was considered the "Lumber Capital of the World," thanks to more than three hundred sawmills operating there.[10] Following an influx of mill laborers that led to sectarian riots in the 1830s, Bangor's leaders saw incorporation of the town as a way to enforce the rule of law and develop the city they called the "Queen of the East." They also "had visions of the Queen City challenging Boston as the industrial and shipping center of New England."[11]

Members of Bangor's affluent society built the Bangor House in 1834 as one of the country's "great palace hotels." They hired British-born architect Richard Upjohn in the 1830s to design their mansions as well as St. John's Church, just before he designed New York City's famed Trinity Church. Residents were also civic-minded, as evidenced by the Bangor Children's Home begun in 1835 to help destitute girls. The city was home to progressive transportation projects such as the first railroad in Maine (1836) and the first ocean-going iron-hulled steamship in the country (1844), intended to take passengers between Bangor and Boston.

Bangor's Mount Hope Cemetery was not formed in reaction to overcrowded conditions at the city's other cemeteries, but rather in response to the city leaders' quest to out-size Boston, though the Panic of 1857 brought an early end to this optimistic goal. Mount Hope was to be Bangor's answer to Mount Auburn in Cambridge.

Mount Auburn was founded by the Boston Horticultural Society, formed in 1829 to teach the latest horticultural techniques and to offer exhibits of locally grown food. Two years later the society bought seventy-two acres on which to build an arboretum, garden, and cemetery; the latter was laid out by General Henry A. S. Dearborn in 1831–32.[12] Following Mount Auburn's lead, the Bangor Horticultural Society was formed in the spring of 1834 with the goal of creating a new cemetery to honor the dead as well as the living, with ponds, trees, shrubs, and other ornamental plants. The society's goal was to "provide a suitable, attractive and tranquil place for quiet reflection."[13]

The horticultural society lasted only a few months, however, and a group of prominent residents then formed the Mount Hope Cemetery Corporation and used in their corporate seal the early Christian symbol of an anchor, which references "hope in Christ beyond this life."[14] The corporation bought fifty acres of farmland about two and one-half miles from downtown on an elevated site north of the Penobscot River. Some of the farmland was used to grow hay and oats to feed the cemetery horses and to sell crops to meet expenses. The founders named the tallest hill at the site Mount Hope, as was done at Mount Auburn.

The corporation hired local architect Charles G. Bryant to plan the new cemetery. Bryant, considered the first person in Maine to call himself an architect, designed and built a variety of structures in Bangor in the 1830s and produced a development plan for the city in 1834.[15] Bryant's plan for Mount Hope no longer exists, but his design set aside land for burial grounds on the highest part of the property, with about two hundred family plots of ten to twelve gravesites. Here are found the cemetery's oldest burial sites. They were auctioned for $25 per lot and, oddly, were numbered randomly according to the order in which they were sold. Only after several hundred lots were sold was a more orderly, logical numbering system adopted for the remaining sites. As was true at other

ABOVE: *A typical family monument in Mount Hope Cemetery.*
OPPOSITE: *Lichen-covered stones, decorative iron fencing, and mature shade trees add to the historic character of Mount Hope Cemetery.*

rural cemeteries, bodies were re-interred at the new, scenic Mount Hope Cemetery.

Bryant's plan also featured a so-called "Garden Lot" for horticultural purposes. Today the "Garden Lot" refers to the area opposite the Superintendent's Lodge, in the southwest corner of the cemetery, and includes the Office Pond, numerous family plots, the plot designated for orphans from the Bangor Children's Home, and the 1864 Civil War monument. Despite its name, this area was always intended for burial sites, but they were to be improved with plantings. Flowers, trees, shrubs, and ornamental fencing made the cemetery more beautiful, rather than simply functional, in keeping with national trends.

As the largest public open space in Bangor, Mount Hope attracted city residents who appreciated its park-like qualities and the chance to visit their family lots. Soon after Mount Hope opened, residents could ride the state's first railroad line (the second in New England) to Mount Hope and disembark at the train station opposite the cemetery's Western Avenue entrance. By the 1870s Bangor also had horse-drawn trolleys, which were replaced by Maine's first electric street railway when it opened for business in 1889.

The corporation continued to annex additional land, and by 1869, the cemetery had expanded from its original two hundred lots to more than 1,300. In 1871 civil engineer Charles E. Green and his assistant, F. E. L. Beale, prepared a new plan, which shows one pond, Western Avenue lined with an allée of trees, and numerous treed spaces within the cemetery. An unnamed stream along the northern border was later dammed to create the five ponds that exist today. The narrow roads, designed for carriages, were laid out in gentle curves and, following a popular trend, were named for trees or landscape features—Laurel, Willow, Cedar, Fir, Lawn, and Riverside.

An additional one hundred acres were acquired in the 1880s, and this area was offered as burial sites about twenty years later. Now known as the Eastern Division, it had no overall plan; roads were laid out and plots assigned as needed, following the character established in the 1871 plan.

The current map of the Eastern Division was prepared in 1962, when a group of college students and their civil engineering professor combined all of the sketches prepared over the years by cemetery staff.

The cemetery went through a period of modernization beginning around 1900. Wooden and iron fencing and decorative iron and granite gates were installed in various sections and new trees were planted to replace old and decaying ones, with about one hundred installed each year in the early 1900s.[16] An elaborate system, with a windmill and standpipes, supplied water for the cemetery from the Penobscot River.

In 1909 a new Superintendent's Lodge with an office, chapel, and waiting room was built to replace the original 1874 lodge. The new building was designed by Bangor architect Wilfred Mansur, who also designed the Penobscot County Courthouse, the Bangor YMCA, and numerous schools and homes in the area. The Tudor-style lodge featured such details as overhanging gables, diagonal window mullions, mixed materials such as stone and stucco, and exposed half-timbers.

Two free-standing waiting rooms were donated in 1928 by Mr. and Mrs. Franklin R. Webber. One of these, the Webber Waiting Room, remains today, located on the cemetery's State Street side. George Mansur, brother of Wilfred, designed a granite and bronze circular building fifteen feet in diameter and roughly twenty feet high. The design featured pink granite from Maine, a cast-iron balustrade, a stone floor, stone bench, bronze ceiling and door, and an electric chandelier.[17]

The cemetery's one hundred-acre Northern Division was surveyed in 1931 but not laid out until 1955. At that time Superintendent F. Stanley Howatt designed it as a "memorial park," with gravestones flush to the ground, in order to reduce maintenance costs. However, the idea proved unpopular and no lots were sold. Landscape architects Grever and Ward of Orchard Park, New York, redesigned this section with above-ground markers in the 1970s and 1980s. Today about fifty acres remain forested and are being held until the need for more burial space arises.

Mount Hope has several war memorials dedicated to those who lost their lives in the Civil War and the Korean War. Despite Maine's distance from the battlefields of the Civil War, that conflict

loomed large in the state. Even today, the names of Harriet Beecher Stowe, author of *Uncle Tom's Cabin*, and Joshua Lawrence Chamberlain, governor, Bowdoin president, and Union general, are well known to residents and tourists. Civil War memorials are prominent at Mount Hope, and the first of these, the Soldier's Monument, is considered the oldest Civil War monument in the country. Dedicated in 1864, the twenty-foot-high obelisk is located in the Garden Lot, near the main entrance off State Street, and is surrounded by soldiers' graves.

The next of Mount Hope's Civil War memorials was added in 1901, when the Grand Army of the Republic Fort was built to mark a new section of the cemetery dedicated to soldiers killed in that conflict. Located near Fort Pond by the Eastern Avenue entrance, the fort features a masonry tower with cannons and flags, with burial sites on the adjacent hillside.

The Second Maine Memorial, located near the main entrance off State Street, was dedicated in 1962 to the men of the Second Maine Regiment of Volunteers in the Civil War. Colonel Luther Peirce of Bangor had served in the Second Maine and other divisions of the Union Army from 1861 to 1868. His 1915 will provided funds for memorial gates and fencing along Mount Hope Avenue and requested that a memorial to the Second Maine be established. The memorial was not installed, however, until the 1960s, when the cemetery added a sculpture designed by Vernon Shaffer of Wisconsin depicting a bronze angel, mounted on white granite, carrying a wounded soldier.

The Maine Korean War Memorial was built in 1995 near the GAR Fort and Fort Pond. The black granite monument is inscribed with the names of 233 men and women from Maine who died or were listed as missing in action in the Korean War. A long granite walkway is lined with flags from countries that supported South Korea in the conflict.

Burials still take place at Mount Hope, with traditional earth burial lots, cremation lots, the Romanesque Columbarium to store cremated remains, or the mausoleum for above-ground burial. In contrast to the original family plots that held ten to twelve gravesites, most lots today are sold in pairs or fours. The cemetery is open to the public seven days a week for strolling, jogging, and quiet reflection; no pets or recreational activities are allowed. In the summer the Bangor Museum and Center for History offers popular guided walking tours and "Ghost Lamp" evening tours.

Visitors to the cemetery may notice the nearby octagon-shaped building that was the cemetery's chapel in the 1800s. When improvements were made in the early 1900s, the corporation sold the chapel, which was moved off site. Today the privately owned building still has its original stained-glass windows, silver metal roof, granite foundation, and ornamental woodwork. Should the building come up for sale in the future, Stephen Burrill, who took over from his father as superintendent, hopes to buy it and return it as an architectural focal point of Mount Hope.

Laurel Hill Cemetery, Saco

*We buried him at Laurel Hill Cemetery, in a spot on the bank of the beautiful river Saco....
There ... on a summer's day, while the stream passes silently by, we will gladly stray, and join-
ing in the mournful melancholy which sweeps over the grave of those we love, we will pay a
kindred offering.* [18] —F. Robie, 1845

Laurel Hill Cemetery, established in 1844, is another of Maine's early rural cemeteries built on the Mount Auburn model. As was typical of cemeteries intended to benefit the living, Laurel Hill rests on a high point overlooking dramatic scenery, in this case the Saco River. The largest, and only active, cemetery in Saco, Laurel Hill contains the graves and monuments of prominent citizens and politicians and is widely known for its extraordinary display of spring-blooming bulbs.

In the 1840s Saco and Biddeford businessmen Joseph Leland, Josiah Calef, James B. Thornton, and others formed an association to create a cemetery "upon the modern plan of Mount Auburn and others, whereby families can be accommodated with private lots, which they can make up and ornament according to their own taste."[19] The new cemetery replaced the old one on the town com- mon (now Pepperell Park), which had become too small and was neglected and no longer used for burials. The new cemetery also followed the national shift to burying the dead in park-like settings away from town centers, and wealthy and prominent citizens buried on the common were soon moved to Laurel Hill.[20]

Leland and his associates bought about twenty-five acres on the Saco River, about one mile from downtown, where gravesites from the 1750s happened to be located; the original cemetery was built around these gravesites. (Today this area encompasses about three hundred feet on each side of the chapel and extends to the riverbank.) The cemetery has two distinct sections separated

Saco, Me., Laurel Hill Cemetery.

by a wide buffer of native woods: the nineteenth-century part with stately oak and linden trees, closely spaced tombstones, and narrow winding lanes; and Deering Park, a twentieth-century addition laid out in a starkly contrasting geometric design.

The Deering family has been involved with the commercial develop- ment of Saco since Joseph G. Deering I founded the family lumber com- pany in 1866. His grandson, Joseph G. Deering II, was a businessman, civic leader, and philanthropist who also served as treasurer of Laurel Hill Cemetery Association for many years. Joseph II's nephew, John Deering, served two terms as mayor of Portland in the 1880s.

The original part of Laurel Hill was laid out by Waldo Higginson, Esquire; little is known about Higginson other than that he was "an experienced engineer." By 1849, trees had been planted along the winding avenues and paths, about 150 lots had been purchased, and the cemetery was described as "an interesting place of resort."[21] A receiving tomb was

built in 1876. Over the next several decades additional parcels were added, with totals of 60 acres by 1899 and 170 acres today.

In 1899 Oliver B. Bradbury, sexton of the cemetery, was given "much credit for the splendid appearance of the grounds."[22] Bradbury had taken over from his father, who had been sexton from 1847 to 1877. Under the Bradburys' direction, the corporation strove to create a park-like setting with shady walks, "fine carriage roads raked smoothly," and "urns and rustic baskets full of rare and beautiful flowers." For the convenience of visitors, vine-covered arbors offered a place to rest, and nearby pumps furnished water to care for flowers. Land overlooking the river was described as "one of the prettiest places in the whole cemetery," and the nearby ravine was also made a "place of beauty" with "artistic rustic bridges" spanning its small stream.

The corporation acquired twenty-four acres of adjacent land for Deering Park in 1919 and held it against future need. Cemetery records show that Deering Park was designed in the late 1930s (but not opened until the 1970s) by Shurcliff, Merrill and Footit. This was a continuation of the firm started in 1905 by Arthur Shurcliff (pp. 149–153), who was most noted for the restoration/re-creation of Colonial Williamsburg. Shurcliff's son, Sidney, had joined the firm in the 1930s and prepared plans for Deering Park at that time. The geometric layout of the Laurel Hill additio n reflects the firm's penchant for Colonial Revival designs.

In the 1950s the Shurcliff firm also oversaw improvements that changed the character of the original cemetery from old-fashioned mounded graves to the rolling, wooded landscape seen today. They added tons of fill and turf between family plots in order to reduce maintenance; the original lanes used by horse and carriage were still visible but were more easily mowed. They also planted numerous trees and shrubs to create a more park-like atmosphere.

The most significant memorial in the historic section of the cemetery belongs to the Fairfield family. John Fairfield was active in Maine politics from 1835 until his death in 1847, as a U.S. Congressman, governor of Maine, and U.S. Senator. In 1956 the cemetery's board of managers erected an elaborate sundial on a circular granite base in memory of the Fairfield family. This monument is aligned on an axis with the Fairfield obelisk and a massive, mature Norway spruce, all providing one of the most formal settings found at Laurel Hill.

The Laurel Hill chapel was designed by Horace G. Wadlin of Reading, Massachusetts. Construction began in 1890. The Queen Anne-style chapel features a combination of granite and shingle cladding and a corner tower with a curving roof. Wadlin designed several buildings in Saco and Biddeford, among them the Pepperell Park Water Tower, Biddeford High School, Thornton Academy, the York Corporation Agent's House, and the Colonial Revival home of Joseph G. Deering I.

Because Laurel Hill has always been privately owned, town records contain little information about its history or use. First the horse-car and then the electric trolley passed by the cemetery on their way to Old Orchard Beach, and today the recently rebuilt Victorian trolley shelter stands near the chapel, but there are no records of how visitors might have enjoyed the cemetery as a strolling destination or park.

For many years following the establishment of Memorial Day in 1868, townspeople marched to the cemetery to decorate graves, sing hymns, and recite patriotic speeches to honor soldiers killed in the Civil War. In 1908 the local newspaper published a roll call of veterans from all of the country's wars who were buried at Laurel Hill.[23] The Deering Park section also features the Saco Veterans Memorial, dedicated in 1987, and a monument built in the 1990s to honor Saco firefighters.

Visitors to Laurel Hill's original section pass through large, wooden gates off Beach Street and emerge under a canopy of mature linden trees, with an expanse of historic gravestones before them. In addition to these traditional burial sites, the landscape includes an unusual arrangement of outdoor "rooms" enclosed by clipped yew hedges. The hedges divide the cemetery into smaller, more intimate burial spaces while also reflecting the formality often associated with cemetery plantings, even in rural cemeteries.

The intent at Laurel Hill has always been to allow and encourage quiet strolling and meditation without the distraction of dogs, bicycles, or other recreational activities, which are not allowed. The cemetery is listed by Saco Bay Trails as a destination for urban walkers, and you can follow a map of prominent burial sites or stroll the peaceful lanes, as do neighborhood residents and bird-watchers. It is also used as a scenic backdrop for high-school prom photographs, and the chapel is popular for weddings. Numerous visitors make a pilgrimage in May to see tens of thousands of daffodils blooming on the river bank, thanks to Joseph G. Deering II. He and landscape architect Sidney Shurcliff reportedly felt that the daffodils would increase the beauty and attraction of the place. Today the cemetery's maintenance crew plants 5,000 tulip bulbs and 14,000 daffodils each year.

ABOVE: *The Queen Anne-style Laurel Hill Chapel was one of several buildings in Saco and Biddeford designed by Horace G. Wadlin.*

EVERGREEN CEMETERY, PORTLAND

The beauty of these grounds, where the harmonies of art are blended with the wildness of nature, sheds the radiance of a heavenly light upon the gloom of death.[24]
— EDWARD ELWELL, 1876

Evergreen Cemetery in Portland is an outstanding example of the rural cemetery movement in Maine and is listed in the National Register of Historic Places. The cemetery was consecrated in 1854. The 239-acre site is the city's largest open space, largest urban forest, and a sanctuary for wildlife and migratory birds. Its extensive collection of historic monuments is set among naturalistic, curving drives, mature trees, and rolling topography.

Portland's existing cemeteries, Eastern and Western, were nearly full by the early 1850s, and the city was growing rapidly. In 1852 the city purchased fifty-five acres for a rural cemetery, about two and one-half miles from downtown Portland, in what was then Westbrook. The new cemetery was to be built on the model of Mount Auburn, as a dignified burial ground as well as a source of comfort for the living. "What could be more desirable than to have a spot resembling Mount Auburn, to which the bereaved might retire for meditation and reflection?"[25]

ENTRANCE TO EVERGREEN-CEMETERY.

ABOVE: *The tree-lined entrance to Evergreen Cemetery, as shown in 1874, led between homes on neighboring properties. In the early 1900s the city bought and razed the homes, and today the drive is framed by lawns.*

LEFT: *The vertical Fobes family monument at Evergreen Cemetery illustrates a common theme of the Victorian period—confidence in a spiritual afterlife. Fobes family graves surround the central monument.*

The site chosen for Evergreen differs from both Mount Auburn and Mount Hope in that it did not have a distinguished high point offering scenic views. In fact, it was heavily forested (hence the name Evergreen) and "sufficiently undulating to present all of those inequalities of surface so necessary to the production of effective contrasts in scenery." Some parts were "open and elevated, from which may be caught glimpses of the mountains upon the one hand and the city upon the other."[26] The property was laced with cow paths and logging trails and had a swampy section suitable for the creation of ponds.

In 1855 civil engineer Charles H. Howe prepared the cemetery's first plan with roughly 680 family burial plots and a combination of curving and grid-like roads based on the existing topography. Roads were for horse-and-carriage travel, while narrower paths allowed pedestrians to reach lots without road frontage. Circular intersections served as focal points; similar circles appear at Mount Hope and Laurel Hill. Sites for a "keeper's lodge," an office, a receiving tomb, and a chapel were shown, along with a mix of naturalistic and formal design elements; two organically shaped ponds (both called "Meadow Pond") were proposed across from a formal circular fountain. Nearby, "Pine Hill" and "Fern Hill" were bordered by informal footpaths. Howe did not make suggestions for grading or planting; these occurred as lots were developed. Most of the earliest work involved clearing the existing forest in order to create gravesites.

Howe oversaw construction of the cemetery, and Portland newswriters praised his work: "The whole plan is conceived and carried out in an artistical [*sic*] manner, and yet the engineer has so admirably executed his work, as to make art secondary to nature…. Mr. Howe has surveyed the ground with the eye of a true artist."[27]

Records beginning in 1856 show that the city regularly purchased trees, shrubs (sometimes more than 1,000 in one year), vines, and thousands of annuals and bulbs for use throughout the grounds. In the 1880s the city installed water lines to assist with the care of plantings.

By 1864, the horse-car street railway was extended to reach the cemetery, allowing even greater access to the general public for recreation, as described in a popular guidebook:

> *We have secured land…within two miles of town, full of attractions, with trees, waters, plentiful shrubbery and the varying undulations of surface, which render natural scenery so attractive. We have laid out winding paths and carriage roads, with hedges and monuments, and beautiful enclosures, of such a character, that the grounds have become a great attraction to visitors, and are often crowded with strangers, hour after hour, toward night-fall; and we have established a line of horse-cars which run thither regularly every half hour.*[28]

A second plan prepared in 1869 by city engineer Charles R. Goodell (who also designed Lincoln Park, pp. 26–28) shows further improvements to Howe's plan, most notably the transformation of Meadow Pond into an unnamed rectangular pool. Goodell also replaced Howe's fountain with a formal, oval pond and proposed about 115 additional family plots and two dozen smaller burial sites. He showed vacant land where Howe had marked Fern and Pine hills.

In the 1870s and '80s, the city purchased several parcels of land, which were designed and developed as needed by city engineers, including Goodell. In contrast to the original section's curvilinear

ABOVE: *The Weeping Lady in Evergreen Cemetery signifies grief and remembrance.*
OPPOSITE TOP: *Burial sites in historic rural cemeteries are typically elevated above adjacent paths.*
OPPOSITE BOTTOM: *The Gould family burial plot displays typical nineteenth-century iron fencing in Evergreen Cemetery.*

layout, much of the expanded area was arranged in a grid pattern. According to architectural historian Kirk Mohney, this new section reflected the transition from the rural cemetery to the lawn cemetery movement, which used grave markers that were set flush with the surrounding lawn.

Today there are four ponds at Evergreen Cemetery, one of which matches the rectangular pool shown on Goodell's 1869 plan. Flanking it are three organically shaped ponds where Goodell had proposed burial plots. The ponds have been a popular destination for visitors since at least the 1870s, when the city first stocked them with several swans and white geese. (In 2006 domesticated ducks and geese were relocated to farms when their caretaker retired; today the ponds are home to wild waterfowl.) In the 1870s the ponds featured wooden bridges, rustic gazebos, and ornamental shrub plantings. The city built a waiting room nearby in 1884.

Evergreen's first office, a handsome wood and stone building with a gabled roof and turret, was built in 1893. The building remains as the existing cemetery office, though it is missing much of the original architectural detail, which was destroyed by fire in 1961.

Portland resident Frederick A. Tompson (p. 33) was responsible for designing much of the cemetery's architecture (although there is no indication that he built the office). Tompson trained with and became a partner of the highly respected architect Francis Fassett. He was most noted for his residential commissions but also designed schools, apartment houses, office blocks, and libraries using the latest building methods. At Evergreen in 1901 he designed a new waiting room for trolley passengers, as well as granite pillars and stone walls at the south entrance; the waiting room was eventually demolished, but the stonework remains.

Tompson also designed the most significant building at Evergreen, the Wilde Memorial Chapel, built in 1902 in English Gothic style. The chapel honors Samuel Wilde, a New York businessman whose wife was from Maine and who summered on the Maine coast. The chapel was used for funerals until the 1940s, when funeral homes gained in popularity. (Today the chapel is used both for funerals and for weddings.) The chapel features Maine materials—white granite from North Jay and roof slate from Brownville—as well as materials supplied by national craftsmen: yellow brick from Philadelphia, stained-glass windows from Boston, a bronze bell from Troy, New York, and furniture from Grand Rapids, Michigan. Following decades of deterioration, the chapel was restored to its original workmanship in 1992.

Evergreen Cemetery has several notable memorials and monuments. The distinctive tomb of Rumford's Hugh Chisholm (pp. 196–199), built in 1913, is a copy of the Maison Carrée in Nîmes, France, which was modeled after the Parthenon. The F. O. J. Smith Tomb, overlooking the ponds, is considered the most significant example of the Egyptian Revival style in Maine.[29] In 1919 the Portland Lodge of the Benevolent and Protective Order of Elks installed their memorial, which features a life-sized bronze elk atop a base of boulders, surrounded by ornamental shrubs. In 1977 the veterans' Court of Honor Memorial was installed.

By the early 1900s the cemetery had a well-established endowment, thanks to perpetual care funds, but city officials diverted the money for other public projects. Interest in Evergreen declined through the 1920s as residents turned to Portland's parks, such as Deering Oaks, for recreation. Over the following decades the cemetery suffered from loss of funding, vandalism, and a general lack of maintenance.

In response, a group of concerned citizens formed The Friends of Evergreen Cemetery in 1991. Their mission was to preserve, protect, and restore Evergreen for past, present, and future generations. Since 1991 the Friends have accomplished numerous projects, such as helping to list the cemetery in the National Register of Historic Places, restoring the Wilde Chapel, and developing a master plan in 1994. The plan by Halvorson Company of Boston outlined the historical character of the cemetery, assessed its condition, and offered suggestions for its future development.

Evergreen remains an active cemetery with burials taking place on a regular basis. As was originally intended, the cemetery continues to serve as valuable public open space within city limits while also maintaining its dignity as a historic burial ground. Portland Trails lists Evergreen as one of twenty-six sites throughout the city where visitors may use the extensive network of gravel lanes, paved roads, and wooded trails, which also connect to Baxter Woods across Stevens Avenue. The Maine Audubon Society conducts spring bird-watching walks at the cemetery, and the Friends of Evergreen offer tours in the spring and fall and have created several brochures for self-guided visits.

ABOVE: *The Greek Revival Baxter family monument is prominent at Evergreen Cemetery both for its architecture and for its historic significance. The monument honors James Phinney Baxter, who is buried here, and his son Percival, whose ashes were dispersed at Mount Katahdin.*

III. PRIVATE ESTATES:
GREAT HOMES AND GARDENS

CHAPTER 8

THE GRAND COLONIAL REVIVAL

The Colonial Revival period, which lasted roughly from 1880 to 1955, evolved from the Centennial International Exposition of 1876, held in Philadelphia to mark the one-hundredth anniversary of the Declaration of Independence. The exhibition was an opportunity for the United States to showcase its latest industrial, agricultural, and engineering inventions: electric lights and elevators powered by the 1,400-horsepower Corliss steam engine, locomotives, fire trucks, printing presses, mining equipment, typewriters, Bell's telephone, and Edison's telegraph. The scale and scope of the fair were unprecedented in this country. It featured 450 acres of exhibition grounds, 30,000 exhibitors, and nearly 200 buildings displaying examples of "Arts, Manufactures, and Products of the Soil and Mine" from around the world. At least fifty countries were represented, and roughly ten million visitors attended during the fair's six-month run.[1]

The Exposition followed a period of rapid urbanization, industrialization, and immigration in the United States, when many Americans looked nostalgically to the past and sought images of simpler and more serene times. Amid the new technological exhibits and machinery, visitors to the fair also toured several buildings that were believed to represent the "colonial" period, from 1600 to 1820. One of the most

popular exhibits consisted of two buildings side by side: the New England Farmer's Home and the Modern Kitchen. The farmer's home was a log cabin with an open-hearth kitchen from the 1770s. Next door, the 1876 version, with clapboard siding and awnings over the windows, featured running water, a cast-iron cookstove, and a hot-water boiler.

Residential architecture of the Colonial Revival period generally fell into two categories: new construction and renovation of existing buildings. New Colonial Revival homes were marked by a symmetrical façade, with windows arranged evenly on either side of a central doorway. The door was often accented with a decorative "crown" that was supported by pilasters (half-columns attached to the wall), or by full columns that formed a small entry porch. The windows were usually double-hung sashes, often in adjacent pairs.[2] Built with the advantages of new technology, many Colonial Revival homes were faithful reproductions that differed from the originals only in their lack of handmade details. This chapter's River House, a stately mansion designed by Guy Lowell for Mary Marvin Goodrich on the York River, illustrates many aspects of Colonial Revival style and has an exceptionally intact Colonial Revival landscape.

The symmetry of Colonial Revival buildings was easily

transferable to the landscape, which may account for the popularity of Colonial Revival gardens. These were known for their geometric, symmetrical layouts of beds and walkways; paths were laid out in simple straight lines, with major axes and minor cross-axes. Often focal points such as sundials and birdbaths punctuated the ends of the axes. Gardens were often furnished with arbors, seats, and garden houses that contributed to the creation of useable outdoor rooms. Sometimes, in an effort to recall the past, gardens featured salvaged parts of old buildings, worn furnishings, and other artifacts. They were typically enclosed with white picket fences, walls, or clipped hedges and often featured specialty gardens such as herb and rose gardens. Overall, Colonial Revival gardens were more decorative, formal, and manicured than those from the true colonial period.

One of the most popular trends of the Colonial Revival period was the renovation or rescue of dilapidated, historic buildings. Hamilton House in South Berwick and Spite House in Rockport, two distinguished homes, were both rescued from deteriorated conditions and renovated with Colonial Revival features. Continuing the theme into the landscape, each was outfitted with elaborate Colonial Revival gardens.

HAMILTON HOUSE, SOUTH BERWICK

In isolation, simplicity, and ripeness, the atmosphere of the whole place breathes of olden days, and might well be taken as a model for the perfect American garden.[3] —LOUISE SHELTON, 1915

Hamilton House, a National Historic Landmark, is a grand Georgian mansion built ca. 1785 by Colonel Jonathan Hamilton. In the 1890s, the twelve-room house was saved from neglect and renovated in the Colonial Revival style. At the same time, the landscape was nostalgically transformed into extensive Colonial Revival gardens. One hundred years later, both house and grounds were returned to their 1920s appearance by the Society for the Preservation of New England Antiquities (SPNEA, known today as Historic New England). Today visitors can tour the mansion and restored formal gardens or follow woodland paths along the Salmon Falls River to Vaughan Woods State Park.

The main focus here is the property's Colonial Revival period from about 1898, but its history began in the late 1700s. At that time, the tidal Salmon Falls River served as the town's highway, as people and merchandise were transported by ship. Elevated dramatically above the river, Colonel Hamilton's mansion displayed the wealth he had gained as a West Indies merchant and ship owner. From his house, Hamilton had scenic views up, down, and across the river. This was also a strategic location, as the new wharves at Hamilton House, located about fourteen miles from Portsmouth Harbor, were as far as ships could navigate on the Salmon Falls River.

The property was sold after Hamilton's death in 1802 and was used as a sheep farm beginning around 1839. Near the end of the century, however, this farm, like numerous others in New England, fell upon hard times when railroads began to bring cheaper foodstuffs from the Midwest. In a state of disrepair, the property was purchased in 1898 by Emily Davis Tyson and her stepdaughter Elise Tyson Vaughan from Boston.[4] The Tysons had learned of Hamilton House through their good friend, Sarah Orne Jewett, who lived nearby and had been fond of the house since childhood. Hamilton House had served as the setting for Jewett's novel *The Tory Lover*.

Emily and Elise Tyson chose architect Herbert W. C. Browne to renovate and make additions to the Hamilton house. Browne and his partner, Arthur Little, were known around the country for their large-scale private commissions in the Colonial Revival style. The Tysons built a new kitchen wing, enlarged the dining room, and added a small bedroom, indoor plumbing, and a partially enclosed piazza overlooking the river. On the exterior of the two wings, Browne designed square trellises, another Colonial Revival motif.

Following popular Colonial Revival trends, the Tysons decorated with antiques, country furnishings, and painted murals. They even reproduced Colonel Hamilton's original wallpaper, which was an unusual practice for the time. They added furnishings with historical references to Hamilton, such as ship models, China Trade objects, maritime prints, hooked rugs with ship scenes, hand-sewn samplers, and prints by Currier & Ives.

Details inside the mansion helped to link architecture and landscape. Artist George Porter

OPPOSITE: *Restored pineapple finials and a garden arbor frame the view of Hamilton House and repeat the lines of the four chimneys.*
BELOW: *Elise Tyson Vaughan photographed Emily Davis Tyson under the pergola at Hamilton House in 1902. The Tysons clipped vines on the pergola to keep open the view of the Salmon Falls River.*

Fernald painted murals over existing wallpaper in two rooms. The parlor mural depicted historic Portsmouth houses lining the Piscataqua riverbank, as well as the ship *The Ranger*, which was associated with John Paul Jones and had been featured prominently in *The Tory Lover*. Fernald's dining room mural romanticized summer life with classical ruins, Italian gardens, and views of the Mediterranean shore. The back parlor's wallpaper was in a garden-like trellis and ivy pattern. In turn, the landscape was linked to the mansion by paths aligned with doorways, views framed by arbors, and window styles of the mansion repeated in the small garden studio.

The Colonial Revival landscape of Hamilton House was most likely designed collaboratively by Herbert Browne and the Tysons. Colonial Revival gardens relied on geometric and architectural forms, both used extensively in the landscape of Hamilton House. The ground around the house was raised and shaped into distinct lawn terraces, and the gardens formed a series of outdoor rooms. The south terrace adjoining the house featured a sitting area backed by the vine-draped mansion, with giant elms towering overhead. New gardens—a Colonial Revival sunken garden, a cutting garden, and a cottage garden enclosed by stone walls—overlooked the Salmon Falls River.

The sunken Colonial Revival garden was perhaps the most ambitious of the Tysons' renovations, as it involved moving a massive barn that stood less than one hundred feet from the mansion. This garden measured about seventy feet by one hundred feet and ran east-west, perpendicular to the river. As with all Colonial Revival gardens, architectural elements played a key role in its design. A long, low garden house on the north side was crowned by finials, trimmed with latticework, and draped with honeysuckle. On the south and part of the west side, a massive vine-covered pergola framed views of the river and created a shady outdoor room for entertaining. At the far end of the pergola was an open-air sitting room under another roof of vines. Paths throughout the garden were arranged at right angles, with the main path aligned with a side door of the mansion. Intersections and endings were punctuated with focal points such as a sundial, marble fountain, birdbath, and classical statues.

Elise Tyson's photographs from 1903 show the sunken garden smothered in greenery: wisteria, trumpet vine, akebia (kiwi), grapes, and ivy. Constant clipping of vines and hedges preserved views to the river. In the geometric beds bordered by formal boxwoods, the Tysons favored plants that recalled colonial times: delphiniums, peonies, roses, lilies, and Canterbury bells, among others. A spirea hedge separated the sunken garden from the adjacent cutting garden. At a break in the hedge, an elegant arbor stood at the top of the granite steps, framing the view back to the mansion and mimicking its Palladian windows.

The sunken garden's geometry was carried into the cutting garden. Here straight grass paths bordered rectangular panels of flowers, and the view to Hamilton House was framed by white columns with pinecone finials. This small garden, at roughly forty feet on a side, was raised above the larger main garden and was enclosed by evergreen hedges.

To the north of the cutting garden were the cottage and its garden. In 1907 architect Herbert Browne designed the cottage using doors, banisters, beams,

paneling, and a fireplace rescued from an eighteenth-century house that was being demolished in Newmarket, New Hampshire; this salvaging of old materials was a notable Colonial Revival trend. The cottage was used for entertaining guests and was comfortably furnished with "early American pieces in maple and pine" and a writing chair with shelf and drawer. Decorations nostalgically recalled the colonial period: a row of old glass bottles threw "shifting color throughout the room," and old wooden spoons and bowls hung on twig hooks taken from the Newmarket house.[5] After Mrs. Tyson's death in 1922, the cottage held her stepdaughter's collection of dolls and miniature furniture. In the 1930s Elise also added two small rooms off the back of the cottage.

The cottage's front yard consisted of a small walled garden, roughly twenty by forty feet, brimming with old-fashioned flowers – phlox, monkshood, Veronica, hollyhocks, sweet Williams, and forget-me-nots, among others. The two planted panels were edged by clipped boxwood, and lilacs lined the outside of the fieldstone wall. A sundial and birdbath completed the old-fashioned theme. On the south side of the cottage, three French doors led to a brick terrace overlooking the river. Elsewhere on the property the Tysons had gardens for cut flowers, vegetables, and reserves for replacement plants.

Elise Tyson Vaughan died in 1949 and left Hamilton House and its gardens to the Society for the Preservation of New England Antiquities, along with a small endowment. The following year a fierce windstorm almost entirely demolished the pergola. Due to limited funds, SPNEA removed the garden's posts, arbors, and fences, which were all in poor condition. To reduce maintenance, they removed some of the hedges and perennial beds and replaced some plants with hardier varieties. This reduction in maintenance costs was relatively common at house museums following World War II. In the 1950s, following national historic preservation trends, SPNEA removed the two wings added by the Tysons in order to bring the building back to its original form.

Elise Tyson Vaughan had left many of the mansion's furnishings when she donated the property to SPNEA. In 1987 curators recreated Emily and Elise's vision of their Colonial Revival mansion based on photographs that appeared in 1929 editions of *House Beautiful* magazine. Curators rearranged the furniture as the Tysons had and prominently displayed their collections, such as colored glass and folk art, in vignettes that recalled the spirit of 1929.

During the 1980s SPNEA also began restoring the gardens to their appearance in the mid-1920s, when they were at their peak. Based on plans developed by landscape preservationist Lucinda Brockway of Past Designs in Kennebunk, Maine, they removed self-seeded trees to restore views and sunny conditions, replanted the lost spirea hedge, and re-created beds for cut flowers and herbs. They built new columns and pinecone finials to replace dilapidated ones and rebuilt a version of Mrs. Tyson's Colonial Revival arbor. On the bank overlooking the river, they removed tangled shrubs and planted sixteen disease-resistant elms that will eventually frame the view of the river, as they did in the 1700s.

Historic New England continues to add details that enhance the landscape's 1920s character. They restored the marble fountain and its water supply and reproduced a unique pot decorated with lion's faces. As shown in historic photos, the lion planter is aligned on axis with the sundial and fountain. Future projects include restoring some of the garden's historic metal furniture.

If you visit Hamilton House today, you drive through a quiet residential neighborhood along a narrow lane and arrive at the large field, the original (relocated) barn, and gravel parking area, all very picturesque and serene. The historic character of Hamilton House extends well beyond the property's fourteen and one-half acres, as a portion of the land is kept in hayfields, and the water view is protected, with no new development visible on either side of the river. The narrow driveway opens up to reveal the mansion, views of the river, and the sunken garden. Guided tours of the mansion begin on the river side of the house, which was the original entrance during Colonel Hamilton's time. After the house tour, you can explore at your leisure some of the best formal gardens, and also best examples of garden restoration, open to the public in Maine. The setting along the river is stunning and is a perfect spot for enjoying outdoor concerts offered by Historic New England during the summer.

Spite House, Rockport

We can enthusiastically concur in the opinion of our director, Mr. Henry Francis du Pont, in calling this one of the great gardens of the country. This greatness extends both into the horticultural interest and the artistic interpretation of the needs of each area.[6] — R. B. Farnum, Horticultural Society of New York, 1963

Spite House is a Federal-style home built by Thomas McCobb in Phippsburg in 1806. Now located in Rockport, this private residence features extensive Colonial Revival gardens that were added between 1926 and 1928. The historic garden overlooking Penobscot Bay is occasionally included in the Camden Garden Club summer tour. Spite House was one of the few Maine residences documented for the Historic American Buildings Survey (1960) and is listed in the National Register of Historic Places (1973).

The name Spite House refers to a disagreement between Thomas McCobb and Mark Langdon Hill, who were stepbrothers; McCobb's father had married Hill's mother. Upon the elder McCobb's death, Thomas expected to inherit the family homestead in Phippsburg. But while he was away at sea in the late 1700s, his deceased father's will was broken, and Mark Hill became the new heir. Thomas then built what became known locally as "the Spite House," which was intended to dwarf the mansion inherited by his stepbrother.

Like Hamilton House, the two-story Spite House with its octagonal cupola also fell into a sad state of disrepair during the late 1800s. In the 1920s Philadelphian Donald Dodge, who had a strong interest in historic architecture, was searching the Maine coast for an old house to move to his new property on Beauchamp Point in Rockport. Part of his reason for choosing Spite House was its proximity to the water, which would make moving it relatively easy. On behalf of Dodge, Captain John Snow purchased a barge in New York to tow the building from Phippsburg. Crews took one month to move the house from its hilltop to the shore, where, minus the kitchen ell, it was loaded onto the barge and moved eighty-five miles to the Dodge property. Under the careful direction of Snow, the house sustained only one cracked window during the trip; amazingly, its four corner chimneys stayed intact.

The original granite foundation blocks were moved by truck and re-assembled in Rockport. Once at the Dodge property, the barge was temporarily sunk to keep it in place during high tide while the house was moved on shore. Snow asked for the barge as payment for this unique project, and Dodge happily agreed, having no further use for it.

For Dodge, Snow also transported the dismantled Stover House (1796) from South Harpswell, with the idea of using the salvaged material in two new wings at Spite House. Architects for the newly relocated Spite House were Tilden & Register of Philadelphia, who added modern improvements, such as mechanical equipment, designed the new wings, and created a uniform exterior between old and new architecture.

In 1925 Dodge hired landscape architect Robert Wheelwright to work with him to design the grounds of Spite House. Wheelwright was also from Philadelphia and summered on the island of

ABOVE: *Wheelwright's historic garden beds are a colorful signature of the Long Garden at Spite House.*

North Haven, Maine. He was nationally known as a founder and editor of *Landscape Architecture* magazine and is considered a pioneer in the field of historic landscape preservation. Wheelwright's biographer, Eleanor McPeck, notes that "Wheelwright shared with Fiske Kimball and others who weathered the Depression years a firm belief in the authority of Colonial tradition as a rich visual resource for both architectural and garden design."[7]

Like the gardens of Hamilton House, those at Spite House illustrated Colonial Revival principles popular at the time. Working closely with Donald Dodge, Wheelwright planned a series of outdoor rooms, sitting areas, and formal flower gardens enclosed by picket fences. Garden paths were long and linear, with framed views, focal points, and cross axes. Donald Dodge was responsible for the design of one of his favorite spaces, the "wild garden." Here he designed meandering paths among the ledge, beds of intricate wildflowers, and displays of lilies mixed with favorites like meadow rue, foxgloves, and spireas. The wild garden also included a large collection of rhododendrons near the border of the neighboring Weatherend estate (pp.156–157). The rhododendrons provided a backdrop to a favorite spot of Dodge's, a small terrace with a sleeping bench where he retreated (armed with mosquito repellent!) after lunch on many summer afternoons.

Closer to the house Dodge had a formal lily garden of several hundred varieties, most of which he ordered from Oregon. He also had a cutting garden edged with boxwood, an herb garden, and a nursery where he grew plants, especially clematis, to be transplanted throughout the gardens.

Dodge took exquisite care of the wild gardens, maintaining them as carefully as he did the formal gardens closer to the house. The high maintenance ended following Dodge's death in the 1970s, and the wild garden's plants gradually declined. In addition, a large number of spruce trees succumbed to "witch's broom" and were removed, creating much sunnier conditions than in Dodge's day. Today's surviving plants include low-bush blueberries, many naturalized spireas, numerous daylilies, and sun-loving ferns.

Spite House itself looks as impressive as it did when Thomas McCobb first built it. The house stands on a high point overlooking the bay to the east and a sloping field to the west. The home has numerous historic details: narrowly spaced clapboards, decorative swags, window shutters, roof balustrade, octagonal cupola, and a handsome main door with a leaded glass fanlight above. At the front entrance, architects Tilden & Register designed semicircular granite steps, a detail repeated elsewhere on the property.

The front yard, as it was called on Wheelwright's plans, is a formal arrangement of lawn panels, brick paths, shade trees, and ornamental picket fences. The paths are laid in traditional herringbone style, a pattern rarely used today because of its cost and difficulty of installation. The yard was once dominated by mature elm trees that, unfortunately, were lost to Dutch elm disease; crabapples and azaleas stood below the elms. Today's simplified but elegant design features two large oaks and two mature birch trees, along with a new border of perennials and annuals backed by Wheelwright's white picket fence.

OPPOSITE: *Oaks and birch trees replaced the original elms in the front yard of Spite House.*
BELOW: *Elms frame the front of Spite House in this ca. 1930 photograph.*

The terrace garden at the back of the house is just as formal as the front yard but smaller and more complicated in its details. In Colonial Revival fashion, the garden's main path and semicircular granite steps, including an old millstone, are aligned with doors to the dining room. Flanking the doors, trellises of square lattice support white clematis, as do nearby picket fences. Brick herringbone paths border small beds of bright-colored annuals. The beds were originally bordered by barberry hedges, per Wheelwright's specifications, clipped to less than twelve inches high. These were replaced by Korean boxwoods, which were damaged recently by a particularly harsh winter; a few specimens survive in a protected location by the house. A handsome stone wall marks the change in grade to the lower gardens.

Below the terrace garden and continuing the axial relationship to the house is the Long Garden, running east/west to the shore. Here are elaborate perennial borders, straight lawn paths, white picket fences, and cross axes to a side garden to the north. At the end of the main axis mature yews frame the view to Penobscot Bay and lead to the historic "cocktailarium."

Donald Dodge was fond of places on his property where he could appreciate views of scenery, sunsets, or the activities of people enjoying themselves. At his South Carolina winter home he had a small brick retreat at the edge of a creek with long views to the distant harbor. The cocktailarium at Spite House was an open-air version tucked below a retaining wall of lichen-covered stones. It looks today much as it did in Donald Dodge's time, with a simple iron railing and granite steps leading to a formal stone terrace perched on a ledge outcrop.

On the north side of the Long Garden is a smaller garden, an intimate lawn panel with benches at each end, bordered by hostas and flanked with mature trees. On the south side is a less formal lawn and an elegant summer house designed by Wheelwright. The summer house is tucked on the edge of the lawn and is protected from the ocean by a backdrop of native trees and shrubs. The summer house is in the same area where Wheelwright showed an oval, geometric cutting garden on the 1925 plan. Today a new cutting garden is located below the fields.

Unlike Hamilton House, Spite House did not suffer a period of neglect during the twentieth century. The house and gardens were downsized in 1993, mainly to reduce maintenance, but thanks to continued stewardship of the Dodge family, the architecture and landscape at Spite House endure as one of Maine's finest Colonial Revival examples.

RIVER HOUSE, YORK

River House, a stately Colonial Revival home in the town of York, was built in 1905 for Mary Marvin Goodrich, widow of tire magnate B. F. Goodrich of Akron, Ohio. Mrs. Goodrich began spending summers in York Harbor in 1891 and a few years later purchased her own property on which to build a summer retreat. Wanting to avoid the foggy conditions so common on the Maine coast, she bought seventy acres of land about two miles upriver from the harbor.

Mrs. Goodrich commissioned Guy Lowell, a talented, Beaux-Arts-trained architect and landscape architect from Boston, to design the mansion. Simultaneously with his work at River House, Lowell designed large estates on Long Island, New York, and in Massachusetts. His practice also included commissions for institutions such as Maine's Cumberland County Courthouse, the Museum of Fine Arts in Boston, and the New York County Courthouse in Manhattan. He also wrote and edited *American Gardens* and helped establish the landscape architecture program at MIT.[8]

Lowell designed the original River House as a large hipped-roof cottage with wings forming a "U" shape. This was his first residential commission in Maine and is an outstanding example of his multiple talents. Lowell located buildings to take advantage of natural landscape features and views from the house, and he was equally concerned about views back to the house from the greater landscape. Interior rooms easily flowed outside onto formal terraces enclosed by walls or hedges. The designed landscape became less formal as one moved away from the house and into the natural landscape beyond.[9]

Unfortunately, Mrs. Goodrich enjoyed River House for only a brief time; she died in 1907, leaving the property to her daughter, Isabella Goodrich Breckinridge. Mr. and Mrs. Breckinridge lived year-round in New York City with their four children. The family traveled extensively, mostly to Europe, but also to China and Japan during World War I. Their travels always brought them back to River House, where they spent part of each summer every year.

In 1929, following the death of her eldest son, Mrs. Breckinridge turned to noted landscape architect Arthur Shurcliff of Boston to design a small family cemetery overlooking the York River.[10] Shurcliff worked in the Olmsted offices before establishing his own practice in 1904. One of his most significant commissions was as chief landscape architect of the re-creation and restoration of Colonial Williamsburg in 1928.[11] The River House cemetery was one of his earliest projects in Maine, and he returned in the 1940s to consult with Mrs. Breckinridge about planting a forested buffer between the house and road below. Other parts of the River House landscape have been attributed to Shurcliff, but the full extent of his involvement is not known.

River House's relationship to the York River is one of the estate's most important features. From the moment you enter the mansion, it is clear how appropriately the property is named. The

front entrance leads to an axial hall, at the end of which a glass door frames the view to the water. Large paired windows in the dining room also overlook the river and meadows just beyond the brick terrace, as do tall arched windows in both the sunroom and the breakfast room.

A stroll through the River House landscape takes you through numerous garden rooms, all unique for their views, intimacy of scale, and choice of plants. The most formal and elegant is the fifty- by fifty-five-foot White Garden, located on a terrace on the west side of the house. The Breckinridge family started the tradition of using only white plants in this garden, a tradition that continues today. The garden reflects the formality of the house with its linear bluestone paths, circular reflecting pool, and brick walls capped with granite. The walls are softened by hedges of upright junipers, which add to the intimate sense of enclosure. The French doors of the drawing room open onto the garden, allowing a seamless flow between inside and outside rooms.

Aligned with the sunroom doors, an opening in the brick wall invites you from the White Garden down a flight of brick steps into the adjacent Round Garden, where a small circular lawn is bordered by beds of fragrant lilacs.

Continuing past the nearby tennis court, the final destination in this series of outdoor rooms is the swimming pool and gymnasium area. In 1909 the Breckinridge family dammed an existing inlet in the river to create a naturalistic pool, affectionately known as the "mudhole." They also built the children's playhouses nearby. The family was committed to personal health and fitness, as shown by improvements to the original pool and with the construction of an adjacent gymnasium in 1915. At the same time they built a handsome pergola to provide shade on a sunny afternoon while enjoying either poolside activity or the tranquility of the river. Finally, in 1922 they settled on the existing circular pool. At about one hundred feet in diameter and nine feet deep in the center, this is one of the largest round saltwater swimming pools in New England.

One of the most prominent Colonial Revival features of River House is the Ramp, a sweeping lawn, about twenty feet wide and 450 feet long, aligned directly on axis with the doors of the Green Room and abutting the White Garden. Historically, an ornate wrought iron gazebo was sited on the distant hill to punctuate the end of the axis. Visitors to the gazebo would in turn have an extended view back up the slope towards the west side of the house. The Ramp is a decidedly formal landscape feature that is softened with the property's gently sloping topography; the land slopes away from the house and up again to the surrounding woodlands. Mature cedars and two rows of rhododendrons, the latter planted in the 1970s, define the edges of the ramp today.

Another Colonial Revival feature is the terrace at the south side of the house overlooking the river. The terrace, running the length of the house, is set with bricks in a historic herringbone pattern. A low brick wall separates the terrace from the adjacent croquet court, which in turn is enclosed by another low brick wall. Wide brick steps make the transition from the court to an unusually formal mowed path that leads to the river about 350 feet away. This is one of the most historic features of the property, appearing in photographs as early as 1908, just three years after the house was built.

The path to the river mimics the concept of the Ramp, with a few modifications. Like the Ramp, the path has a strong axial relationship to the house. In fact, the axis of the path extends all the way through the main hall of the house and into the entrance courtyard. This is a highly formal and rather

unusual addition to a Maine landscape; nothing of a similar scale was discovered at any other property visited during the Survey of Designed Historic Landscapes. Unlike the Ramp's gazebo, there is no formal focal point punctuating the end of this axis; you are drawn to the banks of the river, where you can also appreciate the full view back towards the house. Despite its formality, the path is a subtle element in the surrounding meadow, which is mowed just once or twice a year.

A cart path along the river meanders through a large patch of wisteria that has formed a dense groundcover and leads to the family cemetery, nestled at the edge of the property. The cemetery is surrounded by shady arborvitae and hemlocks and enclosed by a handsome brick wall, short enough to allow a tranquil view of the river. No headstones are present, leaving the simple lawn panel unobstructed; instead, names of Breckinridge family members are listed on the wall itself. Shurcliff's design includes delicate iron gates as well as a curved seat, where visitors could sit in quiet remembrance.

One reason that River House remains historically intact today is due to the vision of another Breckinridge family member, Mary Marvin Breckinridge Patterson, who inherited the property from her mother, Isabella, in 1961. A resident of Washington, D.C., Mrs. Patterson had a great fondness for River House and continued the family tradition of summering there until her death in 2002.

Mary Marvin Breckinridge was one of the most distinguished women of the twentieth century, known around the world as a pioneering filmmaker, photojournalist, and wartime radio broadcaster. She was a major supporter of charitable, cultural, and preservation organizations.[12] In 1973 she donated her beloved River House to Bowdoin College and donated the adjoining Grant House property to the town of York, which established Goodrich Park. For thirty years River House was home to the Breckinridge Public Affairs Center, where the college sponsored conferences and retreats.

Fortunately, the homeowners who purchased the property from Bowdoin have a great appreciation for its historic architecture and landscape. When they acquired River House in 2004, they recognized the intimate link between the house itself and the surrounding historic gardens. Upon close inspection, it was clear that the White Garden, in particular, was suffering from structural and aesthetic problems that would require major restoration. The garden's brick walls were crumbling, the bluestone walk was sunken in places, the circular pool was in need of repair, the original arborvitae hedge was extremely overgrown, and the yew hedge in the rose garden had been ravaged by deer.

It is never an easy decision to remove mature plants that have taken on a vintage character of their own, separate from the designer's original intent. After much deliberation, the decision was made to remove the overgrown and damaged plants and replace them with new ones. It was clear, however, that new plant material could not be brought in until the most deteriorated brick walls were repaired or replaced. Complete reconstruction of damaged walls required documenting their location and height, removing them completely, and finding suitable replacement bricks and mortar to match the historic walls. Many of the original bricks were re-used in the new construction. One of the most surprising discoveries was that the original walls had been built without proper footings, yet had remained standing for almost one hundred years. The new walls retain the character of the historic ones but have the advantage of modern construction methods and machinery, guaranteeing their longevity for decades to come.

Once the outside structure of the garden was restored, the owners addressed the sunken bluestone walks and grading issues in the lawn. Essentially, the garden required a complete facelift, beginning with the walks. Skilled masons removed each stone, carefully numbering them and stockpiling them nearby. They then prepared a proper gravel base and re-laid each stone in its original location.

Only after this hardscape was completed and the beds restored could the new plants be installed. Upright junipers in front of the brick walls help to frame the White Garden, and hardy boxwoods will eventually be clipped into a formal hedge surrounding the rose garden. Fragrant, long-blooming white roses are the focal point inside the boxwood hedges. A summer-blooming Kousa dogwood was added to anchor one corner of the garden. The soil for the lawn panels was re-graded and new sod was planted. The circular concrete pool was repaired, although without its original fish fountain, which has been gone from the property for years. The homeowners are currently in search of a replacement based on historic photographs. Finally, white-blooming perennials and annuals rounded out the seasonal display in the borders.

Following the landscape restoration, in 2005 the owners graciously held an open house to benefit the Old York Historical Society, to celebrate River House's centennial, and to invite the public for one last tour of this magnificent estate. Today, no longer in the public eye, River House is once again a private home. Buffered from the road by mature pines, the ivy-covered mansion still overlooks the rustic meadow and remnants of the apple orchard. As they have for over a century, native trees still line the riverbank, softening the views to the river, surely one of the most serene views in Maine.

ABOVE: *The York River is framed by pergola columns near River House's gymnasium and swimming pool.*

CHAPTER 9

THE NATURALISTIC DESIGNS OF HANS HEISTAD

In creating an American garden in the natural style we follow the Japanese spirit tempered with the English ideal, which is to make an art of improving the scenery and to display its native beauties to advantage.[1]—STUART ORLOFF, 1933

Coastal Maine's bluffs and ledges, salt spray and strong winds, and dramatic views of nearby islands or the open ocean make the area well suited to landscapes in the naturalistic style. In Camden and Rockport, three notable properties designed by Hans Heistad—Weatherend Estate, Beech Nut, and Camden Hills State Park—provide excellent examples of naturalistic trends that evolved as a reaction to formal Colonial Revival landscape designs.

Hans O. Heistad was a Norwegian-born landscape designer who had studied landscape gardening and horticulture in Norway and Denmark. He emigrated to the United States in 1905 and was introduced to Maine through the Olmsted Brothers, working for them at the Bar Harbor estate of Joseph Pulitzer. He provided design services for many summer residences in Camden and Rockport, although very little historical documentation of that work exists today. He also designed the Sagamore area of Camden Hills State Park. In addition to serving as a designer, he was a skilled laborer during installation of the Camden Library Amphitheatre (pp. 58–62) and the Rockport Harbor improvement project under the patronage of Mary Bok.[2]

A 1913 article in *Country Life in America* describes the naturalistic style as:

...the policy of leaving much of the grounds strictly alone, or of merely intensifying natural suggestions, and of carrying out the universal principles of garden design with native materials mingled with old-fashioned flowers long grown throughout New England. [3]

Naturalistic landscapes moved away from formal elements of the Colonial Revival period, such as geometrically arranged perennial beds or focal points at the end of axis lines. Generally, designs were asymmetrical and had curvilinear forms, especially in shrub borders and lawns. Straight lines were usually absent, for "straight is the line of duty, curved is the line of beauty."[4] The goal was to emphasize a site's natural features without imposing geometric formulas on the landscape, as well as to give the impression that the setting was not man-made.

Naturalistic designs were best suited to challenging sites with uneven topography, which would make formal treatment difficult. Dramatic features such as ravines or oceanfront ledge were often incorporated into the design of the grounds, and smaller ledge outcrops were often left exposed in lawn areas. The use of existing topography allowed the garden to "have an individuality that sets it apart from all others."[5]

WEATHEREND ESTATE, ROCKPORT

The story of the Weatherend Estate begins in 1903 with the construction of John Gribbel's Shingle-style summer home. Gribbel, from Philadelphia, was one of the patrons who later donated land for the creation of the Camden Village Green (pp. 52–57). Hans Heistad designed the estate's naturalistic landscape in 1913. The most intriguing aspect of the property is the way in which Heistad skillfully designed the grounds to relate to the architecture as well as to the dramatic, coastal setting. Weatherend is also remarkable for the condition of its landscape, which has survived for almost one hundred years despite the power of wind, sun, water, and the storms that batter the Maine coast.

We do not know the architect who designed Gribbel's 9,000-square-foot home, but we do know that it was built under the direction of Cyrus Porter Brown of Camden. Brown, who built at least thirty summer cottages in the Camden/Rockport area, was a highly respected contractor and builder responsible for "furnishing plans as well as building some of the most pretentious and modernly designed cottages along the shore."[6]

Originally part of a nineteen-acre estate, today the property comprises about four and one-half acres. The home itself is set prominently on a narrow peninsula in Penobscot Bay, from which there is a long view of the ocean to the southeast, views of North Haven and Vinalhaven islands to the east, and Islesboro Island to the northeast. Looking inland, one sees the nearby Camden Hills and Beech Hill, two other sites that feature prominently in Heistad's design legacy.

Heistad transformed the barren, rocky site at Weatherend by building a substantial masonry seawall and adding dozens of truckloads of topsoil behind it. He also created a series of terraced gardens enclosed by stone walls, which buffered the plants from constant winds. Exposed ledge figured prominently in his design, as did rough-cut lawns visible in historic photographs. Along the shore ledge he installed a perimeter walk with wooden bridges, concrete steps, and edging of stone "teeth." The concrete path followed the natural topography of the site, dipping in and out of sight behind ledge outcrops, and featured a rustic pavilion that seemed to emerge from the ledge overlooking the ocean. The pavilion had a sod-covered roof, a Norwegian feature that Heistad used later at Beech Nut.

In addition to his role as landscape designer at Weatherend, Heistad also served as a talented carpenter, designing garden furniture to fit particular outdoor spaces. Curves on his benches matched those of adjacent stone walls, and the curve of an arbor's arch mimicked that on the windows of the 1903 house. We do not know how many pieces Heistad designed for Weatherend, although in the late 1990s about a dozen originals remained.[7] Heistad painted all of his furniture a crisp white, which introduced a sense of formality and created focal points in the naturalistic landscape.

The overall design of Weatherend's landscape was naturalistic, but historic photographs show that the estate also had formal flower plantings. One photograph shows that the narrow beds at the base of stone walls were planted with a single type of edging, reinforcing the horizontal character of the stone wall; a more naturalistic planting would include a greater variety of plants and a less formal edge treatment. Another photograph shows flowers, rather than native plants, bordering the edge

of ledge outcrops. Heistad's role in the planting details is unknown, and we do not know the names of specific plants used at Weatherend.

Today Weatherend remains a private retreat whose historic landscape has seen typical changes over time. The structure of the garden, formed by Heistad's garden walls and sea wall, remains, as does most of the concrete shore path. Not surprisingly, the wooden bridges, railings, and sod-roofed pavilion are gone, although the pavilion's foundation remains. Much less space is devoted to flowers than in the original design, which is true for the majority of historic gardens in Maine. Many of the outdoor furniture pieces are reproductions of Heistad's originals.

The biggest threat to this historic landscape comes from nature: high winds topple trees, drenching rains and waves wash away precious topsoil, deer browse freely during winter, and voles damage the roots of historic junipers. Mature trees and shrubs are highly prized; trees, in particular, must be cabled to the ledge, as shallow topsoil makes it extremely difficult to replant new ones. The massive sea wall receives periodic re-mortaring in its defense against coastal storms.

Beech Nut: Picnics on the Hill

In addition to their dramatic oceanfront peninsula, the Gribbel family owned Beech Hill, which rises more than 500 feet above Weatherend. Here in 1915 Hans Heistad built Beech Nut, a sod-roofed stone hut used by the Gribbels for formal picnics and afternoon tea.

Today the hut and landscape are part of the Beech Hill Preserve, a 295-acre tract owned and managed by Coastal Mountains Land Trust. Also known as the Beech Nut Historic District, the property was placed in the National Register of Historic Places in 2003. The hut itself is open only on special occasions, but the spectacular landscape is open to the public. There are no signs to identify the property, which is accessible from Beech Hill Road in Rockport, but local residents have been coming here for decades, appreciating the gentle three-quarter mile climb as well as the stunning views.

John Gribbel hired Hans Heistad to build Beech Nut during the winter months while Weatherend was under construction; the same crew worked at both places. Beech Nut was inspired by the design of traditional Norwegian mountain cottages known as *hytter*. A long, protected porch, known as a *svalgang*, sheltered the main entrance; terraces enclosed by stone walls flanked the gabled ends. The heavily-timbered roof was constructed of two layers of sod laid back to back, planted with wildflowers. On a traditional Norwegian *hytter*, walls were wood, and stone was used only in the foundation and fireplace. In a break from tradition, Heistad chose to build the entire structure of stone, most likely because his construction workers from Weatherend were skilled in masonry and stone was readily available. [8]

Heistad designed archways on the porch to frame views of the surrounding fields, ocean, and Chickawaukee Pond, and he carried the same detail to the arched interior doorways. The hut was divided into a main dining room, three smaller side rooms, and a very tiny bathroom. One wall of the dining room held a massive stone fireplace; the others featured banks of windows that framed the scenic views. The kitchen held a galvanized cistern for water pumped from a nearby well. Built into the wall of the adjacent room were two naturalistic stone sinks cut from oddly-shaped schist from Beauchamp Point; the same schist was used as accents in the dining room fireplace. All of these features remain today.

Historic photographs show the dining room attractively furnished with an oversized table, decorative benches, a china cabinet with arched windows, a side table with arched trim, and wicker chairs. The furniture and the wooden floor and window trim added warmth to the stone room. The cathedral ceiling sported two round chandeliers, each about the size of a large wagon wheel. The furniture was removed over the years and today the hut is empty.

The trip from Weatherend to the top of Beech Hill was about five miles, a journey of about one-half hour by horse and carriage. To mark the entrance to Beech Hill, Heistad built a timber gateway with masonry wing walls and piers that featured arches similar to those at the hut. We do not know if he had a hand in laying out the scenic carriage drive that leads to the top of the hill.

The Gribbels sold Beech Nut in the 1930s, and over the following decades the hut suffered from vandalism. Windows and doors were removed, and the original sod roof was not maintained,

ABOVE: *A view of Beech Nut from 1916 shows the picnic hut perched on treeless Beech Hill. The driveway allowed visitors arriving by horse and carriage to be delivered to the front steps; arrival today is typically by foot.*

OPPOSITE: *The view to the south at Beech Nut extends to Chickawaukee Pond, with Bear Hill to its left and Dodge Mountain to its right.*

resulting in water damage to the building. Nevertheless, the landscape was spectacular, and in the 1990s the owners placed an easement on the property that prevents subdivision and allows public access and sustainable agriculture. Additional covenants preserve the property's scenic and ecological values. Wanting to see the land conserved and accessible to the public, the owners eventually sold 295 acres surrounding the summit to Maine Coast Heritage Trust, which later transferred the property to Coastal Mountains Land Trust.

After acquiring the property in 2003, the trust launched a campaign to save Beech Nut from further deterioration. Restoration involved removing the original sod roof and rotted floor, beams, and rafters. All cracks in the stone were completely repaired, from the foundation to the chimney top, and a structural concrete crawl space was added to support the weight of the walls.

One of the most unique aspects of Beech Nut was its historic sod roof. Replacing it required an engineered roof capable of preventing leaks and supporting a large amount of weight. The roof is made of several layers: a continuous rubber membrane, a layer of material that protects the membrane from sod roots, a layer of material that allows water to drain, a layer of felt to anchor the sod roots, six inches of topsoil, and finally, the sod itself. Plugs of the original sod were added in recognition of historic continuity and in hopes of quickly re-establishing the sod. The site's extreme conditions, especially regarding wind and rainfall, require regular monitoring of the sod roof to ensure that erosion and die-back do not threaten its structural integrity.

In November 2007 Coastal Mountains Land Trust held an open house at Beech Hill to celebrate the restoration of Beech Nut. In the near future the trust's board of directors will evaluate potential uses for the hut to decide how it will be furnished and used. Meanwhile, the land trust manages the fields as an organic blueberry operation, which keeps them open, maintains views, and provides grassland habitat for native birds. New trails have been opened that allow visitors to enjoy the property without intruding on the natural landscape.

The historic carriage drive, open to pedestrians only, is the most direct (and possibly the most scenic) route to Beech Nut. Walking to the hut, you enjoy a sequence of stunning views while meandering through blueberry fields and meadows. The first is the lovely view of Chickawaukee Pond framed by Dodge Mountain and Bear Hill. Looking inland, you also have the first, tantalizing glimpse of the sod roof's ridgeline.

Farther up the drive is a teasing glimpse of Penobscot Bay, partially hidden by hills. Rounding a corner, you are rewarded with a larger view of the bay. On the inland side, you now see the stone hut's gabled end and elegant stone arches, and from here it is obvious that the hut was sited to frame the view to Chickawaukee Pond. Around the final bend in the road, you come upon an outstanding view of the entire bay and its numerous islands: Vinalhaven, North Haven, Islesboro, and others in the foreground. On the peninsula below is Weatherend, John Gribbel's summer home. Finally, Beech Nut is fully visible on the high point to the left.

The land trust opens the hut for tours several times a year, but you can rest on the porch after your hike and seek respite from the constant wind any time. The return trip provides scenic views of several mountains—Bald, Ragged, Spruce, Pleasant, and Meadow—as well as native birches, bayberry shrubs, sheep laurel, low-bush blueberries, and meadow grasses.

ABOVE: *The newly-restored picnic hut on Beech Hill, as seen from the historic carriage drive, appears to rise from the surrounding blueberry fields.*

CAMDEN HILLS STATE PARK'S LOWER SAGAMORE AREA

Camden Hills State Park encompasses 5,500 acres in the Megunticook Mountain Range at the northern end of the Camden Hills Range. The park is most noted for the scenic vista from atop Mount Battie, with its sweeping views of Camden, Penobscot Bay, and surrounding islands.

By 1936 the National Park Service (NPS) had acquired some 1,500 acres of the current site and began work with the Maine Parks Commissions to develop it as an example of the Park Service's guidelines for park design. Between 1935 and 1939 the NPS created a master plan for the development of the Camden Hills Recreational Demonstration Project. Their guiding principles "began with the premise that any development was a potential threat to natural integrity."[9] Designers were expected to respect the character of the site and to use local materials and indigenous construction techniques in their work. To achieve these goals for the Camden Hills site, the agencies turned to three local professionals: Newell Foster, project superintendent, Lawrence Libby, civil engineer, and Hans Heistad, who served as staff landscape architect from 1935 to 1942.

President Franklin D. Roosevelt's new Civilian Conservation Corps (CCC) played an important role in the development of parks and landscapes throughout the country. When Roosevelt took office in 1933, he was determined to use his New Deal philosophy and landslide victory to improve the lot of the nation's unemployed. The CCC, like the larger Works Progress Administration, was designed to offer workers meaningful, dignified employment that would benefit the nation. Approximately 275,000 young men joined the CCC, which eventually enrolled more than three million participants. Through their labors, many national parks and treasured areas were conserved and developed according to National Park Service guidelines.

Local designers were responsible for creating the details to accompany the NPS master plans. Heistad's interest in naturalistic design made him an excellent choice to serve as primary designer for Camden Hills State Park's Lower Sagamore area, a stretch of fifty acres on the ocean side of Route One.[10] Following NPS approval of his plans, Heistad was given primary responsibility for the development of this day-picnic area. He oversaw the CCC crew as they cleared brush, leveled soil, and built roads and parking areas. They built two miles of hiking trails and rustic footbridges, and planted 7,000 native trees and shrubs. Recalling his work at Weatherend and Beech Nut, Heistad also designed and oversaw construction of numerous stone features: the entrance gate, toll house, picnic shelter, fireplaces

with seats and tables, dams, naturalistic steps along hillside trails, and massive stone benches in the woods. Heistad's proposed amphitheater for 700 to 800 visitors was never built.

Heistad also designed unusual improvements to a stream in the northern part of Sagamore. At the stream's upper elevation he and the CCC crew built a native flower garden and small rock terraces surrounding a large birch tree. Farther downstream they formed a large pool with a stone dam, followed by a series of waterfalls, smaller pools, and rustic footbridges. From here the stream flowed along natural waterfalls towards the ocean.

Much of Heistad's designed landscape, which was intended to look "natural," has disappeared. Trees have filled in the once-open ocean views, invasive species have choked out native plants in places, and areas along the stream have eroded. Nevertheless, Camden Hills is one of the most popular state parks in Maine, and visitors continue to enjoy the Sagamore area for hiking and picnicking along the rocky shore.

HANS HEISTAD AT HOME

Heistad's own home was located on Amsbury Hill, in a residential neighborhood in Rockport overlooking the harbor. The house was in poor condition when he acquired it in 1918, but Heistad, a talented painter and carpenter, renovated it with hand-done murals and detailed woodworking. He added estate-like features to the home's three-quarter-acre lot, including specimen trees, rock gardens, shrub borders, a lily pond, a perimeter walk connecting to the public sidewalk, and an unusual driveway that circled the house. The house accommodated the Heistads and their seven children, and was at some point opened as a guest house for summer visitors.

Heistad's house remains a private residence today, and all that remains of his original landscape plan are the mature shrubs, some specimen trees, and the public sidewalk connection. His legacy remains, however, in his major commissions at Weatherend, Beech Nut, and Camden Hills State Park.

CHAPTER 10

THE MAINE WORK OF BEATRIX FARRAND

Beatrix Jones Farrand was a woman ahead of her time, willing to risk social disapproval by pursuing a career in a male-dominated field; a pioneer who paved the way for other women to follow in her footsteps; and a master at creating formal landscape designs interwoven with native plants. Thanks to her multiple passions—overseas travel; reading, observing, and photographing; an intense knowledge of plants; willingness to be a hands-on gardener; and long-lasting relationships with professional clients—Farrand's career spanned fifty-four years, from 1896 to 1950. She began and ended her career with the Arnold Arboretum in Jamaica Plain, Massachusetts, first studying with Charles Sprague Sargent, founder of the arboretum, and completing her last consultations there when she was seventy-eight years old.

Farrand traveled abroad, frequently with her aunt, Edith Wharton, and based her estate designs on travels to European gardens. Following a European tour in 1895 she became the country's first female professional landscape architect, though she preferred the title "landscape gardener." She was one of the founders, and the only woman member, of the American Society of Landscape Architects in 1899. She completed nearly two hundred commissions, three-quarters of which were private estates. The remainder included the designs of Dumbarton Oaks in Washington, D.C., the East and West gardens of the White House, and the grounds of the Graduate College at Princeton University, among others.[1]

Farrand practiced in eleven states east of the Mississippi River, ventured west to California, and completed her largest number of commissions in Maine and New York. Today on Maine's Mount Desert Island, only a few examples survive of the more than fifty private gardens designed by Beatrix Farrand. Although one of her most famous, Reef Point, no longer exists today, its influence on Farrand's career warrants its inclusion as one of Maine's enduring landscapes.

ABOVE: *At Reef Point, pairs of dwarf Alberta spruce marked the entrance to three paths that led through the heathers (shown here), to the flower garden, and to the shore of Frenchman's Bay. This 1950 view overlooks Bald Porcupine Island.*

REEF POINT GARDENS

The object at Reef Point is to show what outdoor beauty can contribute to those who have the interest and perception that can be influenced by trees and flowers and open air composition. Such interest is never likely to diminish and a taste for gardening can add much to life.[2]
— BEATRIX FARRAND, 1946

New Yorkers Fred and Mary Cadwalader Jones were among the first summer visitors to Bar Harbor, renting a cottage for the first time in 1879, when their daughter, Beatrix, was seven years old. In 1882 Fred Jones bought a two-acre lot in the middle of Bar Harbor along the Shore Path, a long public walkway overlooking Frenchman's Bay. He commissioned Arthur Rotch of the Boston architectural office of Rotch and Tilden to design the shingled cottage, which the family named Reef Point. Mr. and Mrs. Jones divorced before the cottage was completed, and the property was given to Mrs. Jones. She and Beatrix spent every summer there, eventually extending their stay from May to October. They enjoyed months of gardening, entertaining visitors, picnicking, sailing, and social engagements. On Mount Desert Island Beatrix essentially began her study of landscape architecture, photographing and making notes about the intricacies of the natural landscape as well as studying the formal gardens of friends. By the time she was twenty, she was in charge of designing the grounds around Reef Point.

Most of Farrand's early residential commissions came from family and friends, including several on Mount Desert Island. Many others came from the social network of her aunt Edith Wharton, who was one of her greatest supporters. Farrand continued with mainly residential work into her thirties, with more than three dozen projects in Connecticut, Maine, Massachusetts, New York, and Pennsylvania. The projects ranged in size from designing a simple garden seat to creating 135 drawings for a property in Jenkintown, Pennsylvania.[3]

In 1913, at a dinner at the home of Princeton's President John Grier Hibben, Beatrix Jones met Max Farrand, distinguished chairman of Yale's history department. In Max Farrand, Beatrix had found "her ideal partner, a partner of brains, distinction, and kindness, with a passion for the outdoor life to equal her own."[4] Beatrix and Max were married in October of that year, and three years later she received Reef Point as a gift from her mother. Beatrix kept an office in New York, but the Farrands made Reef Point their principal home. By this time the property had grown from two to six acres. Beatrix wrote that "a family tradition of gardening and a growing interest in all plant surroundings caused the owners as they worked over their grounds to consider later development of their little acreage."[5] In 1939 they founded the Reef Point Gardens Corporation for their personal enjoyment and study, for the education of gardeners and students, and for the development of a research center dedicated to horticulture in Maine.

The Farrands wanted the gardens to be practical and useful to the surrounding community. Their professional habits of labeling plants, keeping accurate records, and propagating annuals and perennials provided valuable information to local garden club members, horticulturists, and schoolchildren, who visited with their teachers. Other practical goals included creating a small vegetable garden and an orchard of dwarf fruit trees. In the long term the Farrands planned to offer horticultural lectures, a library, and study rooms in a new building that would replace the original cottage.

The Farrands also wanted to create a place for intimate contact with growing things and for observation of passing seasons. Following a tradition begun by Mary Cadwalader Jones, the Reef Point gardens first and foremost enhanced the natural features of Maine. "Carpets of bunchberries and bearberries are cared for, and native shrubs…are planted where they seem to thrive."[6] Beatrix used stands of native red and white spruce to protect plants from ocean winds. In addition to native plants, she developed trial gardens for cultivated varieties, but she deliberately avoided "a trim lawn stretching unbroken to the sea."[7]

Reef Point had characteristics found in botanical gardens, such as a systematic classification of plants, an herbarium for scientific study, and collections of rare plants, many of which came from the Arnold Arboretum. Beatrix demonstrated which plants grew successfully in various soil types and sun conditions as well as in microenvironments specific to the Maine coast, such as her bog garden. She had an extensive collection of azaleas grouped by color, heath gardens, a rose terrace near the house, and a separate garden of perennials "chosen not merely for attractiveness of flower but for character and beauty of growth and foliage."[8] The gardens contained Arts and Crafts-style

BELOW: *This 1934 view of a terrace at Reef Point shows a birdbath created by Maine potter Eric Soderholtz. Today an exact replica of the birdbath is found opposite the main entrance at Garland Farm.*

ornaments, such as decorative pots and a birdbath built by Eric Soderholtz of Gouldsboro.

Entrances on Atlantic Avenue and Hancock Street provided automobile access to the western half of the property. A narrow service road ran along the outside of the gardens. Main paths were arranged in straight lines that radiated from the house towards ocean views to the east. A circuit of curvilinear paths led through various gardens and gave the illusion of the property being larger than it was, a common practice in landscape architecture.

Max Farrand died in 1945 after a two-year illness. A bereaved Beatrix continued their work at Reef Point, remodeling the house, building additional tool houses, and documenting and rearranging the gardens. She also built a cottage for Lewis Garland, Reef Point's longtime superintendent, and his wife, Amy, chief horticulturist. All of this took a toll on Farrand's personal finances. In addition, the devastating Mount Desert fire of 1947 had greatly reduced the amount of taxable property in Bar Harbor. Although Reef Point was not damaged in the fire, remaining owners such as Beatrix were faced with significantly higher taxes.

In 1955, when she was eighty-three years old, Farrand made the difficult decision to dismantle the house and gardens. As she had been unable to gain a permanent tax exemption from the town of Bar Harbor and was concerned that the property would deteriorate due to rising operating costs, she donated the library, drawings, and herbarium specimens to the landscape architecture department at the University of California at Berkeley. In a poignant letter to George Pettitt, assistant to the president at Berkeley, Farrand wrote, "This place will be left for good next Friday, September 23rd, and the hopes cherished for many years here will be transferred to Berkeley. Reef Point has been sold and the name will perish next April when the new owner takes over. The house which guarded the collections for so many years will be torn down, and probably the gardens will perish also."[9]

The "new owner" was Farrand's long-time friend, architect Robert Patterson, consultant to and director of the Reef Point Gardens Corporation. When the house was dismantled, Farrand

commissioned Patterson to design an addition to the Bar Harbor farmhouse of the Garlands, who had become her caretakers and with whom she lived until her death in 1959.

The gardens also were dismantled, but the plants did not perish as Farrand had predicted. Patterson sold the collection to Charles Savage, one of Reef Point's garden directors and owner of the Asticou Inn. With the help of John D. Rockefeller, Jr., Savage bought the larger trees and shrubs and built two gardens, Asticou Azalea and Thuya (pp. 71–77), to house them.

Patterson divided the Reef Point property into five house lots, one of which included the original gardener's cottage. Today all that remains of Farrand's years of devotion to Reef Point is this cottage and its curving entrance drive, along with the granite gate pillars and finials. The remaining four lots have houses, some of which were designed by Patterson. Farrand's archival collection remains available for review at the Environmental Design Library of the University of California at Berkeley.

John D. Rockefeller, Jr., and Beatrix Farrand at Acadia National Park

This is just a note to tell you how pleased I am with the planting in so far as I have seen it. You cannot know what a relief it is to me to have you giving attention to these matters for it had become quite a burden to me to try to keep up with them on all the roads. Then too, what you do is so much better than anything I could do. Please accept this renewed assurance of my deep gratitude to you for the very real service you are rendering to the National Park and also to me.[10] — Letter from John D. Rockefeller, Jr., to Beatrix Farrand, 1931

Between 1913 and 1940 philanthropist John D. Rockefeller, Jr. built fifty-seven miles of scenic carriage roads, two gatehouses, and sixteen stone masonry bridges at Acadia National Park on Mount Desert Island. Today, the forty-four miles of carriage roads remaining in the park are unique in the country. Although the broken-stone construction technique was common in the early twentieth century, no other examples of comparable length or quality exist today.

For his carriage road project Rockefeller surrounded himself with talented architects, engineers, and landscape architects, including Beatrix Farrand, who designed numerous scenic vistas and roadside plantings. By the late 1920s when Rockefeller hired Farrand, her career was firmly established. Her out-of-state commissions had included designs for country estates in Washington, D.C., New York, and Connecticut, as well as parts of the campuses of Princeton and Yale, among others. Near Acadia National Park, Farrand had designed the village greens in Bar Harbor and Seal Harbor and had designed at least sixteen private gardens on Mount Desert Island, including at Rockefeller's home, The Eyrie.[11]

Rockefeller not only financed the carriage roads, gatehouses, and bridges but also influenced their design. He gained a great appreciation for nature as well as landscape design skills from his father, John D. Rockefeller, Sr., who laid out the grounds of his family estate at Forest Hill, near Cleveland, Ohio. There was a precursor to the carriage roads of Acadia. Rockefeller, Sr., designed and built an extensive carriage road system with rustic bridges, scenic views, and gentle grades that followed natural contours. In 1893, father and son purchased land near Tarrytown, New York, where they eventually established their Pocantico Hills estate known as Kykuit. The younger Rockefeller designed most of the fifty-five miles of carriage roads at Pocantico.[12]

By 1908 John D. Rockefeller, Jr., was married to Abby Aldrich and had two young children, with a third on the way. He rented a shore cottage (near Reef Point) in Bar Harbor, Maine, and two years later purchased 150 acres in nearby Seal Harbor. Here architect Duncan Candler enlarged an existing cottage into the family's summer home, The Eyrie, where Farrand collaborated with Mrs. Rockefeller to create a secluded setting for her collection of Oriental sculpture and to develop English-style flower gardens.

Following the purchase of the Seal Harbor property, Rockefeller also made a life-changing decision to end his career as manager of his father's extensive business interests and devote his life to philanthropy. In 1914 he was asked to join the Hancock County Trustees of Public Reservations in their efforts to conserve land on Mount Desert Island. Through the organization he became friends with George Dorr, who worked ceaselessly with Rockefeller to assemble land that eventually became Acadia National Park. The Hancock County Trustees owned various scenic mountaintops, and Rockefeller bought land that he expected to combine with the trustees' holdings into a national park. Between the early 1930s and 1940s, Rockefeller donated to Acadia National Park more than 6,500 acres of land improved with carriage roads.

Family members recalled that Rockefeller built the roads out of "his deep personal feelings for the earth and its beauty, his conviction that the Divine Presence is revealed in nature, and his belief that nature plays an important role in our lives."[13] In a practical sense, he wanted to provide access to the mountains, valleys, and scenic views by horseback and carriage. He also wanted to make the same areas accessible to larger numbers of pedestrians than those who hiked the narrow woods trails. An avid horseman, he also ensured that automobiles would not interfere with horseback riding or carriage driving; autos were officially allowed on the island in 1915 but banned from the carriage roads. This is still true today.

Rockefeller first laid out the roads by himself until he hired engineer Charles Simpson, who worked for him from 1916 until 1922. Simpson's son, Paul, then took over as chief engineer, working until the roads were completed in 1940. A third engineer, Walters G. Hill, also worked with Paul Simpson.

Building carriage roads to allow access to wilderness resulted in some destruction of the natural landscape, at least temporarily. In the late 1920s, Rockefeller turned to Beatrix Farrand to restore the landscape along the road cuts to as natural a condition as possible, while also creating a park-like setting. Farrand worked closely with Charles Miller, Rockefeller's nurseryman, who propagated thousands of plants for use along the carriage roads. Under Farrand's and Miller's direction, crews removed dead trees and limbs, thinned or removed others to create views from the carriage roads, restored disturbed topsoil, and installed masses of native and naturalized plants in irregular patterns. Farrand studied which plants existed naturally in particular areas and used this information as a guide for restoring disturbed areas. Crews transplanted plants from the wild and bought others to supplement those from Rockefeller's nursery. Today birch trees recommended by Farrand still exist south of "The Tumbledown" on the "Around the Mountain Loop."

Farrand also designed the grounds of the two gate lodges by architect Grosvenor Atterbury. The lodges marked the entrances to the carriage roads and limited automobile access to just what was needed for park maintenance and fire prevention. At the Brown Mountain Gate Lodge, Farrand first suggested screening the driveway and entrance area from view with a mound, an idea that was eventually rejected in favor of plants that would not block the view from the road. At the Jordan Pond Gate Lodge, she suggested placing vines on the exterior of the building, using shrubs and ferns to soften the corners of the buildings, and building a terraced lawn in front of the house in order to save existing trees. She also proposed naturalistic plantings around several of the massive granite bridges, such as those at Bubble Pond, Eagle Lake, and Duck Brook. At the Stanley Brook Bridge she proposed maple and ash trees to frame the arches of the bridge, used trees to frame the approaches to the bridge from the carriage road, and planted mostly native shrubs along the roadsides.

The fire of 1947 destroyed over 17,000 acres on Mount Desert Island, including 10,000 acres in Acadia National Park. Although much of Farrand's work in the northern section of the park was destroyed, her plantings remain throughout much of the carriage road network.

Following Rockefeller's death in 1960, the roads and vegetation received only minimal maintenance from the park service due to limited funds. Nevertheless, the carriage paths, bridges, and gatehouses were listed in the National Register of Historic Places in 1979. The nonprofit Friends of Acadia was founded in 1986 to "preserve, protect, and promote stewardship of the outstanding natural beauty, ecological vitality, and distinctive cultural resources of Acadia National Park and surrounding communities."[14]

In 1989, Rieley & Associates, Landscape Architects, completed a historic resource study on the carriage roads for the National Park Service.[15] The study documented the sequence of the roads' development and construction and made recommendations for their rehabilitation and maintenance. Three years later, the Park Service, with federal construction funds and matching private funds from Friends of Acadia, began the first stage of the restoration of the carriage road system. The top and foundation layers were restored, and drainage ditches and culverts were restored to prevent further erosion. More than one hundred scenic vistas, many first recommended by Farrand, were re-opened.

Coping stones were replaced, and overgrown plants were removed from the roads, shoulders, and ditches. Between 2001 and 2004, all of the bridges received major re-pointing, cleaning, and waterproofing. Friends of Acadia also established a maintenance endowment fund that provides more than $200,000 each year. In addition, volunteers donate thousands of hours each year to clean ditches and culverts, clear brush, and assist park staff with other restoration projects.[16] In 2005 the carriage roads, gatehouses, and stone bridges received a second listing in the National Register of Historic Places, recognized for their national significance as part of the Historic Resources of Acadia Multiple Property Listing.

The carriage roads continue to serve the purpose that Rockefeller intended, mainly as a means of exploring the park's scenic wonders without encountering automobiles; today visitors explore by horseback, horse-and-carriage, bicycle, or on foot. The efforts by Rockefeller and Farrand to transform the scarred, man-made landscapes into healed naturalistic ones also endure today.

Garland Farm, Bar Harbor

ABOVE: *At Garland Farm a Waterer Laburnum blooms in the entrance garden in this 2003 photograph. Farrand's rustic stone bench is located beneath this tree.*
OPPOSITE: *Located near the main entrance to the suites at Garland Farm, this Sargent cherry is fifty feet tall and forty-six feet wide and is listed in the Maine Register of Big Trees.*

In caring for this garden, Mrs. Garland is also perpetuating a most fitting memorial to another great gardener–Beatrix Farrand–who left a legacy of living beauty, not the least of which is this little garden in Eden.[17] – FLOWER GROWER MAGAZINE, 1962

With its 2005 listing in the National Register of Historic Places, Garland Farm joins a handful of distinguished private residences associated with nationally important artists and designers. As the final home and garden of Beatrix Farrand, Garland Farm shares distinction with artists' homes such as the Frederick Law Olmsted National Historic Site in Brookline, Massachusetts; the Augustus Saint-Gaudens National Historic Site in Cornish, New Hampshire; and the home of Daniel Chester French in Stockbridge, Massachusetts, among others. Farrand's last and most intimate garden, Garland Farm was also the only four-season garden that she created in Maine. Here she assembled favorite plants, architectural details, and garden accessories brought from Reef Point. At the end of a career that had lasted nearly sixty years, Farrand created in Garland Farm "a personal statement about her most cherished possessions and design sensibilities."[18] Today Garland Farm is owned by the Beatrix Farrand Society, a non-profit organization dedicated to restoring the buildings and gardens, as well as creating a design and horticultural center modeled after Reef Point.[19]

Farrand lived at Garland Farm from 1955 to 1959, sharing the home of Amy and Lewis Garland, her close friends and managers from Reef Point. Amy Magdalene arrived in New York City from England just after World War I to work for Farrand's mother. Eventually Amy married Lewis, and the two lived with Farrand at Reef Point. When Farrand decided to dismantle her house and gardens, the Garlands made plans for Beatrix and her friend and former maid, Clementine Walter, to live with them in an area of Bar Harbor known as Eden.

The original farm consisted of a ca. 1800 cape, a small ell, a barn, a workshop/garage, and assorted outbuildings, all on about one hundred acres; today the property is just under five acres.

At Garland Farm architect Robert Patterson designed a set of suites for Beatrix and Clementine. When the Reef Point house was dismantled, Farrand kept certain pieces, such as the paneled front door and its matching screen door, French doors, various windows, railings, and light fixtures, which Patterson incorporated into the design of the new home. The one-story addition included two sitting-room suites with bathrooms, a study, an entry hall, a kitchen, a bedroom, and storage rooms. The two suites and the study faced the new terrace garden to the south.

Farrand created gardens at the front and back of the new suites: several lining the driveway, a wild garden, a terrace garden to be seen from the suites, plantings by the barn, and masses of favorite roses, rhododendrons, and azaleas. From Reef Point she also brought garden ornaments, such as chimney pots, millstones, a stone bench, and the Soderholtz bird bath, and transplanted large trees and shrubs around the property; among the unusual specimens were a Korean Stewartia, a dawn redwood, and a Florida dogwood.

Two gardens, enclosed by sections of Reef Point fence, flanked the front walk leading to Farrand's wing. Here formal boxwood hedges bordered the brick and bluestone path to the front door. To soften this formality, Farrand created informal stepping-stone paths that led to a stone bench and to a Chinese ceramic basin. The stepping stones wound through beds of plants native to Asia as well

RIGHT: *A contemporary plan of Garland Farm by Patrick Chassé shows the original farmhouse and ell (right), the Farrand addition with terrace garden (center), the barn (left), and the garage (opposite the barn).*

as Maine, planted below a cypress tree. On the other side of the walk Farrand planted mountain laurel, mountain pieris, and rhododendron below a favored Sargent cherry tree.

In front of the barn Farrand created a shrub garden with plants from Reef Point: forsythia, hawthorn, flowering crabapple, and three golden chain trees. The latter bloomed profusely above the rustic stone bench mentioned above. A narrow gravel path led from the barn's driveway to the terrace garden at the back of the Farrand wing. On the back wall of the barn Farrand planted a climbing hydrangea that she brought from Reef Point.

Outside of the suites and study, Farrand designed a terrace garden made of three formal, rectangular panels, which were further divided into smaller panels. The overall garden was relatively small at forty by forty-four feet, but the panels were packed with Farrand's favorite plants. Outside of her suite she planted perennials in her preferred cool colors of pinks, purples, and blues: columbine, bellflower (*Campanula*), foxglove, bleeding hearts, geranium, iris, phlox, border pinks (*Dianthus*), and thyme, among others. As fillers she used annuals such as *Verbena,* dusty miller (*Artemisia*), other border pinks, clammy campion (*Lychnis viscaria*), dwarf violets, and heliotrope. In the central panels in front of the study she planted anemone, heather, lavender, pasqueflower (*Pulsatilla*), and alyssum. In front of Clementine Walter's suite Farrand used a palette of hot colors that reflected Clementine's favorite yellows, oranges, and reds: Dane's blood (*Campanula glomerata*), yarrow, celandine (*Chelidonium*), Cypress spurge (*Euphorbia*), iris, yellow poppies, and evening primrose, among others. She accented these hot colors with purple iris and white Greek valerian (*Polemonium reptans*) and added annuals as fillers: zinnia, forget-me-nots (*Cynoglossum*), and desert bells (*Phacelia campanularia*).[20]

The terrace garden was built on about eight and one-half feet of fill; on the bank between the terrace and undisturbed ground Farrand planted masses of her favorite single shrub roses. The roses grew behind a wooden fence made of cornice molding salvaged from Chiltern, the summer estate of Mr. and Mrs. Edgar Scott. When Chiltern was razed after World War II, Farrand salvaged several sections of cornice molding, used them at Reef Point, and later brought them to Garland Farm. Chiltern was one of Farrand's early commissions; it is fitting that the molding should end up in her final garden.

Following Beatrix Farrand's death in 1959, Amy Garland continued to care for Clementine Walter until Clementine's death in 1967. Amy lived at the farm for three more years after outliving Beatrix, Clementine, and Lewis. The property was sold twice in 1970, eventually to Jerome and Helena Goff, who were avid gardeners. The Goffs continued to honor and maintain Farrand's work, preparing record plans of the gardens and keeping the main features of the property. New owners bought the farm in 1993 and eventually subdivided it into three lots, offering them for sale in 2002.

Landscape architect Patrick Chassé is a longtime student of the work of Beatrix Farrand. When Garland Farm was placed on the market, Chassé and others interested in saving the property formed the nonprofit Beatrix Farrand Society in 2003. A massive fundraising effort enabled the Society to buy Garland Farm from the estate of the last owner in 2004 and to repair the house and set up an office. Stabilizing historic fences and trees, creating the library, and listing in the National Register of Historic Places took place in 2005. In 2006 Pressley Associates prepared a Cultural Landscape Report, documenting the farm's history and present condition, evaluating its significance, and

BELOW: *Cornice molding from the Scott estate borders heathers in the terrace garden at Garland Farm.*

proposing a plan for rehabilitation from residential to museum use. Since that time the Beatrix Farrand Society has continued to repair the house and outbuildings, prune trees and shrubs, and develop a horticultural study center. In the summer of 2008 the Society began renovating the terrace garden; first steps involved removing, stockpiling, and cataloging plants, to be followed by refurbishing the soil and replanting in Farrand's original beds. Much of this work is based on the garden's description and a planting plan that were published in *Flower Grower* magazine just three years after Farrand's death.[21]

Today, Beatrix Farrand's mission to create a teaching and horticultural institution continues at Garland Farm, although at a much smaller scale than at Reef Point. With the rehabilitation of the Garland farmhouse and gardens, hands-on workshops, guest lectures by noted authors, and a growing library of more than 1,600 books, the Beatrix Farrand society ensures that Farrand's legacy will endure for generations to come.

CHAPTER 11

SKYLANDS: JENS JENSEN'S MAINE MASTERPIECE

I spent four days at Seal Harbor a week or two ago, and went one night at sunset up onto the very top of your very beautiful hill. I do not know when I have seen a more magnificent and stunning view than that which met my eye on every side.[1] —JOHN D. ROCKEFELLER, JR., 1922

John D. Rockefeller's enthusiastic response to Skylands came from a keen observer and dedicated conservationist of Maine's natural landscape. Native woodlands were featured prominently in his own Seal Harbor property, The Eyrie, designed by Beatrix Farrand, and his vision and personal contributions were unequalled in the creation of Acadia National Park. His congratulatory note to Edsel Ford, written in December, must have brought back memories of the Fords' delight in their summer property. The spectacular natural beauty of its setting and its status as a historic property that has been exceptionally well preserved and enhanced make Skylands a stunning example of the best of Maine's designed landscapes.

Skylands, a private estate in Seal Harbor, was originally built for Edsel Ford between 1922 and 1926. The property is significant as the work of landscape gardener Jens Jensen, famous as one of the creators of the Prairie Style of landscape design in the Midwest and one of the earliest advocates of landscape preservation and the use of native plants. Jensen deftly transformed the formal geometry of the Fords' summer home into "a lush woodland, complete with groves, a flowing spring, and a 'mountain meadow.'"[2]

Jens Jensen emigrated from Denmark to the United States in 1884 and settled in Chicago, where he began work for the Chicago West Parks District and started a lifelong study of the prairie countryside landscape and plants native to the Chicago area. His first notable design was for the American Garden in Union Park, Chicago, in 1888. In response to Chicago's rapid growth, which was destroying the native prairie landscape, Jensen became a pioneer in the field of landscape conservation. In 1908 he helped form the Prairie Club, which sponsored walking tours of landscapes threatened by development and also brought Chicago residents closer to nature. In 1913 he inspired the Friends of Our Native Landscape, a group who worked with the Prairie Club to eventually preserve the Indiana sand dunes.

During this time Jensen also developed an extensive reputation as an estate designer. In 1915 he started a lengthy relationship with the Ford family. Jensen was recommended to Henry Ford by the architectural office of van Holst and Fyfe when Fair Lane, Ford's estate in Dearborn, Michigan, was under construction.[3] Jensen continued to work for the Ford family and the company over the next twenty years, designing the grounds of the Henry Ford Hospital, many office buildings and plants, and several homes for Ford executives. Following family tradition, Edsel Ford commissioned Jensen to design the grounds of four homes between 1922 and 1935. One was

Skylands, his summer home in Seal Harbor, and the others were estates in Michigan.

Edsel Ford chose a challenging site on which to build Skylands: a wooded hillside 334 feet above sea level overlooking Seal Harbor. The seventy-four-acre property was covered mainly with young spruce trees, in dark contrast to the sunny prairies and their deciduous trees with which Jensen was familiar. He wrote, "It is far from the prairies of the west to the rocky coast of Maine, to a different landscape with its different beauty—a new world for the prairie mind to understand and to learn to love."[4] Nevertheless, Jensen was familiar with woodlands through his summer properties—both of which he called "The Clearing"—in Ravinia, Illinois, and Ellison Bay, Wisconsin.[5] By the time Jensen arrived at Skylands, the main house, designed by architect Duncan Candler, was under construction. The twelve-bedroom home was built of pink granite quarried on site and featured a dining room ell oriented to take advantage of sunrises and sunsets.

Candler, a New York City architect who had designed numerous properties for the Rockefeller family as well as summer "cottages" in Bar Harbor, followed the popular Beaux-Arts tradition when he proposed a landscape design for the area immediately surrounding the house. Beaux-Arts called for creating clear, orderly outdoor spaces, usually with a main sightline such as a straight path. It also relied on strong vertical planes, such as stone walls, to define outdoor spaces.[6] To conquer the steep slope Candler built massive retaining walls of local granite, on which he proposed three large planted terraces. In keeping with Beaux-Arts formality, he proposed geometric, Italian-style gardens with axes and focal points aligned with the house. Only two of the terraces were built, and the Italian gardens were never installed, due to Jensen's advocacy for a naturalistic landscape.

Jensen did not try to disguise the geometry of Candler's two terraces to the west of the house, nor did he use only native plants. He addressed the larger terrace's formality by proposing a simple panel of turf bordered on each end by informal clumps of sugar maples, with a balustrade planted in bittersweet vines. He softened the linear path to the smaller lower terrace by proposing native shadbush and mountain laurel. For the lower terrace, he suggested another area of turf bordered by non-native white lilacs, with a "bird fountain" as a focal point.

Candler's main terrace was approximately twenty-four feet by seventy feet and was paved with pink granite, carefully cut and fit like a "cracked ice" puzzle. Jensen proposed to soften the granite of the house and retaining walls with Virginia creeper, but the popular kiwi vine was planted instead. The only difference between Candler's and Jensen's plan for the terrace is the addition of tubs of oleander, purple petunias, juniper, and hydrangeas on Jensen's version. For Candler's narrow planter between the house and terrace Jensen suggested delphiniums, hollyhocks, and shadbushes, a rather limited plant palette for such a large space. He proposed buffalo berry, a groundcover native to Canada, for the other planting beds surrounding the main terrace.

Candler's east terrace, near the service wing, was intended to be as formal as the west terraces. He proposed a simple square garden with flower beds, grass paths, and a border of shrubs, all aligned on axis with the dining room. The University of Michigan's Bentley Library has a copy of Candler's plan on which Jensen drew large "Xs" through Candler's formal garden and adjacent laundry yard. To create his garden on such a steep slope, Jensen built a massive granite retaining wall, roughly twenty-five feet high. Instead of Candler's formal design, Jensen proposed a naturalistic garden with a curving path, a "mountain meadow" of heather and shrubby St. Johns-wort, a campfire ring bordered by yews, a granite waterfall and pool (labeled "Fountain" on the plan), and extensive rockwork, including boulders aligned to mimic a stream. Jensen proposed pine needle paths, an interesting detail given that pines are common in the surrounding forests but seldom occur in groves, where pine needle duff could easily be collected.

The mountain meadow was one of Jensen's signature pieces, appearing in many of his landscape designs as representative of his beloved prairie.[7] At Skylands, the mountain meadow was the most heavily planted of Jensen's gardens. Here he proposed almost exclusively trees, shrubs, and groundcovers native to the eastern United States. Most grew naturally in the Maine landscape: shad, viburnum, sumac, alder, dogwood, winterberry, blueberry, ferns, partridgeberry, and lambkill, among others. He proposed native hemlocks to screen the garden from the service area and laundry yard and to provide a backdrop at the top of the massive retaining wall. Native sugar maples, red maples, mountain ash, and a rock elm would provide interesting fall color. Jensen was not a purist, however, and his design included non-native shrubs such as Savin juniper and Smilax, along with perennial delphiniums, harebells, and Siberian iris.

Duncan Candler's plan shows a "foreturn" in the driveway leading to the house's entrance hall, and this was built as proposed. The circular turnaround was quarried from the granite bedrock, leaving one large cliff exposed. Candler did not address the cliff, proposing only a narrow border of flowers along the east side of the circle. In contrast, Jensen listed native trees and shrubs, such as pitch pine, mountain ash, shad, and withe-rod viburnum, to break up the view of the cliff and soften the granite.

OPPOSITE: *The granite waterfall and pool designed by Jensen remain today in the mountain meadow, surrounded by numerous plants native to the eastern U.S.* BELOW: *The council ring at Skylands was reconstructed based on Jensen's original design. A granite-capped seating wall surrounds a raised fire pit set on a floor of crushed pink granite.*

Jensen proposed a variety of plants along woodland trails as well. Again, he used native shrubs, ferns, and wildflowers, such as pink and yellow moccasin flowers (lady's slippers), dogtooth violets, columbine, and asters. Typically at summer estates a designer would select plants that would flower when the client was in residence, but this does not seem to have been the case at Skylands. Many of these native plants bloomed in the spring, when the Fords were presumably not at their summer home.

Skylands remained in the Ford family until 1980, when it was sold to a family from Texas who continued to enjoy it as a summer home into the 1990s. Ownership changed again following a dinner party that included guest Martha Stewart. Although the harbor view was blocked by overgrown spruces and hemlocks, Martha was captivated by the powerful sense of place formed by architecture and landscape.[8] Surprised to find Skylands for sale, Martha bought the property in 1997. Together with landscape architect Patrick Chassé, who has extensively researched Skylands' history, she has preserved the soul and structure of Jensen's landscape.

Jensen's plan for the garden near the mountain meadow called for a council ring, another signature piece, which his biographer, Robert Grese, describes as a simple, circular stone bench with a fire pit in the center. Council rings resembled the kivas of the Pueblo Indians in the American Southwest[9] and were considered a symbol of democracy by Jensen:

> *In this friendly circle, around the fire, man becomes himself. Here there is no social caste. All are on the same level, looking each other in the face. The fire in the center portrays the beginnings of civilization, and it was around the fire our forefathers gathered when they first set foot on the continent.*[10]

Jensen incorporated council rings in designs throughout the Midwest, in parks, where they were intended to hold as many as 150 people, as well as in private estates. In fact, for Edsel Ford's year-round home in Detroit, he designed a council ring that apparently saw little use; the Fords chose not to build one he designed for Skylands for that reason.

In 1998, Martha Stewart decided to build Jensen's council ring on the site of the former laundry yard. Patrick Chassé, in collaboration with master stone mason Jeff Gammelin, reconstructed the ring based on Jensen's original design, including the inscribed "glyph" decoration on the seat's surface and the front faces. The council ring is a circular stone wall with a granite seat cap, surrounding a raised granite fire pit. The ring is sunken into the grade and surrounded by ledge-like weathered irregular granite blocks and softened with masses of Japanese painted ferns. The floor of the circle is of crushed pink granite. The entire setting is as Jensen intended, a meditative gathering spot where one may appreciate all of nature's offerings—the stars, the woods, the wind, or "the brotherhood of all living things."[11]

The series of terraces at Skylands provide unique opportunities for viewing the landscape from above. Near the main terrace overlooking the harbor, massive stone steps bordered by Kenilworth ivy lead to the woodlands below. On the way down, in a moss garden backed by a quarried granite wall, Martha has added "La Rivière," a large bronze sculpture of a woman by Aristide Maillol of France. La Rivière was cast between 1938 and 1943.

Bar Harbor M.E. Seal Harbor, Maine.

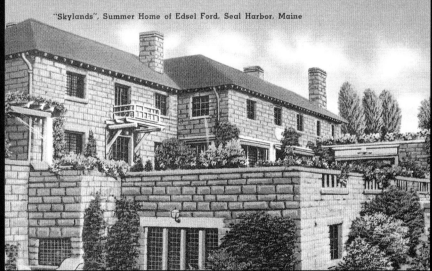

"Skylands", Summer Home of Edsel Ford, Seal Harbor, Maine

ABOVE: (CLOCKWISE FROM TOP LEFT): *In this 1950 view at Skylands, kiwi covers the pergola, as it does today. A vintage postcard shows cottages along the shore at Seal Harbor. Artistic license was used in this hand-colored postcard of the main terrace at Skylands; note the pergola's kiwi on the left, shown in pink. In this hand-colored view of the mountain meadow, note the granite framed by tree trunks; stones match those shown in the photo on page 178.*

With his naturalistic design philosophy, Jens Jensen intended nature to take its course. At Skylands this has meant a shift in plants as the landscape matured. The driveway foreturn no longer has the variety of plants suggested by Jensen, but its numerous ferns and young spruces mimic the surrounding native woods. The quarried ledge, originally camouflaged with vines trained on wires, has weathered over the last eighty years and is softened by mountain laurel, blueberries, viburnum, and ferns at the base. Mature sugar maples flank the main entrance, with young spruce trees in the understory. Lush moss covers the ground, and a stone path leads to what was once the children's entrance to the house. Over the door an unpainted wooden arbor matches one found on the guest cottage elsewhere on the property.

Working with Patrick Chassé, Martha Stewart has gradually restored parts of Jensen's plan, including returning flowing water to the granite pool in the mountain meadow. She has planted woodland favorites that suit this now-shady glen—purple trillium, bugbane, foam flower, wild ginger, and orchids. She has also restored the harbor view from the terrace with careful pruning of mature evergreens and has designed numerous pots to overflow with vividly-colored, patterned, and textured annuals.[12] The granite-capped terrace walls are partially covered by kiwi vines planted in the 1920s; the same vines with their deep green leaves soften the granite walls of the house. On the western end of the house the original, rough-hewn pergola forms the ceiling of an outdoor dining room. In the woods below the terrace, Martha maintains Jensen's pine needle paths, which are bordered by a groundcover of ferns, bunchberry, and haircap moss. The narrow paths wind through the native woods, passing by a dramatic ravine near the guest house site.

During initial construction of Skylands, the Bar Harbor *Times* reported: "Landscape work of the highest type is being carried on there in one of the most beautiful of modified naturalistic schemes…"[13] A few months later, the *Boston Transcript* declared, "Out of the native granite [Ford] has built himself a mansion that will withstand the test of time."[14] Thanks to the stewardship of current owner Martha Stewart, Jens Jensen's vision for Skylands and its landscape continues to stand that test well. The seamless integration of this designed landscape into its natural Maine environment makes Skylands a model for future landscapes.

ABOVE: *Colors and textures of annuals on the main terrace offer an elegant contrast to the surrounding native landscape of Skylands.*
OPPOSITE: *The main terrace at Skylands features a "cracked ice" paving pattern. The terrace overlooks Seal Harbor, out of view to the left.*

IV. EXPANDING THE LANDSCAPE

CHAPTER 12

HISTORIC SUBDIVISIONS: CREATING NEW NEIGHBORHOODS

If... the lots are small, the houses necessarily close to the street so that no broad naturalistic effect is possible, then the beauty to be sought must be of quite another kind – a beauty of harmonious but diversified houses, of tree-shaded streets, with pleasant curves or with pleasantly broken straights, a beauty consisting largely in a general air of decency and well being.[1] – HENRY VINCENT HUBBARD AND THEODORA KIMBALL ON LAND SUBDIVISION, 1917

There must be few communities in the United States today without a neighborhood of Sears homes dating from 1908 to the 1940s, or tract homes from the 1950s and '60s, or clusters of today's condominium developments and mini-mansions. When we think of subdivisions, we probably picture these familiar housing options. However, divisions of land for residential use have occurred throughout the country since the early 1800s, when developers bought land, hired surveyors to map existing topography, and created plans showing house lots and roads. Later, typical landscape improvements included grading roads and house sites, addressing storm-water drainage issues, adding sidewalks and utilities, and planting street trees.

The proliferation of neighborhoods, suburbs, industrial housing, and new towns was a national phenomenon as the population of the United States grew rapidly in the mid-nineteenth century. "The early residential suburbs fostered an emerging American aspiration for life in a semi-rural environment, apart from the crowded city, but close enough to the city for commuting daily to work."[2]

Two residential subdivisions are recognized as prototypes of the modern subdivision. The first was Llewellyn Park, initiated in 1857 by New York businessman Llewellyn Haskell and architect Alexander Jackson Davis. Located in Orange, New Jersey, Llewellyn Park was built in response to the degraded living conditions, poor air quality, and unsanitary conditions of New York City, twelve miles away. In addition to curving streets in a park-like setting, Llewellyn Park featured winding paths, streams, and ornamental trees, shrubs, and flowers.

The second prototypical planned community was Riverside, Illinois, designed by Frederick Law Olmsted, Sr., and Calvert Vaux and built in 1869. Riverside is a community of tree-lined curving streets, open spaces, and a handsome village center located about nine miles from downtown Chicago. The construction of the railroad in 1863 opened the surrounding countryside to wealthy Chicagoans seeking relief from unsanitary urban conditions, many caused by the largest stockyards in the world.[3]

Of course, conditions in Maine's smaller, less industrialized cities were not as dire, but Portland's Great Fire of 1866 indirectly caused movement to the suburbs. When the city was rebuilt following the fire, downtown land was at a premium, lots became smaller, and houses were built closer together, prompting development into the surrounding countryside. This was especially true following improvements in public transportation that allowed convenient access to and from

Looking from Mountain View Park.

Greetings from Casco Bay.

urban areas, a trend seen nationwide.

Nationally, the first public transportation systems used horse-drawn cars operating on rails of primitive iron strips laid on stone blocks or wooden stringers. By the 1860s such systems were in place in New York, Baltimore, Philadelphia, and Boston, as well as in Portland, Maine. The cars were restricted to a fixed route and traveled at roughly six miles per hour, pushing the limits of residence for city dwellers to about four miles from downtown places of employment.[4] The change to the faster electric streetcar, introduced by Frank Sprague in Richmond, Virginia, in 1887, brought the radius of residences to about eight miles.

During this period, the City Beautiful movement also influenced city planning and the location and design of residential suburbs. The movement began with Chicago's World's Columbian Exposition of 1893 and continued into the 1920s. Reformers addressed deteriorating urban conditions—pollution, crime, and over-population—through sanitation and through beautification projects such as broad, tree-lined boulevards and monumental civic buildings. In newly emerging residential parks and garden suburbs, developers and designers used "a general plan of development, specifications and standards, and … deed restrictions … to control house design, ensure quality and harmony of construction, and create spatial organization suitable for fine homes in a park setting."[5]

Promoters of Maine suburbs offered the promise of a combination of modern amenities and stunning scenery. In the Portland subdivisions, developers stressed natural features such as "some of the most beautiful trees in Maine" or "the shores of beautiful Capisic Pond."[6] Advertisements promoted water from Lake Sebago, "sanitary plumbing," hot water heat, new city hydrants for increased fire protection, electricity, and telephone lines as attractions to draw residents away from city centers.

Historic Greater Portland Neighborhoods, 1899–1921

The Greater Portland area was home to the largest number of subdivisions designed and built in the state between the 1860s and World War I. Several of the most successful of these early suburban developments have remained and retain much of their original landscape and architectural features. They provide good examples of neighborhoods built along national trends adapted to the native Maine landscape.

Portland's horse-drawn trolley cars were replaced with electric streetcars in 1891, greatly increasing pleasure travel as families, church groups, and social clubs rode the cars into the countryside for picnics and to visit newly established amusement parks. Trolley companies built three pleasure parks to draw weekend visitors and increase revenues. These were Riverton Park (1896) on the Presumpscot River in Portland, the ocean-front Cape Cottage Park (1898) in Cape Elizabeth, and Underwood Springs (1899), also on the ocean in Falmouth Foreside. Tourists and residents flocked to the casinos, theaters, dance halls, picnic grounds, and rustic pavilions, eager to escape the summer heat of the city. The trolleys not only passed through scenic, rural landscapes but opened them up for development as well.[7]

Outside Portland, Cape Elizabeth saw some of the earliest neighborhood developments, some of which began as summer colonies. Ottawa Park, developed in 1899 by C. B. Dalton & Company, was conveniently located on the trolley line, which went as far as Cape Cottage Park. Before the site was subdivided, it housed the rambling Cliff Cottage, a summer hotel built in 1860. The original hotel was destroyed by fire in 1873 but was soon rebuilt. Extensive remodeling in 1900 created one hundred rooms, and the hotel owners enticed visitors with "electric lights, an orchestra, unsurpassed cuisine, perfect sanitary arrangements, salt and fresh water baths, large ocean frontage, [and a] fine beach."[8] The hotel's popularity with Canadian tourists may have prompted the choice of "Ottawa Park" as the name of a new subdivision surrounding the hotel. Harry Taylor Harmon, a Portland civil engineer, designed fifty-six house lots (most of which have houses today) along the newly laid Seaview, Crescent, and Glen avenues. Harmon noted on his plan that he revised the streets "to better fit the contour of the ground," a detail that remains today. These curving streets surrounded Cliff Cottage, which was destroyed by another fire in 1914. Taylor also proposed an area called "Public Grounds," which gave neighborhood residents access to the ocean.

Like other historic subdivisions, Ottawa Park appears to have been developed in stages. Most of the roads were built as designed in 1899, although Sea View Avenue is not a through road, as originally intended. The first twenty-five homes were located on the highest ground with the best ocean views. Lots in lower elevations with more tree cover were developed later, as were the lots on Montgomery Terrace, which occupies the former Cliff Cottage site. Neighborhood residents still have access to the "Public Grounds" leading to the ocean.

Directly opposite Ottawa Park is Mountain View Park, developed by Portland resident George Washington Brown in 1900. Brown created the Suburban Realty Company to develop and market the properties and hired Charles Fenn, a civil engineer and surveyor from Portland, to lay out the lots. Fenn's plan shows fifty house lots neatly arranged on curving roads with scenic names: Ocean View, Island View, Forest, Summit, and High Ridge. These tree-lined streets exist today as designed by Fenn. Homes were built on most lots, with a few houses sited on double lots. A second neighborhood entrance, marked by handsome stone pillars, was added later on Island View Road.

George Washington Brown went to great lengths to advertise Mountain View Park's scenic views. He claimed that one could see the White Mountains from the site's most prominent elevation, and he built an observation tower that rose 165 feet above sea level for a view of the mountains and ocean. He reportedly used the tower for promotional purposes and placed a brilliant electric beacon on top, which was removed when the Coast Guard declared it a "navigational menace."[9]

Driving through Mountain View Park today, one sees only a few

OPPOSITE: *Homes in Mountain View Park subdivision, with Casco Bay in the distance, are seen in this ca. 1915 postcard. The tallest building on the right is Cliff House (Cliff Cottage), part of the neighboring Ottawa Park subdivision.*
BELOW: *This vintage postcard shows the Cape Casino at Cape Cottage Park, an amusement park owned and operated by the Portland Railroad Company. In the 1920s the park was subdivided into a residential neighborhood of the same name. The casino was substantially reduced in size and is a private residence today.*

houses at a time, which increases a sense of privacy and spaciousness, enhanced by narrow streets, mature maples, and a mix of Arts and Crafts bungalows and Colonial Revival and shingle-style homes.

The expansion of Cape Elizabeth neighborhoods continued along the electric trolley line. Adjacent to Mountain View Park is Cottage Farms, a neighborhood of more than twenty house lots designed in 1909 by civil engineer F. H. Files of Cape Elizabeth. The nearby neighborhoods of Birch Knolls and Shore Acres (both designed in 1911), Pillsbury Bluffs (ca. 1914), and Oakhurst Park (1917), continued this trend, and others followed.

NEW ROADS LEAD TO NEW NEIGHBORHOODS

No transportation system had a greater effect on suburban development than the automobile, which freed commuters from the timetable and limited routes of the trolleys. A law passed by the Maine legislature in 1901 offered $100 to any town that agreed to spend $200 for the improvement of a main thoroughfare to be designated as a state road. By 1915, Mainers had become so entranced with "motoring" that they passed legislation and a $2,000,000 bond issue beginning an "excellent highway system." The automobile allowed access to areas of potential development as well as to scenic wonders, as summed up in 1915: "You owe it to yourself and to Maine to see the state in the intimate way you can from the seat of an automobile."[10] A real estate advertisement also boasted of newly paved roads "offering auto owners a most delightful ride to and from the city...."[11]

One Portland neighborhood that developed directly out of a road project is Boulevard Park, located just under a mile from the city's center, between Forest Avenue and Back Cove. Designed in 1912 while construction of Baxter Boulevard (pp. 34–37) was under way, Boulevard Park was one of Carl Rust Parker's major commissions during the period of his solo practice in Maine and is one of the few historic subdivisions in Maine designed by a landscape architect. Later, as a member of the Olmsted firm, Parker designed several public landscapes in Augusta (pp. 41–51).

Mayor James P. Baxter wrote that, following completion of Back Cove Boulevard, "The high ground which surrounds the Back Bay, and which is now of insignificant value, will afford hundreds of fine building sites and make this the most attractive portion of the Back Bay region. With this park completed and connected with the promenades and Deering's Oaks, Portland and its suburbs will offer advantages for residence unequalled by any city in New England."[12] Baxter's expectations for the land surrounding the boulevard came true; today homes along Baxter Boulevard are some of the city's most highly valued.

At Boulevard Park Parker proposed about 110 house lots and two small parks with paths and trees. What distinguishes his plan from the hundreds of others in Maine is that he also proposed sidewalks and grassy esplanades lined with street trees; very few historic subdivision plans showed such attention to landscape details. A 1912 newspaper advertisement describes Boulevard Park as "the latest and most desirable residential development in the City. Completed streets with granolithic

ABOVE: *In this ca. 1921 postcard, a trolley car crosses the Fore River on the "Million Dollar Bridge." The bridge and expansion of trolley service led to development of subdivisions south of Portland.*

curbing, sewers, and granolithic sidewalks. All improvements free to lot buyers. Prices are reasonable. 50 cents per foot for choicest lots."[13]

Today Boulevard Park seems to have the best of all worlds. It is close to downtown Portland but also buffered from Forest Avenue's commercial congestion by shade trees. Views across Baxter Boulevard to Back Cove are some of the most scenic in the city. Historic architecture contributes to the charm of the neighborhood, with homes of similar scale with period details such as hipped roofs and dormers. Today the neighborhood consists of about forty homes; many along Forest Avenue were replaced with commercial buildings, and Preble Street Extension caused the loss of others.

Over the Bridge to Sylvan Site

> *[Sylvan Site] should in no way be considered the same as the usual building or development projects with which most cities are familiar...It is a residential section of fine type.*[14]
> — Lewiston Journal, 1928

In 1916 the newly built "Million Dollar Bridge" from Portland made outlying areas even more accessible and contributed to land speculation. A 1915 newspaper article predicted that "certain real estate will double its present value when the new Portland Bridge is completed.... People now owning real estate... are holding on to their property... and South Portland realty is very difficult to obtain."[15] One of the developments that began following construction of the bridge was Sylvan Site, a neighborhood of thirty-seven homes on Richards, Adelbert, Clifford, and Sawyer streets in South Portland. This location differs from the historic subdivisions above, in that it had no special scenic views or unusual topography and was laid out in a rectangular grid pattern.

The unique appeal of Sylvan Site is in the architecture designed by politician and developer Frederick Wheeler Hinckley. A native of Princeton, Maine, Hinckley was admitted to the bar in 1901, and began a notable career in Portland two years later. He was elected to the Maine Legislature in 1918, became mayor of South Portland in 1919, served in both the Maine House and Senate in the 1920s, and ran unsuccessfully for governor in 1927. In 1909 he bought about twenty acres of land in South Portland on which he designed and built his home, "Clyfdale Villa," at 925 Sawyer Street. He shared this Southern Colonial-style brick mansion with his wife, Blanche Richards; the two had no children. In 1919 Hinckley bought the adjacent one hundred acres in order to prevent less expensive homes from being built nearby. He started developing Sylvan Site in 1921, investing more than $700,000 over the next decade, and designing and building the "finest type of homes, designed for people of means."[16] He envisioned creating two hundred homes in Sylvan Site, but that plan was derailed by the Depression.[17]

ABOVE: *Frederick Wheeler Hinckley was a lawyer, politician, and self-taught designer of homes and landscapes, as shown in his Sylvan Site subdivision.*
BELOW: *This shingled craftsman-style cottage in Sylvan Site illustrates Frederick Hinckley's knowledge of architectural styles popular in the early 1900s.*

Hinckley was a talented amateur architect who designed each home to be unique, based on his knowledge of a variety of architectural styles. The neighborhood is a sampler of Spanish, Colonial, Tudor, Italianate, and Arts and Crafts architecture. Each home's roofline is distinct; some have multi-level eaves or multiple gables, while others are hipped or steep and curving. Hinckley also embellished his designs with details such as roof balustrades, patterned windowpanes, and contrasting quoins. Many of the homes have deep verandas to provide a transition from outdoors to indoors. In addition Hinckley was concerned with practical comfort and modern conveniences; all homes had oil burners, modern plumbing, and electric lights. Addressing the increased availability of the automobile, Hinckley provided many homes with matching two-car garages.[18]

The name "Sylvan," referring to a wooded landscape, still suits the neighborhood today; streets are shaded by mature, purple-leaved Norway maples, though originally the land was treeless and was most likely open farmland. The Norway maples are planted in grassy esplanades between the sidewalks and roads and create a dramatic sense of arrival from Sawyer Street. The trees are a major character-defining feature of the neighborhood, although they have a reputation as an invasive species, which creates a challenge for maintaining the historic character. Residents have worked with the city of South Portland to select appropriate replacements for the aging maples.

A common element of architecture and landscape is the neighborhood's extensive stonework. The stone came from Hinckley's nearby quarry on Sawyer Street and was used in foundations, exterior chimneys, porch columns, and the formal stone walls bordering many homes.

There is no indication that Hinckley influenced the landscapes of individual homes, which were as varied as the architecture. In contrast to paved asphalt driveways of today, some of Sylvan Site's early driveways featured narrow concrete paths with grass center strips. Historic photographs show backyards with Colonial Revival-style lattice fences, arbors, benches, and planters, as well as square lattice trellises attached to homes. Ivy climbed the walls of some houses, and shrubs were dotted around foundations.

Preservationists and contemporary planners have a great interest in the study of historic American suburbs, and much work has been done to document their development. Exemplary sites such as Llewellyn Park and Riverside are listed in the National Register of Historic Places, and state historic preservation offices have documented lesser-known sites across the country. To guide future research and encourage surveys of historic neighborhoods, in 2002 the National Park Service (NPS) published *Historic Residential Suburbs–Guidelines for Evaluation and Documentation for the National Register of Historic Places*, as well as *Suburbanization of Metropolitan Areas in the United States, 1830–1960.*[19]

Although the NPS documents have raised public awareness about historic suburbs, these neighborhoods face complex challenges from intrusions on their borders, road and sidewalk improvements, and nature itself. Residents of Portland's Boulevard Park successfully prevented construction of a gas station at the neighborhood's entrance. But following sidewalk improvements, the city planted street trees that will stay below power lines and that will not heave sidewalks. Although these are a practical choice, over time the neighborhood will lose its canopy of lindens, one of its character-defining features.

Subdivisions have always been for-profit business ventures. Those that have the advantage of beautiful natural sites and thoughtful landscape planning have much to contribute to the look and livability of our urban and suburban environment.

OPPOSITE: *Norway maples are one of Sylvan Site's most distinguishing features. Once widely planted, the maples now have a reputation as an invasive species, presenting challenges to maintaining historic character.*

BELOW: *The Sylvan Site neighborhood originally was open and treeless, as shown in this 1920s view. In the front yard note the unusual plantings, neither a formal garden nor a trim lawn. The driveway with concrete driving lanes and a grassy center leads to the porte-cochère.*

CHAPTER 13

New Town Plans: Utopian Experiments

The town of Rumford, Maine, has long been overlooked as just another mill town, subject to the boom-and-bust cycles of the paper industry. Rumford's industrial history began in the late 1800s when entrepreneur Hugh Chisholm sought to attract loyal mill-workers with modern neighborhoods, cultural amenities, and access to the wild scenery of the Maine woods. Eyeing the massive mill buildings, railroad yards, and enormous piles of pulp wood today, few would suspect that the town was carefully designed according to European and national industrial models.

New England is considered the birthplace of industrialization in the United States. The first successful water-powered cotton spinning mill in the United States was built along the Blackstone River in Pawtucket, Rhode Island, in 1793. Twenty years later, the country's first completely mechanized cotton mill was built on the Charles River in Waltham, Massachusetts. By the early 1800s, mills along New England's other powerful rivers supplied the country with tools, fabrics, leather goods, and numerous other materials and finished products. The mills and their accompanying dams, canals, and villages forever changed the character of New England's rural landscape.

Throughout New England the early mill villages developed haphazardly, with new mills constructed as need arose. The importation of mechanized technology from Great Britain greatly increased production and started a new phase in mill construction in the United States. The Waltham mills required more power than could be supplied by the Charles River, so mill owners moved to the Pawtucket Falls on the Merrimack River and established the city of Lowell, Massachusetts. Lowell is considered the country's first large-scale factory town, noteworthy because it was planned as "an industrial community of unprecedented size" even before the first mill was constructed. Mills in Lowell were built in an orderly fashion, arranged in a single row facing the canal, and worker housing was laid out in rows on a rectangular plan. Lowell was also famous for its Utopian social system that attracted farm girls to work in the mills by offering good wages, "strictly proper and carefully managed boardinghouses," and amenities such as a church, a library, a lyceum, and a savings bank.[1]

In their first decades, the Lowell mills were successful because they had the market to themselves; they competed against material made by hand. By the 1840s, however, as increasingly mechanized mills became more widespread, the market had become saturated. Wages dropped, and immigrants were willing to accept lower wages than those paid to farm girls. In the following decades, as demand for manufactured goods

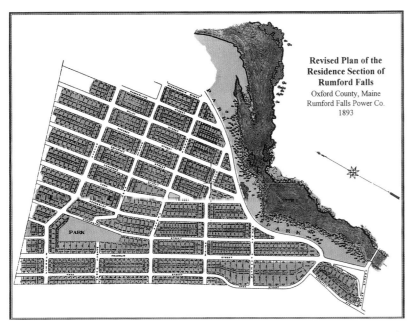

Revised Plan of the Residence Section of Rumford Falls
Oxford County, Maine
Rumford Falls Power Co.
1893

grew again, additional mills were built, causing congested living and working conditions and leading mill owners to abandon ideas of Utopia.[2] Conditions were further stressed following the Civil War, when workers flocked to factory jobs in cities, looking for a better life. They worked for low wages and crowded into unhealthy urban tenements.

One response to such conditions came from N. O. Nelson, a manufacturer of plumbing goods in St. Louis, Missouri. Nelson experienced firsthand the plight of workers after serving as arbitrator during a railroad strike in 1886, and he vowed to improve conditions in his own factories. Following visits to industrial villages in New England and Europe, he relocated his company to a rural area across the river in Illinois. There in 1890 he created the ideal model community of Leclaire and provided exemplary working and living conditions—spacious manufacturing buildings with natural light, fresh air, and modern conveniences such as electric lights and a sprinkler system. He offered workers and their families low-cost housing in tree-lined neighborhoods, progressive education, a guest-speaker series, a library, and recreational facilities. Now part of the city of Edwardsville, Leclaire is listed in the National Register of Historic Places.[3]

THE NEW TOWN OF RUMFORD, MAINE: THE PROGRESSIVE WILDERNESS

The power here available exceeds that of the three largest manufacturing cities of New England. The plan of development of the power secures to the manufacturer a steady flow the year round, a great variety for choice of mill sites, secure foundations, and ample transportation facilities.[4] – SCENIC GEMS OF MAINE, 1898

Lightly populated Maine may seem an unlikely location for a new, industrial town in the 1890s, but Canadian entrepreneur Hugh Chisholm had a vision to harness the industrial power of the Androscoggin River. Chisholm purchased over 1,400 acres surrounding Great Falls with the intention of transforming Rumford Falls into a model, working-class town unrivaled in Maine. Even before the last parcel was purchased, he hired Boston civil engineer Edward A. Buss to survey and lay out the new town.

Rumford Falls was one of several villages in the greater town of Rumford, where about 1,000 people lived in the 1880s. The main village of East Rumford was home to three lumber mills, a shovel handle factory, a grist-mill, a cheese factory, a starch factory, and "other manufactories common to villages."[5] At the confluence of the Swift and Androscoggin rivers, the elevation drops 177 feet in one mile, creating the greatest waterfall drop east of Niagara Falls. The region's dramatic natural scenery was a great attraction in the development of the town.

Here at Rumford Falls are the purest of mountain breezes laden with that life-giving ozone that Oxford's forest-clad hills alone can give. The scenery has all the happy combinations in broad, level intervals, hillside farms, mountain pasture, woods, and fertile fields. It is surrounded on all sides by beautiful drives, rivers, lakes, and streams for boating and fishing, abundance of forest and wild game for the huntsman's chase, interesting rocks and minerals and wonderful formations to interest the student of nature. [6]

With his interests in paper and water companies, banks, steamboats, and railroads, Hugh Chisholm was the dominant industrial developer in Maine in the late 1800s. He was the primary founder of International Paper Company, which brought together seventeen pulp and paper mills in New York, Massachusetts, New Hampshire, Vermont, Maine, and Canada. He formed the Rumford Falls Power Company and created an ambitious plan for the town: thirty mill sites along the river; dams and canals to supply water to the mills; more than 1,000 house lots; and land set aside for parks, schools, churches, and public buildings.

The power company first built dams, canals, and mills and then connected the railroad to Portland and northern points where pulpwood was located. The water and transportation connections led Chisholm to promote Rumford as the new industrial center of New England, and several industries were established in the early 1890s—Rumford Falls Paper Company, Rumford Falls Sulphite Company, and the Electro Chemical Company, among others. [7]

In his new town, Chisholm capitalized on Rumford's natural scenic amenities for both the working class and for business owners and detailed these advantages in his "Prospectus of Rumford Falls Power Company." [8] For town residents, "Ample breathing spaces have been reserved at various portions of the property, including those commanding views of the falls, and among them the highest knoll on this property, which is the park on Knox St." He also set aside "park reservations" to preserve the "wildest and most commanding portion of the property." As for the business owner, Chisholm stated: "The manufacturer can here find the opportunity of building a summer home convenient to the factory, and still possessing all the charms of river, mountain, and valley view which many travel long distances to reach."

Chisholm discouraged boardinghouse and tenement blocks but recognized the need for temporary housing for the rapid influx of mill workers. He conveyed a small section near the river to several companies, "to enable them to meet the temporary demand for boarding places, while the help are becoming established and acquainted with the property." Skilled workers lived in the boarding houses, while day laborers (typically European immigrants) set up camp in shanties and sod huts.

Chisholm disapproved of the boxed tenement housing found elsewhere in New Hampshire and Massachusetts and refused to follow their models. To address Rumford Falls' dramatic housing shortage and to attract manufacturers and workers, Chisholm offered special pricing and payment options to "mechanics wishing to become householders." House lots were as small as thirty by one hundred feet but were practical; conforming to Rumford's numerous hills, all had "…a good outlook and situation, none of them being in sags which would leave them hemmed in by higher ground on all sides." Roads were engineered to follow existing contours as closely as possible and the "laying

of streets was studied with the special reference to economical grading of the house lots."

Chisholm's ambitious plans for Rumford were not without criticism. He bought his 1,400 acres through a local agent, and many of those who sold land did not understand the magnitude of his plan. Chisholm also had a monopoly on the major transportation facilities in and out of Rumford. He controlled two banks, and "the Power Company purchased lands and rented property within sight of the smoke belching mills at increasingly burdensome prices."[9]

During the 1890s, the supply of housing in Rumford Falls could not keep up with demand. In 1901 Hugh Chisholm opened the Oxford Paper Company's Rumford mill and, in response to the severe housing shortage, formed the Rumford Falls Realty Company to build homes for mill executives and line workers. The result was the construction of Strathglass Park, home to some of the most elegant company housing in New England.

STRATHGLASS PARK: "IDEAL HOMES FOR WORKINGMEN"

To see Hon. Hugh J. Chisholm of New York inspecting the progress of affairs at Strathglass Park, Rumford Falls, is to see him happily astride his favorite hobby. "I actually think," said a business man recently, "that Mr. Chisholm is more interested in the successful development of the park than he is in the financial results of his paper mill connections." [10]
—LEWISTON JOURNAL, 1902

Strathglass Park, a neighborhood of fifty-one brick duplex houses, is a commanding sight in the middle of Rumford. The subdivision was built in 1901–1902 as rental housing for employees of the Oxford Paper Mill and was generously supported by mill owners. Although the appearance of the town has deteriorated following declines in the paper industry, Strathglass Park stands today as a tribute to Hugh Chisholm's philanthropic approach to community planning.

Before building Strathglass Park, Chisholm visited and studied industry housing neighborhoods in the United States and overseas, where he discovered the European approach toward progressive worker housing. Chisholm adopted the philosophy of the European reformers, who raised working-class housing standards in order to cultivate company loyalty and increase profits. [11] But he also genuinely cared for his skilled workers, providing places to gather in the neighborhood through "a handsome little casino, with reading, billiard, and pool rooms, and a hall with a goodly stage, where amateur theatricals may be presented." [12] He also offered employees modern conveniences at affordable prices:

He is beautifying this portion of Rumford Falls for the working men. The houses, uniformly of brick, and slate roofed, are comfortable and commodious. Modern improvements will include city water, steam heat, electricity, bath rooms, hot and cold water, and a laundry in the basement. Each tenement has a furnace and set range. For these conveniences, an unusually low rent is charged. [13]

Strathglass Park Rumford Maine

Chisholm hired architect Cass Gilbert of New York to design the duplexes, which had seven different exteriors. Features such as turreted roofs, dormers, and Dutch gables in several forms helped avoid the sterile character found in typical industrial housing.

The Park's "landscape gardening" was planned by W. W. Gay of Boston, whose design called for trees on both sides of the main streets and a hedge to "enclose the tract." Historic photographs show ivy-covered front entrances, precisely graded slopes on front lawns, neat walkways or concrete steps leading to public sidewalks, and grass esplanades planted with street trees. Homes looked onto a central open space with a grove of pine trees, offering privacy between opposite sides of the streets. Streets were named after Scottish castles, to honor Chisholm's family heritage.

Chisholm's Oxford Paper Mill provided a generous maintenance fund for the upkeep of the brick residences for the first several decades. Financial support ended

in 1948, however, when the Rumford Falls Realty Company ceased operation. Many residents purchased their duplexes at reduced costs, but the neighborhood gradually fell into disrepair without company support. Rumford's gradual population loss because of declines in the paper market and pollution issues caused further neglect of the historic buildings and grounds. Nevertheless, Strathglass Park was listed in the National Register of Historic Places in the 1970s. The next decades saw no movement toward preservation or restoration, and, in 2005, the neighborhood was listed by Maine Preservation as one of the state's ten most endangered historic properties.

Rumford is unique in that it never went through a period of urban renewal. Although its neighborhoods are not in prime condition, most retain their historic architecture and character today. The paper mill, which has changed hands several times since 1967, continues to dominate the town, although there has been a dramatic decrease in air and water pollution.

In the mid-2000s, a revitalization effort began throughout Rumford. Town officials and residents gathered information about local history, studied preservation challenges, and explored ideas for adapting Rumford properties to modern needs while preserving their historic character. They commissioned a cultural assessment report, created *A Guide to Arts and Culture in the River Valley*, and adopted a revitalization and redevelopment plan that capitalizes on Rumford's strengths. In 2008 the Strathglass Park Property Owners Association was formed as the first step in revitalizing that neighborhood. The group is seeking non-profit status, which may result in the development of a restoration plan and funding assistance from the Maine Historic Preservation Commission. Although much work lies ahead, Hugh Chisholm's legacy lives on in Rumford's heritage as a model new town plan.

CHAPTER 14

SHIPYARD HOUSING: GARDEN CITIES FOR WORKERS

They were considered intelligent, even if hurried, experiments on a large scale, directed toward securing the best obtainable results in the way of comfortable, healthful, pleasant living conditions for persons of limited means.[1] – FREDERICK LAW OLMSTED, JR., 1919

Bath, Maine, is known as the City of Ships, with a shipbuilding heritage that dates to the 1740s; since then the city has been home to more than 200 shipbuilding firms. By the mid-1800s Bath was the fifth largest seaport in the United States, and its clipper ships traveled around the world. Bath Iron Works, named for an iron foundry from the 1830s, was founded by Thomas W. Hyde in 1884. Over the past 125 years, Bath Iron Works has built more than 400 military and merchant ships at its facility on the Kennebec River.

With its long history of shipbuilding, the city of Bath was a logical place for a surge in government contract work during World War I. Accompanying the demand for more ships was a new program for wartime industry housing. Two such communities survive today—the North End Project (known locally as the Brick Project) and the Lincoln Street Project (known locally as the White Project). Both offer a notable example of another chapter in town and landscape planning in Maine.

During World War I the United States began an unprecedented effort to establish a merchant fleet at sea and to replenish ships lost to German submarines. The demand for ships was staggering; to fully supply the American army in France in 1918 required "seventy ships to be loading all the time at American ports, seventy to be un-loading at European ports, and four-hundred and twenty to be crossing the Atlantic each way, continually." With allowances for the sinking of six ships per week, about thirteen hundred ships had to operate continually in order to feed, clothe, and supply the American army.[2]

In record time the government established new shipyards and entire towns to support them. Hog Island near Philadelphia was the largest, with fifty shipbuilding stations, housing for 30,000 workers, a hospital, YMCA, hotel, cafeteria, trade school, and restaurants.

In addition, the government pressed existing shipyards into wartime production, but lack of housing for the influx of thousands of workers in existing communities was a major hindrance to the war effort. In response, the government created two temporary federal agencies to address housing concerns: the Emergency Fleet Corporation and the United States Housing Corporation.

Numerous town planners, engineers, and landscape architects fulfilled their wartime obligation by designing emergency housing communities for industrial workers. The Housing and Fleet corporations sent designers to England to study the new garden cities of Sir Ebenezer Howard. Based on

200

Howard's model of creating self-sustaining villages near industrial work areas, dozens of neighborhoods of artistically pleasing homes for low-income workers were built in the United States.

In 1918 the United States Housing Corporation prepared *Suggestions to Town Planners*, which outlined principles of design for the new neighborhoods. In addition to practical matters—making maps and figuring cost estimates, reducing construction costs, and prioritizing which parts of a project should be built first—the manual addressed less tangible aspects. Designers were advised to make their projects compatible with surrounding neighborhoods, orient houses to receive sunlight at both the front and back, and ensure that "the summer fair-weather breeze shall blow through the houses and not along the street only."[3]

Frederick Law Olmsted, Jr. was manager of the Town Planning Division of the U.S. Housing Corporation. In a 1919 report summarizing the work completed under his supervision and the lessons learned from the program, he referred to the "inability of many war industries to obtain sufficient workers because of lack of housing facilities within easy access of the factory."[4] In some cases, workers from three different shifts shared the same room, and additional beds were added in already cramped conditions. Poor housing conditions were one of the key reasons for an excessively high turnover rate for workers, leading to an unacceptable decrease in factory production. Olmsted summed up the situation by saying:

> *No urge of patriotism or high wages could compensate for the overloaded accommodations for individual and family life. Inadequate access not only to sleeping places but to food, merchandise, recreation, and everything relating to family and social life outside of working hours, put a limit on production far below the maximum capacity of the increased plants.*[5]

The federal government allocated funds to enlarge factories but lagged behind in funding worker housing. In March of 1918, eight months before armistice, "Congress authorized the expenditure of $50,000,000 by the United States Shipping Board for accelerating the production of housing facilities in connection with shipyards."[6] Since it was impossible to fully meet the demand for wartime housing, projects were geared toward essential workers, "generally married men with families, the strength of American industrial life," who were difficult to retain under bad living conditions. These workers, Olmsted noted, "are normally able and willing to pay for decent and comfortable living conditions, schooling and play opportunities for their children, and all reasonable essentials of civilized life for themselves and their families."[7]

One of the first projects built was Atlantic Heights in 1918, located in Portsmouth, New Hampshire. The neighborhood of 150 houses was designed in just ten days and built in eight months for employees of the Portsmouth Naval Shipyard in Kittery.[8] Over the next two years, the government built the two housing projects in Bath. These communities exist today as excellent examples of wartime housing built according to the progressive design standards of the day.

The North End Project

When the World war [sic] was in progress, and Uncle Sam was calling for ships and more ships, it was but natural that Bath, a shipbuilding city for many generations, should respond to the call and filled its yards with construction of craft designed to help win the war.[9]
– The Bath Daily Times, 1922

Bath's population swelled during World War I, when the shipyard was called into service. The 1910 Census listed Bath's population as 9,396–slightly higher than the current figure of about 9,200. By 1920 the population had jumped to 14,731.[10] In a 1936 history of Bath, Henry Owen recalled that:

Every existing house was filled to its utmost capacity, and the overflow made use of whatever shelter could be extemporized. On the water front there grew up villages of houseboats. On the vacant lots people put up tents. Sheds, barns and other outbuildings were converted into temporary homes. And hundreds who came to Bath to work overflowed into neighboring towns.[11]

One of Bath's wartime shipbuilders was the Texas Steamship Company, which operated on about four acres at Clapp's Point in the North End and is thought to have been owned by Texaco. Prior to the government housing program, the Texas Steamship Company bought vacant lots and built duplexes for its principal employees. In addition, a worker named Louis Gagne started what became known as the Tented City (near today's North and Gerald streets). By June of 1918 the neighborhood consisted of twenty-one cabins, a dining tent, and a large number of tents where workers and their families lived.[12] The federal government offered relief in the form of the North End Project and the Lincoln Street Project, although they were not completed until after the war.

The North End Project was built by the Emergency Fleet Corporation for workers of the Texas Steamship Company. Built on the site of the Hagan hayfield at today's

High and Oliver streets, the project consisted of sixty-seven brick houses with 109 units for rent. The architect for the North End Project was R. Clipston Sturgis of Boston, who served at various times as president of the Boston Institute of Architects, the American Institute of Architects, and the Society of Arts and Crafts Boston.

Sturgis designed three types of brick houses for the North End Project: 1½-story single-family bungalows, 1½-story semi-detached houses (duplexes), and 2-story dormitories with a kitchenette and three bedrooms on each floor. The compact bungalow style was popular among "families of moderate incomes.... As regards appearance, the main demand is that the house shall look like an attractive, comfortable home lived in by a happy family."[13] There was very little open space, and no playgrounds were built at the North End Project, but sidewalks lined both sides of the streets. Children walked to the community school, known as the Dike Schoolhouse, which was built jointly by the city and federal government and intended to match the character of the brick houses. A 1922 newspaper article lists the construction price of the North End Project at $1.5 million.[14]

The war was in full force when construction started in August; no one could predict that armistice was three months away. North End's speed of construction was remarkable. A 1918 newspaper article noted that "Building 65 good-sized brick houses in 97 days is some achievement!" Construction involved a swarm of men with picks and shovels, thirty teams of horses, steam shovels, great motor trucks, and a "monster trench digging machine." Many workmen lived on site in a nearby bunk house and ate meals in the company-provided mess hall. "But because of this rapidity of action, it must not be supposed that these buildings have been thrown together. They are substantially built and are modern in every respect."[15]

Construction continued for another month after the armistice. The Texas Steamship Company left Bath around 1921, and most of the residents of the North End Project moved out; by 1922 only about six houses were occupied. The project had been conveniently located for the Steamship workers but was too far from other industries to be of much use after the war. The first efforts to auction individual homes failed when the U.S. Shipping Board refused to accept the bids. In 1923 the entire parcel was sold at auction to Arthur G. Spear, who struggled for the next twenty years to rent or sell the homes. A local dairy farmer mowed the yards of numerous vacant homes to keep the neighborhood presentable. A second influx of shipyard workers in World War II brought new residents to the North End Project; Spear finally sold the last house in 1943.[16]

The North End Project is an overlooked gem in the city of Bath. The entire neighborhood exists as it was designed in 1918, minus a proposed street extension that was never built. The Dike Schoolhouse operated until 1980 and was renovated a few years later to house community services such as a senior center and daycare, which continue today. As in many historic neighborhoods, some homes have seen more wear and tear than others, but the unique sense of community has not waned in almost one hundred years.

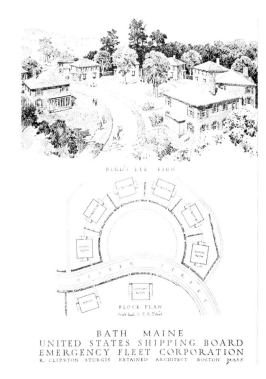

BIRD'S EYE VIEW

BLOCK PLAN

BATH MAINE
UNITED STATES SHIPPING BOARD
EMERGENCY FLEET CORPORATION
R. CLIPSTON STURGIS   RETAINED   ARCHITECT   BOSTON MASS.

ABOVE: *This 1919 drawing for Oliver Street in the North End Project includes four dormitories and two dining halls bordering a circular open space, one of the few open spaces in the development. The bird's eye sketch shows large shade trees and a lawn in the open space.*

OPPOSITE: *A modern view of two former dormitories (now private homes) on Oliver Street in the North End Project. The buildings border the central lawn, as shown above.*

Detail - Lincoln Street Project
Bath, Maine
Loring Underwood, Town Planner
Parker, Thomas & Rice, Architects
Weston & Sampson, Engineers
1919

ABOVE: *A detail of the Lincoln Street Project plan shows the original Russell farmhouse overlooking the proposed Flaherty Park (center, in green). The neighborhood contained mainly single-family homes, with four apartment buildings next to the park.*

THE LINCOLN STREET PROJECT

The houses were small individual dwellings of wood which still form a village within the city quite distinct in appearance from any other section of the place.[17] —HENRY OWEN, 1936

Following the North End Project, a second neighborhood of distinction was built for the war effort. The Lincoln Street Project was built by the U.S. Housing Corporation for employees of Bath Iron Works and the Hyde Windlass Company. The project was built on about twenty-four acres of the Russell Farm and was located just three-quarters of a mile from Bath Iron Works. The old Colonial farmhouse was left standing to be used as a community building, and new homes and duplexes were designed by architects Parker, Thomas, & Rice of Boston.

The Lincoln Street Project consisted of seventy-four single-family homes and four apartment buildings described as semi-detached two-flat houses. The individual homes in the development were compact, just twenty-two feet square, but were described as "…excellent in design…. Whether one views front or side or inspects the details of doorways and porches, one realizes that the designers were thoroughly conversant in what is called 'colonial' architecture."[18] However, a summary report lists two major faults with the development as a whole. First, all of the houses seemed to be set too high out of the ground, due to clay soil which made the cellars hard to drain. In addition, there was "an unfortunate repetition of forms" among the buildings. The architects planned only two types, one with the front gable facing the street and the other with the gables turned sideways, but they attempted to break up the repetition with four different arrangements of front doors and piazzas. They also suggested that the size of front yards should vary, in order to relieve any monotony. Construction materials were simple: concrete block foundations, porches built on posts rather than concrete footings, clapboard siding, and green asphalt roofs. The report notes that, "[as] in many developments, the general woodwork is not of first grade nor is the hardware in good taste, due to the war conditions, which necessitated the use of material of a secondary quality."[19]

The Lincoln Street Project was fortunate to have the planning services of Loring Underwood, a landscape architect and a proponent of and lecturer on the City Beautiful movement, who wrote, "Beautiful and clean cities attract desirable citizens and real estate values increase. Clothes don't make the man, but they come pretty near making the city."[20]

The landscape plan of the Lincoln Street Project showed sidewalks and dozens of trees lining all four new streets, and the land immediately surrounding the historic farmhouse was listed as open space. A park of just over one-tenth of an acre was proposed in front of the farmhouse. Named Flaherty Park, reportedly after a Bath native who was killed in World War I, this rectangular parcel eventually became privately owned and was used for parking; Flaherty Park was relocated to a more visible intersection nearby. A 1918 drawing showed an attractive street scene with formal hedges, lattice fences, and vine-covered arbors above side windows. Street trees were aligned with property lines, where they would not obscure views to or from the homes' front entrances.

After the war, the Lincoln Street Project fared better than the North End one, mainly because of its close proximity to Bath Iron Works. The homes sold relatively quickly in 1921 to private owners, and most were occupied by the following year.

At the time of their construction, war housing projects saw an influx of workers "from away," many of whom were expected to be temporary residents at best. But the small waterfront city of Bath, with its attractive neighborhoods and steady employment, led many residents to remain after the war. There has been a surprising sense of longevity at both the Lincoln Street and North End projects, and indeed throughout Bath, with a majority of homes bought between the 1920s and '40s remaining in the same families today. During recent road improvements in the Lincoln Street Project, the city replaced street lights with new ones resembling the originals, thanks to residents who had stored them in basements for decades.

The city of Bath is a Preserve America community, dedicated to protecting, celebrating, and encouraging local appreciation of its rich heritage. The Lincoln Street and North End projects are a major part of this heritage and continue to serve as vibrant villages within the city.

LEFT: *Illustrations from the U.S. Housing Corporation's 1919 report offer an "example of effect of planting and minor architectural details" at the Lincoln Street Project. Landscape details included street trees in grass esplanades, formal hedges, and vine-covered trellises and arbors.*

ABOVE: *A recent view in the Lincoln Street Project shows that homes were built as illustrated in the U.S. Housing Corporation's 1919 report, shown to the left.*

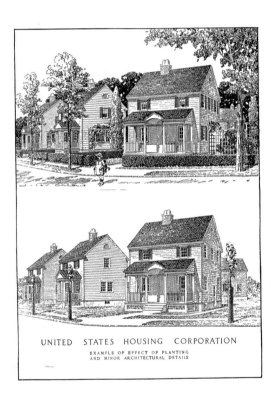

UNITED STATES HOUSING CORPORATION
EXAMPLE OF EFFECT OF PLANTING AND MINOR ARCHITECTURAL DETAILS

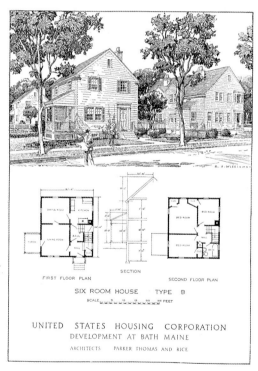

SIX ROOM HOUSE   TYPE B

UNITED STATES HOUSING CORPORATION
DEVELOPMENT AT BATH MAINE

ARCHITECTS   PARKER THOMAS AND RICE

ACKNOWLEDGMENTS

Five years ago board members of the Maine Olmsted Alliance made plans to produce a small guidebook to the properties visited during the Survey of Designed Historic Landscapes. Early in our planning, we approached Tom Morgan of Blue Design, who convinced us that we had enough material to create a much larger, well-illustrated book, one that would share the unique stories of Maine landscapes with a broad audience; we are deeply grateful to Tom for his foresight and artistic talent as book designer. Our thanks go to the many individuals and organizations who helped make this concept a reality.

As current and former presidents of the Maine Olmsted Alliance, Charlton and Eleanor Ames are to be commended for their extraordinary support for and devotion to historic landscapes over the past eighteen years, as well as for their enthusiastic support during the creation of *Designing the Maine Landscape*. Neale Sweet, former publisher of Down East, greatly encouraged our early efforts; John Viehman has continued to support our project in his current position as publisher. We have greatly enjoyed working with Michael Steere, editor at Down East Books, and we appreciate his experience and calming presence.

Noted Olmsted scholar Charles E. Beveridge provided an engaging foreword to *Designing the Maine Landscape*, as well as comments on early drafts; his knowledge of Olmsted's influence on the profession was invaluable and set the context for both the national and Maine scenes. We are indebted to Earle G. Shettleworth, Jr., director of the Maine Historic Preservation Commission (MHPC) and state historic preservation officer, for his thoughtful preface, for his assistance and support during all phases of the survey, and for sharing a vast collection of historical material. Kirk Mohney, assistant director of MHPC and deputy state historic preservation officer, provided survey management expertise. Elizabeth Igleheart, formerly with MHPC, initiated the statewide survey and served as a resource to its consultants, Shary Page Berg, Theresa Mattor, and Pamela Griffin.

Charles Birnbaum, president and founder of the Cultural Landscape Foundation, has been an avid supporter of the Alliance's mission. Initial funding for the survey came from the National Park Service, with additional support from local benefactors such as Joan Burns, who heartily supported the unusual (for the time) task of documenting historic landscapes. We are also grateful to the Davis Family Foundation and Rebecca Rundquist of the Quimby Family Foundation for their generous contributions.

We are greatly indebted to Patrick Chassé, landscape architect and Beatrix Farrand scholar, without whom many Mount Desert Island properties could not have been included, either in the survey or in *Designing the Maine Landscape*. Many thanks go to Patrick for sharing his wealth of knowledge and materials gathered over decades of intense study of MDI's historic landscapes.

Past and present members and advisory trustees of the Maine Olmsted Alliance for Parks and Landscapes generously donated their time to research historic properties; others wrote substantive articles in the *Journal* of the MOAPL that often provided the basis for our chapters. Thank you to Eleanor Ames, Shary Page Berg, Charles Beveridge, Constance Bloomfield, Patrick Chassé, Nano Chatfield, Martha Deprez, Ann Gibbs, Pamela Griffin, Elizabeth Igleheart, Robin Karson, Regina Leonard, Arleyn Levee, Rebecca Linney, Isabel Mancinelli, Mary Louise McGregor, Susan Merrow, Stephen Mohr, Marta Morse, Linda Murnik, Marion Pressley, Helen Rollins, and Tatyanna Seredin.

With his technical skills and photographer's eye, Greg Currier captured the essence of these historic landscapes today. Supplementing Greg's work are photos by a number of other professional photographers, landscape firms and architects, and homeowners. (For specific photo credits, please see the book's endnotes.)

Thank you to all who provided background material, historic photographs, and first-hand knowledge of historic properties for this book. For help with Portland, we thank: Nan Cummings, Portland Trails; Alissa Lane, Maine Historical Society; Phillip Labbe, formerly of Portland Parks & Cemeteries; Paul Loring; Todd Richardson and Meghan Rochefort, Richardson & Associates Landscape Architects; Abraham Schechter, Special Collections, Portland Public Library; Stephen Mohr, Tatyanna Seredin and Patty Jewell, Mohr & Seredin Landscape Architects; Jeffrey Tarling, Parks Operation manager, City of Portland; and Kay White and Pete Thaxter, Boulevard Park.

For Augusta: Karen Baldacci; James Goulet, Augusta Parks, Cemeteries, and Trees Bureau; Lester Kenway, Maine Conservation Corps.; and Marion Pressley, Lauren Meier, and Melissa Braun, Pressley Associates Landscape Architects.

For Bath: Brenda Cummings, Bath assessor; Peter Goodwin, Patten Free Library; and Al Smith, community development director.

For Camden and Rockport: Heather Bilodeau, Camden Public Library; Scott Dickerson, Coastal Mountains Land Trust;

Christopher Glass, architect; Justin Hicks, manager, Weatherend; Robin Karson, Library of American Landscape History; Judy McGuirk, Camden Garden Club; David Jackson, Harbor Park and Amphitheatre committee; and Elizabeth Moran, retired director of the Camden Public Library.

For Mount Desert Island properties: Letitia Baldwin; Patrick Chassé and James Fuchs, Beatrix Farrand Society; Karen Jania, Bentley Library, University of Michigan; Carole Plenty, Mount Desert Land & Garden Preserve; Martha Stewart and her executive assistant, Eliad D. Laskin; and Joanna Young Graphic Design, Bangor.

For assistance with the campus chapter: for Berwick Academy, Diane Field, Tracey Kelly, and Rachel Saliba; Terry Heller, Sarah Orne Jewett Text Project. For Bowdoin College, Richard Lindemann, Caroline Moseley, and Daniel Hope, George J. Mitchell Department of Special Collections & Archives; Michelle Henning, Bowdoin College Museum of Art; and Scott Hood, Andrea Richards, and Cecelia Greenleaf, Office of Communications. For Colby College: Stephen B. Collins and Laura Meader, Office of Communications, and Anna Graves, Special Collections, Miller Library. For Bates College: H. Jay Burns, editor of *Bates Magazine*, and Pat Webber, Muskie Archives & Special Collections Library. For the University of Maine: Mac Collins, Brian Foley, Sara Martin, Kathleen McIntyre, and Margaret Nagle, and Elaine Smith and Brenda Steeves in the Special Collections Dept., Raymond H. Fogler Library.

For golf courses: Deborah Gray, University Press of New England, for Poland Spring permissions; Eleanor Ames, Megunticook Golf Club; David Closson, Kebo Valley Golf Club; Tatyanna Seredin, Mohr & Seredin Landscape Architects.

For cemeteries: Stephen G. Burrill, Mount Hope Cemetery Corporation and Crematory; Dana Lippitt, Bangor Museum and History Center; David Little, Kirk Mohney, and Peter Morelli, Evergreen Cemetery; Marie O'Brien, Saco Museum; Jeffrey I. Richman, Green-Wood Cemetery, Brooklyn; William Tate, Laurel Hill Cemetery; and staff of Dyer Library and McArthur Library.

Our deep thanks to these owners of private residences for allowing us to feature their historic landscapes and for providing background information and historic photographs: Eddie and Sylvia Brown; Charles W. H. and Marylee Dodge; Daniel J. Hartigan and Mark E. Toney; and Martha Stewart, who also generously allowed us to use some of her personal photographs of Skylands. Many thanks to

Helen Rollins, archivist (retired), Piscataqua Garden Club, for her assistance with River House. For Hamilton House from Historic New England: Emily Novak-Gustainis and Lorna Condon; Susanna Crampton; Arleyn Levee; Peggy Wishart; and Gary Wetzel.

The initial survey took place over a decade and would have required many more years without the assistance of these volunteers. Our thanks to Eleanor Ames, Gail Berneike, Constance Bloomfield, Margaret Bonarrigo, Sarah Braik, Phil Carey, Patrick Chassé, Robert Cram, John Denvir [sic], Josephine Hildreth Detmer, Clementine Earle, Joel Eastman, Blythe Edwards, Carol Kneedler Edwards, Thomas Farmer, Christian Fasoldt, Ann Gibbs, Rosalee Glass, Elizabeth Igleheart, Norma Johnson, Gudrun Heistad Kononen, Rebecca Linney, Isabel Mancinelli, Elizabeth Mattor, Paul Mattor, Mary Louise McGregor, Kirk Mohney, Ann Montgomery, Linda Murnik, Kim Myers, Albert Nickerson, Diane Nolan, Gladys O'Neil, Sally Rand, Mimi Rice, Todd Richardson, John Robbins, Jr., Helen Rollins, Patricia Scull, Tatyanna Seredin, Lynn Shafer, Deborah Stabor, Henry Tonole, Susan Wales, Clyde Walton, Ametta Wetherhead, Doug Whitney, and Katherine Whitney.

Working together on this book has been a great pleasure. We have become very fond of the places in *Designing the Maine Landscape* and are delighted to share them with you.
—Theresa Mattor and Lucie Teegarden

Special thanks go to Kenneth Helphand of the University of Oregon for introducing me to the study of historic landscapes. I greatly appreciate the talents of Nano Chatfield as editor of my earliest articles for the Olmsted Alliance *Journal*. For many years I have been greatly inspired by the friendship and kindness of Charlton and Noni Ames, without whom this book would not exist. Peter Monro, long-time friend and mentor, offered enormous encouragement during this book's challenging times and helped celebrate successes along the way. To Paul and Riley go my love and gratitude for being patient and self-reliant, but especially for enduring.
– T.M.

I am grateful for the ongoing interest of family and friends and especially for my mother, Lucie Dowling Giegengack, a gardener, artist, and poet, and for my architect brother, Richard Giegengack. Their interests, shared conversations, and beautiful designs gave me an appreciation for landscape architecture long before I came to this project.
– L.G.T.

BIBLIOGRAPHY

Following are useful, readily available sources of information for readers who may want to study landscape types and architects in greater detail.

PRESERVING HISTORIC LANDSCAPES

Birnbaum, Charles A., and Christine Capella Peters. *The Secretary of the Interior's Standards for the Treatment of Historic Properties with Guidelines for the Treatment of Cultural Landscapes*. Washington, D.C.: U.S. Department of the Interior, National Park Service, Cultural Resource Stewardship and Partnerships, Heritage Preservation Services, Historic Landscape Initiative, 1996.

Birnbaum, Charles A., Cheryl Wagner, and Jean S. Jones, eds. *Making Educated Decisions: A Landscape Preservation Bibliography*. Washington, D.C.: National Park Service, Department of the Interior, Historic Preservation Services, Historic Landscape Initiative, 1994. [2000 2nd edition also available.]

Additional information can be found online at the Web site of the National Park Service. Available resources include bulletins and brochures on a variety of topics, nomination forms and technical assistance for historic properties and landscapes, and a variety of books and videos. See http://www.nps.gov/history/nr/publications/index.htm

In addition, the index of *APT Bulletin: The Journal of Preservation Technology*, published by the Association for Preservation Technology International, is accessible at http://www.apti.org/publications/bulletin.cfm. Articles are available through subscription or at participating libraries.

MAINE ARCHITECTURE AND LANDSCAPE

Anderson, Patricia McGraw. *The Architecture of Bowdoin College*. Brunswick, Maine: Bowdoin College Museum of Art, 1988.

Baldwin, Letitia. *Asticou Azalea Garden: The Work of Charles K. Savage* and *Thuya Garden: Asticou Terraces & Thuya Lodge*. Seal Harbor, Maine: Mount Desert Land and Garden Preserve, 2008.

Bold Vision: The Development of the Parks of Portland, Maine. Edited by Theo H. B. M. Holtwijk and Earle G. Shettleworth, Jr. West Kennebunk, Maine: Phoenix Publishing, 1999.

Bryan, John M. *Maine Cottages–Fred L. Savage and the Architecture of Mount Desert*. N.Y.: Princeton Architectural Press, 2005.

Calhoun, Charles. *A Small College in Maine: Two Hundred Years of Bowdoin*. Brunswick, Maine: Bowdoin College, 1993.

Clark, Charles E. *Bates Through the Years*. Bates College: Lewiston, Maine, 2005.

Emmet, Alan. *So Fine A Prospect–Historic New England Gardens*. Hanover, N.H.: University Press of New England, 1996.

Journal, Maine Olmsted Alliance for Parks & Landscapes, 1991–2007. Available from MOAPL, 18 Pleasant Street, Portland, ME 04101, 207-761-8081.

Labbance, Bob, and David Cornwell. *The Maine Golf Guide*. Stockbridge, Vermont: New England Golf Specialists, 1991.

Lamb, Jane. *The Grand Masters of Maine Gardening*. Camden, Maine: Down East Books, 2004.

Maine Forms of American Architecture. Edited by Deborah Thompson. Camden, Maine: Down East, 1976.

Murphy, Kevin D. *Colonial Revival Maine*. New York, N.Y.: Princeton Architectural Press, 2004.

Richards, David L. *Poland Spring–A Tale of the Gilded Age, 1860–1900*. Durham, N.H.: University of New Hampshire Press, 2005.

Roberts, Ann Rockefeller. *Mr. Rockefeller's Roads–The Untold Story of Acadia's Carriage Roads and Their Creator*. Camden, Maine: Down East Books, 1990.

Scee, Trudy Irene. *Mount Hope Cemetery: A Twentieth-Century History*. Bangor, Maine: Mount Hope Cemetery Corp., 1999.

Smith, Earl H. *Mayflower Hill: A History of Colby College*. Hanover and London: University Press of New England and Colby College, 2006.

Thayer, Robert. *Acadia's Carriage Roads*. Camden, Maine: Down East Books, 2002.

BOOKS ABOUT LANDSCAPE DESIGNERS

Balmori, Diane, Diane Kostial McGuire, and Eleanor M. McPeck. *Beatrix Farrand's American Landscapes–Her Gardens & Campuses*. Sagaponack, N.Y.: Sagapress, Inc., 1985.

Beatrix Jones Farrand (1872–1959)–Fifty Years of American Landscape Architecture. Edited by Diane Kostial McGuire and Lois Fern. Washington, D.C.: Dumbarton Oaks / Trustees for Harvard University, 1982.

Beveridge, Charles E. and Paul Rocheleau; David Larkin, ed. *Frederick Law Olmsted: Designing the American Landscape*. New York: Universe Publishing / Rizzoli, 1998.

Biographical Dictionary of Architects in Maine. Edited by Earle G. Shettleworth, Jr., and Roger Reed, associate editor. Augusta, Maine: Maine Historic Preservation Commission, Vols. I–VII, 1984 – 1995.

Brown, Jane Roy. *The Gardening Life of Beatrix Jones Farrand, 1872–1959*. New York, N.Y.: Viking Penguin, 1995.

The Bulletins of Reef Point Gardens. Edited by Carol Betsch. Bar Harbor, Maine: The Island Foundation, 1997. (Reprint of Beatrix Farrand's bulletins from 1946 to 1956.)

Grese, Robert E. *Jens Jensen–Maker of Natural Parks and Gardens*. Baltimore, Md.: The Johns Hopkins University Press, 1992.

The Master List of Design Projects of the Olmsted Firm 1857–1979. Edited by Lucy Lawliss, Caroline Loughlin, and Lauren Meier. Washington, D.C.: National Association for Olmsted Parks, National Park Service, and Frederick Law Olmsted National Historic Site, 2008 – Second Edition.

Pioneers of American Landscape Design. Edited by Charles A. Birnbaum and Robin Karson. New York: McGraw-Hill, 2000.

OTHERS OF INTEREST

America's National Park Roads and Parkways–Drawings from the Historic American Engineering Record. Edited by Timothy Davis, Todd A. Croteau, and Christopher H. Marston. Baltimore & London: The Johns Hopkins University Press, 2004.

Ames, David L., and Linda Flint McClelland. *Historic Residential Suburbs–Guidelines for Evaluation and Documentation for the National Register of Historic Places*. U.S. Department of the Interior, National Park Service, 2002.

Girling, Cynthia and Kenneth I. Helphand. *Yard–Street–Park: The Design of Suburban Open Space*. New York: John Wiley & Sons, Inc., 1994.

Richman, Jeffrey I. *Brooklyn's Green-Wood Cemetery: New York's Buried Treasure*. Brooklyn, New York: The Green-Wood Cemetery, 1998.

Turner, Paul Venable. *Campus, An American Planning Tradition*. Cambridge, Mass.: The Architectural History Foundation/MIT Press, 1984/1987.

COLLECTIONS OF DESIGNERS' PAPERS

Beatrix Jones Farrand Collection, University of California at Berkeley, Environmental Design Archives.

Architectural Drawings of Jens Jensen, Bentley Library, University of Michigan.

Warren H. Manning Papers, Special Collections Department, Iowa State University.

John Nolen Papers, Division of Rare and Manuscript Collections, Cornell University Library.

Papers of Frederick Law Olmsted and Olmsted Associates (two separate collections), Library of Congress, Washington, D.C.

Papers of John Charles Olmsted, Special Collections, Frances Loeb Library, Harvard University Graduate School of Design.

Olmsted Archives, Fredrick Law Olmsted National Historic Site, Brookline, Massachusetts.

Golf Course Drawings of Donald Ross, Tufts Archives, Given Memorial Library, Pinehurst, North Carolina.

Papers of Arthur and Sidney Shurcliff, Special Collections, Frances Loeb Library, Harvard University Graduate School of Design.

Fletcher Steele Manuscript Collection, State University of New York at Syracuse, College of Environmental Science and Forestry.

ENDNOTES

Photography: All contemporary photography by Greg Currier except as otherwise noted.

CHAPTER 1: THE PORTLAND PARK SYSTEM, PAGES 16–39

Historic images: pp. 18, 19, 30, 36, 37, private collections; pp. 21, 23, 28, 29, 31, Jeffery Tarling; p. 27, Portland Public Library; pp. 21, 22, 23, 35, National Park Service, Frederick Law Olmsted National Historic Site.

1. *Auditor's Report* (Portland, Maine: City of Portland, 1881–1882).

2. James P. Baxter, *The Park System of Portland* (Portland, Maine: City of Portland, 1905), p 5

3. *Auditor's Report* (Portland, Maine: City of Portland, 1907).

4. *Eastern Argus*, Portland, Maine, June 2, 1836, as cited in *Bold Vision: The Development of the Parks of Portland, Maine*, ed. Theo H.B.M. Holtwijk and Earle G. Shettleworth, Jr. (West Kennebunk, Maine: Phoenix Publishing, 1999), p. 39.

5. *Eastern Promenade Master Plan*, Walker-Kluesing Design Group, Boston, Mass., 2004, Chronology section.

6. Mayor's address, March 1877, as quoted in *Eastern Promenade Master Plan*, p. 15.

7. Letter from George Fernald, Commissioner and City Engineer, City of Portland, to Olmsted Brothers, Nov. 15, 1904. Manuscript Division, Library of Congress.

8. Letter from J. C. Olmsted to James P. Baxter, May 22, 1905. Manuscript Division, Library of Congress.

9. Letter from Carl Rust Parker of Olmsted Brothers to James Baxter, August 26, 1905. Manuscript Division, Library of Congress.

10. *Eastern Promenade Master Plan*, Walker-Kluesing Design Group, Boston, Mass., 2004, with Gillon Associates, Transportation Engineers, Norwood, Mass.; Ocmulgee Associates, Structural Engineers, Ipswich, Mass.; Carl Cathcart Arboriculture, Maynard, Mass.

11. *The Dedication of Lincoln Park Being the Public Exercises Held in the Payson Memorial Church and at Lincoln Park, February 12, 1909, in Observance of the One Hundredth Anniversary of the Birth of Abraham Lincoln* (Portland, Maine: City of Portland, 1909), p. 34.

12. *The Dedication of Lincoln Park*, p. 31.

13. *The Daily Eastern Argus*, March 11, 1911, as reported in Lincoln Park National Register of Historic Places Registration Form, Sec. 8, p. 1–2.

14. *The Dedication of Lincoln Park*, p. 36.

15. *Auditor's Annual Report of the Receipts and Expenditures of the City of Portland*, 1879–80.

16. *Bold Vision*, pp. 74–77.

17. *Deering Oaks, Portland, Maine, Master Plan*, The Halvorson Company, Boston, Mass., May 1994.

18. *Deering Oaks, Portland, Maine, Master Plan*, p. 18.

19. James P. Baxter, "The Story of Portland," *The New England Magazine*, Vol. 19, Issue 3,

November 1895, p. 370. Cornell University Library, *Making of America* online collection, http://cdl.library.cornell.edu/cgi-bin/moa/moa-cgi?notisid=AFJ3026-0019-56

20. Olmsted, Olmsted & Eliot, *Landscape Architect's Report on the Improvement of Back Cove* (Portland, Maine: The Thurston Print, 1896).

21. *Bold Vision*, p. 210.

22. *Baxter Boulevard Improvement Plan*, 1998. Prepared by Portland City Planning staff; Baxter Boulevard Advisory Committee; Richardson & Associates, Landscape Architects; T.Y. Lin International, Engineers; Eleanor Ames, Landscape Historian; Bartlett Tree Experts, Arborists.

CHAPTER 2: AUGUSTA: CAPITAL CITY ON THE KENNEBEC, PAGES 41–51

Historic images: pp. 45, 46, 47, Maine Historic Preservation Commission (MHPC); pp. 42, 48, National Park Service, Frederick Law Olmsted National Historic Site

1. Letter from Olmsted Brothers to Lewis Burleigh, Chairman, State Park Commission, October 6, 1920. Manuscript Division, Library of Congress.

2. LD 1991 HP1488. http://janus.state.me.us/legis/lio/history120R2/finald-isp-423.htm

3. Friends of the Blaine House, http://www.blainehouse.org/History.html

4. Elizabeth Igleheart, *The Blaine House–A Brief History and Guide* (Augusta, Maine: Maine Historic Preservation Commission, 1994), p. 27.

5. Letter from Carl Rust Parker to Carl Milliken, September 24, 1920. Manuscript Division, Library of Congress.

6. Maine Library Bulletin (Augusta, Maine: Maine State Library, 1930), p. 83.

7. "The Blaine Memorial," *Kennebec Journal*, November 27, 1920.

8. Maine Library Bulletin, 1930, pp. 82-83.

9. Blaine Memorial Visit by Carl Rust Parker, July 10 and 11, presumably 1920. Manuscript Division, Library of Congress.

10. "Begin Work on Blaine Park–Memorial to Statesman Will Be Beauty Spot of Pine Tree State," *Boston Sunday Advertiser*, August 21, 1920.

11. Olmsted Brothers, "Planting List to Accompany Plan #6" for Blaine Memorial, Augusta, Maine. Revised November 29, 1920. Manuscript Division, Library of Congress.

12. Blaine Memorial Visit by Carl Rust Parker.

13. Letter from Carl Rust Parker to Carl Milliken, September 1, 1920. Manuscript Division, Library of Congress.

14. Letter from the Olmsted firm to Mrs. Blaine Beale, August 15, 1921. Manuscript Division, Library of Congress.

CHAPTER 3: CAMDEN'S HISTORIC GEMS: THE VILLAGE GREEN, THE CAMDEN AMPHITHEATRE, AND HARBOR PARK , PAGES 52–65

Historic postcards and images, p. 54, private collection; p. 55, National Park Service, Frederick Law Olmsted National Historic Site; pp. 58, 59, 61, Camden Area History Center; p. 65, Marta Morse.

1. Louise Dickinson Rich, *The Coast of Maine*, 3rd Edition (New York: Crowell, 1970), p. 265.

2. Letter from Mary Louise Bok to Frederick Law Olmsted, Jr., May 9, 1927. National Park Service, Frederick Law Olmsted National Historic Site, Job # 7808, Camden Village Green, Camden, Maine.

3. Letter from Mary Louise Bok to Frederick Law Olmsted, as cited.

4. Summarized from Charles Beveridge, "In Search of Camden's Harborside Park," *Maine Olmsted Alliance for Parks & Landscapes Journal*, Autumn, 1999.

5. Report of Visit–Camden Public Park, Leon Zach, June 7, 1927. Frederick Law Olmsted National Historic Site, Job # 7808, as cited.

6. Camden Green–Report of Visit by F. L. Olmsted, October 6, 1928. Frederick Law Olmsted National Historic Site, Job # 7808, as cited.

7. Fletcher Steele, Interview, *Town and Country*, 1926, as quoted in Robin Karson, "Fletcher Steele's Design for the Camden, Maine, Amphitheatre," *The Official Newsletter of the Maine Landscape and Nursery Association*, Vol. 9, No. 3, September 2006, p .7.

8. "The Conservancy for Camden Harbor Park and Amphitheatre," publicity brochure, ca. 2006.

9. Robin Karson, "Fletcher Steele and the Camden Public Library Amphitheatre," *Maine Olmsted Alliance for Parks & Landscapes Newsletter*, Spring 1992, p. 4.

10. Karson, "Fletcher Steele and the Camden Public Library Amphitheatre," p. 4.

11. Karson, "Fletcher Steele and the Camden Public Library Amphitheatre," p. 5.

12. Maine Historic Preservation Commission Web site, National Register of Historic Places, *High Street Historic District (Additional Documentation: Bok Amphitheatre), Camden, 1929*. http://www.maine.gov/tools/whatsnew/index.php?topic=mhpc_recent_listings&id=26387&v=article

13. *Historic Landscape Report, Preservation Treatment Plan*, 1997. Prepared for Camden Public Library Board by Heritage Landscapes with landscape historians Robin Karson and Charles E. Beveridge.

14. The Conservancy for Camden Harbor Park and Amphitheatre has been replaced by the Harbor Park and Amphitheatre Committee, which reports to the Library Trustees.

15. National Historic Landmark Program, http://www.nps.gov/history/nhl/

16. Information about Harbor Park is summarized from Charles Beveridge, "In Search of Camden's Harborside Park," *Maine Olmsted*

Alliance for Parks & Landscapes Journal, Autumn 1999.

17. Robin Karson, "Fletcher Steele's Design for the Camden, Maine, Amphitheatre," *The Official Newsletter of the Maine Landscape and Nursery Association*, Vol. 9, No. 3, September 2006, p. 7.

CHAPTER 4: NORTHEAST HARBOR: A LEGACY OF KINDRED SPIRITS, PAGES 66–77

Historic images, pp. 67, 69, 74, 77, Mount Desert Land & Garden Preserve, Seal Harbor, Maine; p. 75, Patrick Chassé,

1. History of Acadia Web site: http://www.acadia.net/anp/w95026ap.html

2. Letitia Baldwin, *Asticou Azalea Garden: The Work of Charles K. Savage* and *Thuya Garden: Asticou Terraces & Thuya Lodge* (Seal Harbor, Maine: Mount Desert Land and Garden Preserve, 2008).

3. Curtis chose to use the phonetic rather than the botanical spelling of *Thuja*.

4. Paula Deitz, " 'Open to All Real Plant Lovers': Beatrix Farrand's Invitation to Reef Point Gardens," *The Bulletins of Reef Point Gardens*, ed. Carol Betsch (Sagaponack, N.Y.: Sagapress, Inc., 1997), p. xxii.

5. "Concept paper," Charles Savage, 1954/55, as quoted in *A Framework for Future Decision Making: A Cultural Landscape Assessment for the Thuya Garden and Asticou Terraces*, Richardson & Associates, 2007, p. 16.

6. Richardson & Associates, p. 4.

7. Richardson & Associates, p. 16.

8. Charles K. Savage, letter to John D. Rockefeller, Jr., 1956, as quoted by Letitia Baldwin in *Thuya Garden: Asticou Terraces & Thuya Lodge*, p. 30.

9. "Asticou–History of an Inn & an Era," http://asticou.com/history.html

10. Patrick Chassé, "A Dream Transplanted," *Garden Design*, Vol. 7, No. 1, Spring 1988, p. 30.

11. Excerpt from the Trustees Report developed by Charles Savage, 1964–65, as quoted in Richardson & Associates, p. 24.

12. Richardson & Associates, p. 24.

13. Richardson & Associates, p. 29.

14. Richardson & Associates, p. 29.

CHAPTER 5: EDUCATIONAL ADVANCEMENTS: MAINE'S HISTORIC DESIGNED CAMPUSES, PAGES 80–105

Historic painting, p. 81, Bowdoin College Museum of Art, Brunswick, Maine, Gift of Harold L. Berry, Class of 1901.

1. Paul Venable Turner, *Campus, An American Planning Tradition* (Cambridge, Mass.: The Architectural History Foundation/MIT Press, 1984/1987), p. 3.

2. Turner, pp. 9-15.

3. Charles Calhoun, *A Small College in Maine: Two Hundred Years of Bowdoin* (Brunswick, Maine: Bowdoin College, 1993), p. 3.

4. Calhoun, *A Small College in Maine*, Appendix I, p. 206.

BERWICK ACADEMY

Historic photos: p. 83, private collection; all others courtesy of Berwick Academy.

5. Sarah Orne Jewett, "My School Days," *The Berwick Scholar*, Vol. I, No. 1, October 1887. Sarah Orne Jewett Text Web site, Terry Heller, Coe College, manager, http://www.public.coc.edu/~theller/soj/una/berwick.html.

6. http://www.state.me.us/education/150yrs/150part1.html.

7. Sarah Orne Jewett, "The Old Town of Berwick," *New England Magazine*, July 1894. Sarah Orne Jewett Text Web site, http://www.public.coe.edu/~theller/una/berwick.html.

8. Jewett, "The Old Town of Berwick."

9. Wendy K. Pirsig, "Rum, Murder and Arson: South Berwick's Struggles of 1845–1855," Old Berwick Historical Society Web Archives, http://www.obhs.net/Rum1.html.

10. Wendy K. Pirsig, "Renaissance Woman: In a Maine mill town, windows shed light on a once-prominent Victorian artist," Nov. 7, 2001. National Trust for Historic Preservation Online, http://www2.preservationnation.org/Magazine/archives/arch_story/110701.htm

11. Betty S. Smith, "Sarah Wyman Whitman: Brief life of a determined artist: 1842–1904," *Harvard Magazine*, January-February 2008, pp. 32-33, http://harvardmagazine.com/2008/01-pdfs/0108-32.pdf

BOWDOIN COLLEGE

Photos: p. 86, Bob Handelman; lithograph, p. 89, Bowdoin College Office of Communications, photo by Dennis Griggs; historic photos, pp. 87, 88, George J. Mitchell Department of Special Collections & Archives.

12. *Brunswick (Maine) in Letters; by a Gentleman from South Carolina, to a Friend in That State*, 1820; Letter III, March 29, 1820. George J. Mitchell Department of Special Collections & Archives, Bowdoin College.

13. Calhoun, *A Small College in Maine*, p. 10.

14. Leland M. Roth, *A Biographical Dictionary of Architects in Maine: McKim, Mead & White*, Vol. II, No. 5 (Augusta, Maine: Maine Historic Preservation Commission, 1985), p. 3.

15. Minutes of the Governing Boards Committee on Buildings and Grounds, October 1929. George J. Mitchell Department of Special Collections & Archives, Bowdoin College.

16. Report of the Committee on Buildings and Grounds, March 19, 1930. George J. Mitchell Department of Special Collections & Archives, Bowdoin College.

17. Patricia McGraw Anderson, *The Architecture of Bowdoin College* (Brunswick, Maine: Bowdoin College, 1998), p. 76.

18. Carol R. Johnson Associates Inc., *Bowdoin College Landscape Master Plan Report*, 1996, pp. 6-7.

COLBY COLLEGE

Contemporary photos: Colby College. Larson plan and historic images, pp. 90–93, Special Collections, Miller Library.

19. Earl H. Smith, *Mayflower Hill: A History of Colby College* (Hanover and London: University Press of New England and Colby College, 2006), p. 47.

20. Smith, p. 7.

21. Smith, p. 31.

22. Smith, p. 61.

23. Thomas C. Jester, *A Biographical Dictionary of Architects in Maine: Jens F. Larson*, Vol. VI (Portland, Maine: Maine Citizens for Historic Preservation, 1991), [p. 5].

24. Jester, *Jens F. Larson*, [p. 5].

25. Smith, p. 48.

26. Jester, *Jens F. Larson*, [p. 5].

27. Reed Hilderbrand Landscape Architects, *Proposed Landscape Framework and Colby Green Concept Design*, October 2002.

28. Shepley Bulfinch Richardson and Abbott, *Colby College Campus Plan, District Studies*, December 2000, p. 4.

BATES COLLEGE

Photos: Bates College. Contemporary photos by Phyllis Graber Jensen. Historic images, pp. 95, 98, 99, courtesy of Muskie Archives and Special Collections Library.

29. James Leaman, "A Historical Essay," Bates College Web site: http://www.bates.edu/x72163.xml.

30. Charles E. Clark, *Bates Through the Years* (Bates College: Lewiston, Maine, 2005), p. 20. Further information from H. Jay Burns, editor, *Bates: The Alumni Magazine*.

31. Clark, p. 20.

32. Clark, p. 23. First black graduate, Henry Chandler, class of 1874; first black woman graduate, Stella James, class of 1897.

33. Clark, p. 24. A requirement that the president and a majority of the trustees should be Free Baptists lasted from 1891 to 1907 but did not endure.

34. Rebecca Corrie, "Coram Library 1902: When Manhattan Came to Lewiston," Bates College Inaugural Symposium: Sense of Place, October 2002.

35. Corrie, as cited.

36. Turner, *Campus, An American Planning Tradition*, p. 165.

37. Corrie, as cited.

38. John Nolen, "Note to Accompany General Plan for the Reconstruction and Future Development of Bates College, Lewiston, Maine," December 24, 1914. Bates College, The Edmund S. Muskie Archives and Special Collections Library.

39. John Nolen, "Proposal for consulting services." Bates College, The Edmund S. Muskie Archives and Special Collections Library.

40. Betsy Kimball, "A Campus Plan for Now and the Future," *Bates: The Alumni Magazine*, Spring 1993, p. 5.

THE UNIVERSITY OF MAINE, ORONO

Historic images, pp. 102, 103, 104, Special Collections Dept., Raymond H. Fogler Library, University of Maine.

41. President M. C. Fernald, "A History and Description of Maine State College," *The New England Magazine*, Volume 5, Issue 30, April 1887, p. 547. From The Nineteenth Century in Print: Periodicals, American Memory, The Library of Congress, http://memory.loc.gov/cgi-bin/query/D?ncps:1:./temp/~ammem_lsqf::.

42. President M. C. Fernald, "A History and Description of Maine State College," pp. 546-557.

43. "About the Land-Grant System," University of West Virginia Extension Service, http://www.wvu.edu/~exten/about/land.htm#why.

44. Charles E. Beveridge and David Larkin, *Frederick Law Olmsted: Designing the American Landscape* (New York: Universe Publishing / Rizzoli, 1998), p. 8.

45. Turner, p. 141. See also Beveridge, p. 188.

46. *University of Maine–Orono Historic Preservation Plan*, SMRT Architects Engineers Planners, March 2007, p. III-6. The decision may have been influenced by Abraham Lincoln's vice president, Bangor resident Hannibal Hamlin, after Orono, Bangor, and Oldtown pledged $50,000 in funding.

47. *Historic Preservation Plan*, p. III-6, quoted in Stephen L. Goodale, "The State Agricultural College," *Agriculture of Maine*, 2nd Series (A27.1: 1865), 238.

48. *Historic Preservation Plan*, p. III-11.

49. *Historic Preservation Plan*, III-14.

50. *Historic Preservation Plan*, III-24.

51. University of Maine Web site: http://www.umaine.edu/president/magazine-maine-alumni.htm

CHAPTER 6: HISTORIC GOLF COURSES: PURE AIR AND INSPIRING SCENERY, PAGES 107–117

Historic images: pp. 108, 111, private collection; p. 112, Maine Historic Preservation Commission; p. 115, *Glimpses of Camden* (Newtonville, Mass.: John R. Prescott, 1916).

All references to *New York Times* articles are from New York Times Article Archive, http://www.nytimes.com/ref/membercenter/nytarchive.

1. http://en.wikipedia.org/wiki/Golf#History

2. http://baharris.org/historicpolandspring/PolandSpringHouse/Activities/activities.htm

3. Earle G. Shettleworth, Jr., "Turn-of-the-Century Architecture: from about 1880 to 1920," *Maine Forms of American Architecture*, ed. Deborah Thompson (Camden, Maine: Down East Books, 1976), p. 206.

4. David L. Richards, *Poland Spring–A Tale of the Gilded Age, 1860–1900* (Lebanon, N.H.: University of New Hampshire Press, 2005), p. 55.

5. Richards, pp. 205–206.

6. Richards, pp. 205–206.

7. *Outings Monthly Review of Amateur Sports & Pastimes*, May 1898, Vol. XXXII No 2 p. 191. www.la84foundation.org/SportsLibrary/Outing/Volume_32/outXXXII02/outXXXII02p.pdf

8. Kevin R. Mendik, National Park Service, "The Challenges of Restoring a Classic American Golf Course," presented at Preserve and Play: Preserving Historic Recreation and Entertainment Sites, Chicago, May 2005. http://www.golfclubatlas.com/opinionmendik.html

9. "Golf Courses Enlarged–Many Local Clubs Extending Their Links to Eighteen Holes for This Season's Games," *New York Times*, March 20, 1898.

10. W.A. Whitcomb, "Now New England Beckons," *The American Golfer*, Vol. 37, Issue 9, 1934, p. 62. www.la84foundation.org/SportsLibrary/AmericanGolfer/1934/ag379x.pdf

11. *New York Times*, July 8, 1900.

12. Kebo Valley Golf Club Web site, http://www.kebovalleyclub.com/history.html

13. Joseph H. Curtis, "Plan of the Grounds of the Kebo Valley Club and the Surrounding Land of the Acadia Park Company," 1888.

14. Saint Andrews Golf Club Web site, http://www.saintandrewsgolfclub.com/

15. Summarized from Betsy Fahlman, *A Biographical Dictionary of Architects in Maine–Wilson Eyre (1858–1944)*, Vol. III, No. 12 (Augusta, Maine: Maine Historic Preservation Commission, 1986).

16. "Kebo Valley Golf Players–A. Howard Hinkle of Cincinnati Wins the First Tournament," *New York Times*, July 9, 1899.

17. John M. Bryan, *Maine Cottages–Fred L. Savage and the Architecture of Mount Desert* (New York: Princeton Architectural Press, 2005), pp. 158 and 162.

18. "Bar Harbor Season Opened," *New York Times*, July 5, 1901.

19. Author unlisted. *The Spirit of Kebo: The Kebo Valley Club, 1888–1988*, pp. 19 and 37.

20. Author unlisted. *The Kebo Valley Club, Bar Harbor, Maine: 1888–1948: Sixtieth Anniversary Year*.

21. *Scenic Gems of Maine* (Portland, Maine: George W. Morris, Publisher, 1898).

22. Elizabeth Igleheart and Kirk Mohney, "National Register Registration for Megunticook Golf Club," prepared by Maine Historic Preservation Commission, 1993, p. 2.

23. Kevin R. Mendik, National Park Service, "The Challenges of Restoring a Classic American Golf Course," as cited. There were 24 golf courses and/or clubhouses listed in the NRHP. See also NRHP database, http://www.nps.gov/history/nr/about.htm

24. *The Bangor Historical Magazine*, Vol. VII, July 1891–June 1892 (Bangor, Maine: Joseph Porter, editor & publisher), p. 112.

25. "National Register Registration for Megunticook Golf Club," p. 2.

26. "Designs Associated with Charles Brigham," http://www.davidjrusso. com/architecture/brigham/buildings/ DesignList.php

27. "National Register Registration for Megunticook Golf Club," Sec. 8, p. 5.

28. Warren Manning Papers, Iowa State University, http://www.lib.iastate.edu/ spcl/manuscripts/MS218/MS218.2.html

29. Mohr & Seredin, *Landscape Treatment Report, A Plan for the Rehabilitation of the Golf Course Vegetation at the Megunticook Golf Course*, 1988.

CHAPTER 7: RURAL CEMETERIES: LANDSCAPES FOR THE LIVING AND THE DEAD, PAGES 119–135

Historic images: pp. 120, 121, 125, 127, Mount Hope Cemetery Corporation; p. 128 Dyer Library/Saco Museum, Saco, Maine; p. 131, *Portland Illustrated* (Portland, Maine: W.S. Jones, 1874); p. 134, Maine Historic Preservation Commission.

1. Allan I. Ludwig, *Graven Images* (Middletown, Conn.: Wesleyan University Press, 1966), pp. 52–58.

2. Jeffrey I. Richman, *Brooklyn's Green-Wood Cemetery: New York's Buried Treasure*. (Brooklyn, N.Y.: The Green-Wood Cemetery, 1998), p. 4.

3. Richman, p. 7.

4. http://www.paris.org/Expos/ PereLachaise/pl.history.html

5. http://europeforvisitors.com/paris/arti-cles/pere-lachaise-cemetery.htm

6. National Register Bulletin #41, *Guidelines for Evaluating and Registering Rural Cemeteries & Burial Places*, U.S. Department of the Interior, National Park Service, Cultural Resources, Interagency Resources Division, 1992. http://www.nps.gov/ history/nr/publications/bulletins/nrb41/ nrb41_5.htm

7. National Register Bulletin #41, as cited.

8. Richman, Green-Wood Cemetery, p. 16.

9. Mount Hope Cemetery Web site, http:// www.mthopebgr.com/history.html

10. Bangor History, http://bangorinfo.com/ history.html

11. Bangor in Focus Web site, "The Bangor House," http://bangorinfo.com/Focus/ focus_bangor_house.html

12. http://en.wikipedia.org/wiki/ Massachusetts_Horticultural_Society

13. Bangor in Focus Web site, "Mount Hope Cemetery," http://bangorinfo.com/Focus/ focus_mount_hope_cemetery.html

14. Ralph F. Wilson, "Anchor as an Early Christian Symbol," http://www.jesuswalk. com/christian-symbols/anchor.htm

15. *Handbook of Texas Online*, s.v. Bryant, http://www.tsha.utexas.edu/handbook/ online/articles/BB/fbrcb.html. Accessed December 11, 2007.

16. Trudy Irene Scee, *Mount Hope Cemetery: A Twentieth-Century History* (Bangor, Maine: Mount Hope Cemetery Corp., 1999), pp. 23-24.

17. Scee, p. 43.

18. Crystal Fount and Rechabite Recorder, Vol. 5–6 (Independent Order of Rechabites, 1845–1846); original from Harvard University, digitized March 28, 2008.

19. *Saco & Biddeford City Directory* (Saco, Maine: Cowan & Hanscom, 1849) p. 24.

20. Diana Allen, "Those Who Were Left Behind: Pepperell Park, Saco's Abandoned Cemetery 1844–Present," University of Southern Maine history thesis, 1999.

21. *Saco & Biddeford City Directory*, p. 24.

22. "A Journal Reporter's Ramble through Saco's Beautiful Cemetery," *Biddeford Weekly Journal*, August 9, 1889, p. 3.

23. "Roll Call of Soldiers Buried in the Cemeteries of Saco," *Biddeford Weekly Journal*, June 19, 1908. Note that Laurel Hill was the only cemetery listed.

24. Edward H. Elwell, *Portland and Vicinity* (Portland, Maine: Greater Portland Landmarks, 1975; facsimile of 1876 and 1881 editions).

25. *Portland Advertiser*, June 4, 1835. Research by Peter Morelli on Evergreen Cemetery in *Bold Vision: The Development of the Parks of Portland, Maine*, ed. Theo H.B.M. Holtwijk and Earle G. Shettleworth, Jr. (West Kennebunk, Maine: Phoenix Publishing, 1999).

26. *Portland Transcript*, June 18, 1853. Research by Peter Morelli for *Bold Vision*.

27. *The Portland Eclectic*, November 12, 1853. Research by Peter Morelli for *Bold Vision*.

28. John Neal, *Portland Illustrated* (Portland, Maine: W.S. Jones, 1874), p. 92.

29. Kirk Mohney, "National Register of Historic Places Registration Form for Evergreen Cemetery," prepared by Maine Historic Preservation Commission, 1992, Sec. 7, p. 3.

CHAPTER 8: THE GRAND COLONIAL REVIVAL, PAGES 138–153

Historic images: pp. 141 (Elise Tyson Vaughan), 142, 144 (Paul Weber), Historic New England; p. 147, Mr. & Mrs. Charles W. H. Dodge; contemporary photos of Spite House, pp. 139, 145, 146, 148, Kevin Shields; p. 150, private collection.

1. University of Delaware Library Special Collections Department, *Progress Made Visible–The Centennial Exhibition, Philadelphia, 1876*. http://www.lib.udel. edu/ud/spec/exhibits/fairs/cent.htm

2. Virginia & Lee McAlester, *A Field Guide to American Houses* (New York: Alfred A. Knopf, 1988), pp. 321–335.

3. As quoted by Richard C. Nylander. "Garden Ornaments Past and Present." *Historic New England Magazine*, Winter/Spring 2005. http://www.historicnewengland.org/ NEHM/2005WinterSpringPage08.htm

4. Alan Emmet, *So Fine A Prospect* (Hanover, N.H.: University Press of New England, 1996), p. 179.

5. Edith Kingsbury, "Suggesting Long Holidays–'The Cottage' at Hamilton House in South Berwick, Maine," *The House Beautiful*, LXVI, No. 6, December 1929, pp. 691–695.

6. Letter to Mr. and Mrs. Donald D. Dodge from R. B. Farnum, executive director of the Horticultural Society of New York, July 31, 1963, following a tour of gardens in New Hampshire and Maine. Courtesy of Mr. and Mrs. Charles W. H. Dodge.

7. Eleanor M. McPeck, "Robert Wheelwright 1884–1965," *A Biographical Dictionary of Architects in Maine*, Vol. 7, Earle G. Shettleworth, Jr., ed., Roger Reed, associate editor (Portland, Maine: Maine Citizens for Historic Preservation, 1995).

8. Jeffrey A. Harris, "Biography of Guy Lowell, *Biographical Dictionary of Architects in Maine*, Vol. 7 (Augusta, Maine: Maine Historic Preservation Commission, 1995).

9. Kimberly Alexander Shillen, "Guy Lowell (1870-1927)," *Pioneers of American Landscape Design*, ed. Charles Birnbaum and Robin Karson (New York: McGraw-Hill, 2000), pp. 230–233.

10. *Alternative Sketches for Gates in Wall* by Arthur Shurtleff [sic], May 24, 1929. Private collection.

11. Elizabeth Hope Cushing, "Arthur Asahel Shurcliff (Shurtleff) (1870-1957)," in *Pioneers of American Landscape Design*, eds. Birnbaum and Karson, pp. 351–356.

12. "In Memory of Mary Marvin Breckinridge Patterson," Business Network, Health Care Industry Web site, http://findarticles. com/p/articles/mi_qa4050/is200301/ ai_n9199571

CHAPTER 9: THE NATURALISTIC DESIGNS OF HANS HEISTAD, PAGES 155–163

Historic images: p. 159, *Glimpses of Camden* (Newtonville, Mass.: John R. Prescott, 1916); p. 162, Maine Olmsted Alliance for Parks and Landscapes collection; portrait p. 163, Maine Historic Preservation Commission.

1. Stuart H. Orloff, L.A., *Informal Gardens* (New York: Macmillan Co., 1933), p. 8.

2. Information about Heistad's biography and his work at Weatherend and Beech Nut is summarized from Elizabeth Igleheart, "The Design Legacy of Hans Heistad," *Maine Olmsted Alliance for Parks & Landscapes Newsletter*, Fall 1991.

3. Phil M. Riley, "Adapting the Italian Villa to the Maine Coast," *Country Life in America*, Vol. XXIV, August 1913, p. 31.

4. Riley, p. 31.

5. Riley, p. 31.

6. Camden Area History Center, Cyrus Porter Brown Collection. Undated newspaper article, Catalog # CAHC 2006.1.1.

7. Interview with caretaker, summer 2007.

8. "The History of Beech Nut" http://www. coastalmountains.org/protecting_land/ active_campaigns.html#beech_hill

9. Pamela Griffin, "National and State Parks: A Brief Overview of Design Development," *Maine Olmsted Alliance for Parks & Landscapes Journal*, Winter 2001, pp. 1 and 3-6.

10. Information about Heistad's work at Sagamore is summarized from Pamela Griffin's *Camden Hills State Park Landscape Report*, c. 1997.

CHAPTER 10: THE MAINE WORK OF BEATRIX FARRAND, PAGES 164–175

Historic images: pp. 164, Archives of the Beatrix Farrand Society, Cousins Collection; pp. 165, 166, 167, 168, 172, 173, 174, 175, Patrick Chassé; contemporary Acadia photos, pp. 169, 170, Gloria Steiger.

1. Jane Roy Brown, *The Gardening Life of Beatrix Jones Farrand, 1872-1959* (New York: Viking Penguin, 1995), "List of Commissions," pp. 203–216.

2. Beatrix Farrand, *The Bulletins of Reef Point Gardens*, a reprint of *Reef Point Gardens Bulletins*, Vol. I, Numbers 1–17, 1946–1956 (Bar Harbor, Maine: The Island Foundation, 1997). Citation is from Vol. 1, No. 1, August 1946, p. 2.

3. Brown, *The Gardening Life of Beatrix Jones Farrand*, pp. 203–216.

4. Brown, *The Gardening Life of Beatrix Jones Farrand*, p. 102.

5. Farrand, *The Bulletins of Reef Point Gardens*, Vol. I, No. 1, p. 2.

6. Farrand, *The Bulletins of Reef Point Gardens*, Vol. I, No. 1, p. 3.

7. Farrand, *The Bulletins of Reef Point Gardens*, Vol. I, No. 1, p. 10.

8. Farrand, *The Bulletins of Reef Point Gardens*, Vol. 1, No. 3, p. 15.

9. Letter from Farrand to Pettitt, September 19, 1955. Web site of the University of California–Berkeley and Jepson Herbaria Archives–Correspondence, http://ucjeps. berkeley.edu/main/archives/correspon-dence.html

10. Ann Rockefeller Roberts, *Mr. Rockefeller's Roads–The Untold Story of Acadia's Carriage Roads and Their Creator* (Camden, Maine: Down East Books, 1990), p. 127. Original source: Rockefeller letter to Farrand, 7/21/1931, Rockefeller Archive Center, Tarrytown, N.Y.

11. Inventory of Beatrix Farrand's Maine Work by Patrick Chassé.

12. Ann Rockefeller Roberts, Chapter 1: The Making of a Landscape Artist.

13. Ann Rockefeller Roberts, p. 2.

14. Friends of Acadia Web site, http://www. friendsofacadia.org/

15. *Historic Resource Study for the Carriage Road System, Acadia National Park, Mount Desert Island, Maine*, prepared for U.S. Department of the Interior, National Park Service, North Atlantic Regional Office, by William D. Rieley and Roxanne S. Brouse, Rieley & Associates, Landscape Architects, Charlottesville, Va., 1989.

16. National Park Service Web site, *Acadia's Historic Carriage Roads*, http://www. nps.gov/acad/historyculture/historicca-rriageroads.htm

17. Mary Alice Roche, "A Perfect Dooryard Garden," *Flower Grower: The Home Garden Magazine*, April 1962, p. 63.

18. Pressley Associates, *Beatrix Farrand at Garland Farm – Cultural Landscape Report*, July 5, 2007, p. 1.3.

19. Sources for this section include: "Garland Farm Background," an essay from the Save

Garland Farm Web site, http://members. aol.com/savegarlandfarm/; *Beatrix Farrand Society News* published by the Beatrix Farrand Society, 2006 to 2007; interview with Patrick Chassé and site visit, August 2006; "Beatrix Farrand's Secret Garden," by Anne Raver, *New York Times* House & Home section, November 27, 2003, p. D1.

20. Pressley Associates. *Beatrix Farrand at Garland Farm–Cultural Landscape Report*, July 5, 2007. See Appendix C: Analysis of Plant Lists for the Terrace Garden.

21. Roche, "A Perfect Dooryard Garden," p. 63.

CHAPTER 11: SKYLANDS: JENS JENSEN'S MAINE MASTERPIECE, PAGES. 176–183

Historic images: p. 180, photo of Jens Jensen, The Morton Arboretum, Lisle, Illinois; p. 181, Maine Historic Preservation Commission, Patrick Chassé, and private collection. Contemporary photos on pp. 177 and 183 by Martha Stewart.

1. Letter from John D. Rockefeller, Jr. to Edsel Ford, December 21, 1922, as quoted by Jane Roy Brown, "Skylands–A Jens Jensen Landscape in Maine," *Journal of the New England Garden History Society*, Vol. 10, Fall 2002, p. 21.

2. Brown, "Skylands–A Jens Jensen Landscape in Maine," p. 23.

3. Robert E. Grese, *Jens Jensen–Maker of Natural Parks and Gardens* (Baltimore and London: The Johns Hopkins University Press, 1992) p. 100.

4. Jens Jensen, *Siftings* (Chicago: Ralph Fletcher Seymour, 1939), pp. 76-77, as quoted by Jane Roy Brown in "Skylands–A Jens Jensen Landscape in Maine," p. 20.

5. Grese, pp. 136-140.

6. The Gardens at Kykuit, The Rockefeller Estate in Hudson Valley, N.Y. http://www.hudsonvalley.org/web/kyku-gard.html

7. Brown, "Skylands–A Jens Jensen Landscape in Maine," p. 27.

8. Susan Heeger, "Jens Jensen at Skylands," *Martha Stewart Living*, March 2002, p. 213.

9. Grese, p. 176.

10. Jens Jensen, 1939, as quoted in Robert E. Grese, *Jens Jensen–Maker of Natural Parks and Gardens*, p. 139.

11. Grese, p. 176.

12. Heeger, pp. 216-217.

13. *Bar Harbor Times*, January 20, 1926.

14. *Boston Transcript*, May 22, 1926.

CHAPTER 12: HISTORIC SUBDIVISIONS: CREATING NEW NEIGHBORHOODS, PAGES 186–193

Historic images: pp. 188, 189, 190, private collection; pp. 191, 193, Maine Historical Society.

1. Henry Vincent Hubbard and Theodora Kimball, *An Introduction to the Study of Landscape Design*, revised edition (Boston: Hubbard Educational Trust, 1967), p. 278.

2. David L. Ames and Linda Flint McClelland, *Historic Residential Suburbs: Guidelines for Evaluation and Documentation for the National Register of Historic Places*, U.S. Department of the Interior, National Park Service, National Register of Historic Places, September 2002, p. 3.

3. DePaul University History Department online exhibit, "History of Chicago: The Origins of the Stockyards," http://condor.depaul.edu/~history/chicago/packorig.html

4. William D. Middleton, *The Time of the Trolley* (Milwaukee, Wisconsin: Kalmbach Publishing Co., 1967), p. 77.

5. Linda Flint McClelland, David L. Ames, and Sarah Dillard Pope, *National Register of Historic Places, Multiple Property Listing, Historic Residential Suburbs in the United States, 1830 1960*, U.S. Department of the Interior, National Park Service, 2002, pp. E-14 and 16, http://www.nr.nps.gov/multiples/64500838.pdf

6. *Portland Sunday Telegram*, March 28, 1915.

7. The use of trolleys in Maine declined in the 1920s and '30s following construction of new roads and increased availability of automobiles and buses. Service to Cape Cottage Park ended in 1940. See Edwin B. Robertson, *Remember the Portland, Maine, Trolleys* (Portland, Maine: Robertson Books, 1982).

8. William B. Jordan, Jr., *A History of Cape Elizabeth, Maine* (Portland, Maine: House of Falmouth, Inc., 1965), p. 152.

9. Jordan, p. 335.

10. "Motor Car Aids in Development–State of Maine," *Portland Sunday Telegram*, January 3, 1915.

11. Real estate advertisement for Wildwood subdivision, Falmouth Foreside. *Portland Sunday Telegram*, May 30, 1915.

12. James P. Baxter, "The Story of Portland," *The New England Magazine*, Vol. 19, Issue 3, November 1895, p. 370.

13. *Portland Sunday Telegram*, July 7, 1912.

14. "Persistence Characterizes State Senator Hinckley, Aspirant to Governor's Chair," *Lewiston Journal*, Magazine Section A-1, May 26, 1928.

15. Real Estate and Building Notes, *Portland Sunday Telegram*, June 13, 1915.

16. "Persistence Characterizes State Senator Hinckley," *Lewiston Journal*, as cited.

17. "Vision of a Model Community," *Portland Press Herald*, March 3, 2006.

18. Barbara Duff, "Sylvan Site: Frederick Wheeler Hinckley's Model Community," Greater Portland Landmarks *Observer*, July-August 1983, pp. 10-11.

19. Guidelines cited are accessible at http://www.nr.nps.gov/multiples/64500838.pdf and http://www.nps.gov/history/nR/publications/bulletins/suburbs/Suburbs.pdf]

CHAPTER 13: NEW TOWN PLANS: UTOPIAN EXPERIMENTS, PAGES 195–199

Historic images: p. 197, 198, Maine Historic Preservation Commission; p. 196, Rumford town plan from Oxford County Registry of Deeds.

1. Summarized from Randolph Langenbach, "From Building to Architecture, The Emergence of Victorian Lowell," *Harvard Architecture Review*, Vol. 2, Spring 1981, (Cambridge, Mass.: MIT Press,, 1981) http://www.conservationtech.com/rl%27s%20resume&%20pub%27s/rl-publications/milltowns/1981-LOWELL(Harv-Arch-Rev).htm

2. Summarized from Langenbach.

3. Summarized from "History of Leclaire Village," Edwardsville / Glen Carbon Chamber of Commerce Web site, http://www.edglenchamber.com/visit/leclaire.asp. Original source: "Historic Tour of Leclaire Village," Edwardsville Economic Development Commission and Edwardsville Historic Preservation Commission, no date given.

4. *Scenic Gems of Maine: Illustrating Many of the Most Beautiful and Interesting Places in the State of Maine* (Portland, Maine: Geo. W. Morris, Publisher, 1898), p. 130.

5. George J. Varney, "History of Rumford, Maine," *Gazetteer of the State of Maine* (Boston, Mass.: B. B. Russell, Publisher, 1886), http://history.rays-place.com/me/rumford-me.htm

6. *Scenic Gems of Maine*, p. 131.

7. Jason Stone, "Chisholm's Folly," *Down East*, 1992 Annual, pp. 55–59.

8. *Prospectus of Rumford Falls Power Co.* (Boston, Mass.: Press of H. G. Collins, 1891), p. 19.

9. Randall H. Bennett, "Bowler versus Chisholm, and the Ill-fated Bethel-Rumford Electric Railway," The Bethel Historical Society *Courier*, Volume 30, No. 2 (2006). http://www.bethelhistorical.com/Bethel-Rumford_Electric_Railway.html

10. "The Strathglass of Maine–Ideal Homes for Workingmen as Being Realized in Wonderful Paper Town of Rumford Falls," *Lewiston Journal*, Illustrated Magazine Section, June 14–19, 1902.

11. Summarized from Jennifer Stowell-Norris, "The History of Strathglass Park," 2004. http://growrumford.com/Strathglashistory.pdf

12. "The Strathglass of Maine," *Lewiston Journal*, as cited.

13. "The Strathglass of Maine," *Lewiston Journal*, as cited.

CHAPTER 14: SHIPYARD HOUSING: GARDEN CITIES FOR WORKERS , PAGES 200–205

Historic images: p. 201, *The History of Bath* (cf. note 11); p. 203, *Beautiful Bungalows of the Twenties* (cf. note 13); p. 204, redrawn detail of plan at Sagadahoc County Registry of Deeds; p. 205, *Report of the United States Housing Corporation* (cf. note 18).

1. Frederick Law Olmsted (Jr.), "Lessons from Housing Developments of the United States Housing Corporation," *Monthly Labor Review*, 8 (May 1919), pp. 27-38, http://www.library.cornell.edu/Reps/DOCS/olm19.htm#Return%20to%20top

2. "Sea Lift in World War I," http://www.globalsecurity.org/military/systems/ship/sealift-ww1.htm

3. "Suggestions to Town Planners," *Report of the United States Housing Corporation, December 3, 1918*, U.S. Department of Labor, Bureau of Industrial Housing and Transportation, United States Housing Corporation, (Washington, D.C.: Government Printing Office, 1919), Appendix Ix, August 26, 1918. http://www.library.cornell.edu/Reps/DOCS/ushcorp.htm

4. F. L. Olmsted (Jr.), "Lessons from Housing Developments of the United States Housing Corporation," pp. 27-38.

5. F. L. Olmsted (Jr.), as cited.

6. F. L. Olmsted (Jr.), as cited.

7. F. L. Olmsted (Jr.), as cited.

8. J. Dennis Robinson, "Atlantic Heights Was Architecture for the Poor," 2006. http://www.seacoastnh.com/History/As_I_Please/Atlantic_Heights_was_Architecture_for_the_Poor/

9. "Houses Built by Uncle Sam during the Great World War," *The Bath Daily Times*, 25th Anniversary Pictorial Section, August 14, 1922.

10. Historical U.S. Census Totals for Sagadahoc County, Maine, http://en.wikipedia.org/wiki/Historical_U.S._Census_Totals_for_Sagadahoc_County,_Maine#1910

11. Henry Wilson Owen, *The History of Bath* (Bath, Maine: The Times Co., 1936), p. 323.

12. Juliana L'Heureux, "Louis Gagne's 'Tented City' in Bath," *The Times of Bath, Maine: A Publication of the Bath Historical Society*, Victoria Jackson, ed., April 1999.

13. *Beautiful Bungalows of the Twenties*, (Mineola, NY: Dover, 2003), p. 4. Unabridged reprint of *Beautiful Bungalows* (Building Age Publishing Corporation, 1923).

14. "Houses Built by Uncle Sam During the Great World War," *The Bath Daily Times*, 25th Anniversary Pictorial Section, August 14, 1922.

15. *Bath Daily Times*, December 23, 1918.

16. Arthur G. Spear, *I Bought a White Elephant in Maine–an Adventure in Homes.* Privately published.

17. Henry Wilson Owen, *The History of Bath*, p. 337.

18. *Report of the United States Housing Corporation*, Volume II: *Houses, Site-planning, Utilities*, Washington, D.C.: U.S. Department of Labor, Bureau of Industrial Housing and Transportation, 1919, p. 105.

19. *Report of the United States Housing Corporation*, p. 106.

20. Alex Krieger, "Between The Crusader's Jerusalem and Piranesi's Rome: Conflicting Ideals for the City," *Modernism and History: Essays in Honor of Eduard F. Sekler* (Cambridge, Mass.: Harvard University Press, 1996), http://www.chankrieger.com/cka/essays/crusaders.pdf

A Legacy of Designers

Since the late 1800s, some of the country's most revered landscape architects have left their signature in Maine. Following is a short list of designers, their relevant projects featured in *Designing the Maine Landscape,* and notes about their contributions to the field of landscape architecture, including a few key projects outside of Maine.

Browne, Herbert W. C. (1860–1946), architect

Project: Hamilton House (pp. 141–144)

Home/Practice: Little and Browne, Boston. Partner Arthur Little; known around the country for large-scale private commissions in the Colonial Revival style. Firm's buildings were a prominent feature of the World's Columbian Exposition of 1093.

Bryant, Charles Grandison (1803–1850), architect

Project: Mount Hope Cemetery (pp. 121–127)

Home/Practice: Bangor, Maine. Considered first person in Maine to call himself an architect. Designed and built numerous structures in Bangor in the 1830s. Worked as an architect in Galveston, Texas, after 1839.

Curtis, Joseph Henry (1841–1928), landscape designer, civil engineer

Projects: Thuya Lodge; Asticou Terraces; Asticou Terraces Landing (pp. 66-77)

Home/Practice: Boston. In 1870s worked with F. L. Olmsted, Sr., re new location of McLean Asylum, Belmont, Massachusetts. In Maine designed Plan of Cottage Lots (1883), Hancock Point, and Plan of the Club Grounds of the Kebo Valley Club (1888), Bar Harbor.

Farrand, Beatrix (1872–1959), landscape architect/landscape gardener

Projects: Reef Point; Carriage Roads of Acadia National Park; Garland Farm (pp. 164–175)

Home/Practice: New York City and Maine. One of eleven founders (the only woman) of American Society of Landscape Architects, 1899. Completed nearly 200 commissions, three-quarters private estates, most in Maine and New York. Designed Dumbarton Oaks, Washington, D.C.; East and West gardens of the White House; and parts of campuses of Princeton (1912–43) and Yale (1923–46). In Maine, designed more than fifty private gardens on Mount Desert Island, including the Abby Aldrich Rockefeller Garden; and village greens in Bar Harbor (1921–22) and Seal Harbor (1924).

Fenn, Arthur (1857–1925), golf course designer

Project: Poland Spring Golf Course (pp. 108–111)

Home/Practice: Waterbury, Connecticut; resident golf professional and course supervisor. Summered at Poland Spring; wintered and taught golf in Palm Beach, Florida. Master athlete in numerous sports; championship golfer. Designed West End Golf Links, Waterbury, Connecticut (c. 1895), and Abenaqui Country Club, Rye Beach, New Hampshire (1903).

Heistad, Hans (1871–1945), landscape architect

Projects: Weatherend, Beech Nut, Camden Hills State Park's Lower Sagamore Area, Hans Heistad Residence (pp. 155–163)

Home/Practice: Rockport, Maine. Born in Brevik, Norway; emigrated to U.S. in 1905. Introduced to Maine in 1910 through Olmsted Brothers, working at Bar Harbor estate of Joseph Pulitzer, and at General Henry Knox home ("Montpelier") and Rockport Harbor Improvement Project, both 1931.

Jensen, Jens (1860–1951), landscape architect

Project: Skylands (pp. 176–183)

Home/Practice: Chicago, Illinois, and Ellison Bay, Wisconsin, where he established The Clearing, "a center of learning for artists and other students." Emigrated from Denmark to U.S., 1884. Student of native prairie landscapes and pioneer in field of landscape conservation. Formed Prairie Club (1908) and Friends of Our Native Landscape (1913), leading to preservation of Indiana sand dunes. Extensive reputation as designer of estates throughout Midwest; designed grounds of Henry Ford Hospital, office buildings and plants, and homes for Ford executives.

Larson, Jens Frederick (1891–1981), architect

Project: Colby College (pp. 91–94)

Home/Practice: Hanover, New Hampshire, and New York. Practiced with Harry Artemus Wells (Larson and Wells), 1919–1925. Began career as designer of college campuses in 1919 as architect in residence at Dartmouth College. Designed master plans and buildings for more than thirty academic institutions. Official architect of Association of American Colleges. Wrote *Architectural Planning for the American College,* 1933, one of first and most influential books on the subject.

Leeds, Herbert Corey (1855–unknown), golf course designer

Project: Kebo Valley Golf Course (pp. 112–115)

Home/Practice: Boston, Massachusetts. Redesigned original nine holes at Myopia Hunt Club, South Hamilton, Massachusetts (1896) and completed nine-hole extension, 1901. Expanded original nine holes to eighteen at Bass Rocks Golf Club, Gloucester, Massachusetts (1913).

Lowell, Guy (1870–1927), architect, landscape architect, educator

Project: River House (pp. 149–153)

Home/Practice: Boston and New York. Helped establish landscape architecture program at MIT in 1900. Commissions included private estates and public, academic, and commercial buildings, as well as Charles River esplanades in collaboration with Charles Eliot. Designed Maine's Cumberland County Courthouse, Museum of Fine Arts in Boston, and New York County Courthouse. Wrote and edited books on American and Italian residential gardens.

Manning, Warren Henry (1860–1938), landscape architect, horticulturist, planner

Project: Megunticook Golf Course (pp. 115–117)

Home/Practice: Cambridge, Massachusetts. Worked for F. L. Olmsted, Sr., and Charles Eliot, specializing in horticulture and planting design, 1888 to 1896; supervised about 100 projects with Olmsted firm. One of eleven founding members of American Society of Landscape Architects. Client list of more than 1,700 jobs, with some forty commissions in Maine. Wrote articles on botanic gardens, town planning, and office practice.

NOLEN, JOHN (1869–1937), landscape architect, planner

Project: Bates College (pp. 95–101)

Home/Practice: Cambridge, Massachusetts. Completed more than 450 projects: parks, parkways, comprehensive plans in twenty-nine cities, and plans for twenty-seven new towns. Served on advisory committee of Emergency Fleet Corporation's Housing Division for World War I. Wrote numerous books and articles on city planning; heavily influenced next generation of city planners.

OLMSTED, FREDERICK LAW, SR. (1822–1903), landscape architect, author, lecturer

Projects: Back Cove, Portland (pp. 34–38); University of Maine, Orono (pp. 101–105)

Home/Practice: New York, New York. As Olmsted, Vaux, & Co. from 1857 in partnership with Calvert Vaux. Permanent home and office in Brookline, Massachusetts as of 1883. In partnership with stepson, John Charles Olmsted, 1884, as F.L. & J.C. Olmsted. In 1889 with Henry Sargent Codman added, as F.L. Olmsted & Co. As Olmsted, Olmsted & Eliot in 1893 with addition of Charles Eliot. F. L. Olmsted, Sr., considered forefather of landscape architecture in U.S. Won Central Park design competition with Calvert Vaux, 1858. Designer of all aspects of landscapes throughout U.S.: scenic reservations, urban parks, parkways, park systems, residential communities, campuses, government buildings, and country estates. Site planner of World's Columbian Exposition, Chicago, 1893. Olmsted, Sr., retired from practice in 1895.

OLMSTED BROTHERS:
JOHN CHARLES OLMSTED (1853–1920), landscape architect;
FREDERICK LAW OLMSTED, JR. (1870–1957), landscape architect, educator, author

Projects: Portland Park System (pp. 16–38); Capitol Park; Blaine House; Blaine Memorial Park (pp. 41–51); Camden Village Green (pp. 52–57); Harbor Park (pp. 63–65); University of Maine, Orono (pp. 101–105)

Home/Practice: Brookline, Massachusetts. Frederick Law Olmsted, Jr., added to partnership in 1898; firm name of Olmsted Brothers. Name changed to Olmsted Associates in 1961. Both Olmsted brothers were founding members of the American Society of Landscape Architects. Completed more than 3,000 commissions in the U.S. and Canada (1895–1950), trained many landscape architects practicing in the early 1900s. F. L. Olmsted, Jr., wrote numerous articles and edited his father's correspondence, reports, and biographical notes into two books: *Frederick Law Olmsted: Landscape Architect, 1822–1903* (1922) and *Forty Years of Landscape Architecture–Professional Papers of Frederick Law Olmsted, Vol. 2: Central Park* (1928).

PARKER, CARL RUST (1882–1960), landscape architect

Projects: Capitol Park, Blaine House, Blaine Memorial Park (pp. 41–51); Boulevard Park (pp. 190–191), University of Maine at Orono (pp. 101–105)

Home/Practice: Massachusetts with Olmsted Brothers (1901–1910); private practice in Portland, Maine (1910–1917); returned to Olmsteds following World War I; partner 1950–1960. Responsible for all aspects of landscape design: residences, subdivisions, campuses, parks, memorials, cemeteries, and grounds of major institutions. Other Maine projects: Yarmouth Village Green (ca. 1910); Elmhurst / John S. Hyde Estate in Bath (1913); and Good Will-Hinckley Home and School for Boys and Girls in Fairfield (ca. 1915).

ROSS, DONALD (1872–1948), golf course designer

Project: Poland Spring Golf Course (pp. 108–111)

Home/Practice: Pinehurst, North Carolina, with oversight of additional designers and offices. Designed or revised more than 400 golf courses in U.S. and Canada, eleven in Maine. Nationally known courses are Pinehurst No. 2, North Carolina, Seminole in Florida, and Oakland Hills near Detroit. Founding member of American Society of Golf Course Architects, 1947.

SAVAGE, CHARLES KENNETH (1903–1979), landscape designer, woodcarver, innkeeper

Projects: Thuya Lodge and Garden; Asticou Terraces and Landing; Asticou Azalea Garden (pp. 66–77)

Home/Practice: Northeast Harbor, Maine. Owner/innkeeper of Asticou Inn. Friend of Beatrix Farrand; one of several directors of Reef Point Gardens Corporation. Trustee of Joseph Curtis properties. Purchased Farrand's Reef Point plant collection and designed Thuya and Asticou Azalea gardens.

SHURCLIFF, ARTHUR ASAHEL (SHURTLEFF) (1870–1957), landscape architect, planner, educator

Project: River House (pp. 149–153)

Home/Practice: Massachusetts with Olmsted Brothers (1896–1904); opened private practice in Boston in 1904. Helped F. L. Olmsted, Jr., establish Harvard's landscape architecture program, the first in U.S., in 1900. Served as chief landscape architect of re-creation and restoration of Colonial Williamsburg, 1928. Worked on numerous public parks, dams, reservoirs, and college campuses in Boston area. Designed hundreds of private gardens in New England.

A LEGACY OF DESIGNERS (CONT.)

SHURCLIFF, SIDNEY NICHOLS (1906–1981), landscape architect
Project: Laurel Hill Cemetery (pp. 128–130)
Home/Practice: Boston. Joined father Arthur Shurcliff's firm in 1930s; continued firm under the name Shurcliff, Merrill and Footit. Sample projects include a roof garden for the New England Merchants National Bank in Boston (1969) and a report on the recreational needs of Andover, Massachusetts (1970).

STEELE, FLETCHER (1885–1971), landscape architect, author
Project: Camden Amphitheatre (pp. 58–62)
Home/Practice: Cambridge, Massachusetts, in office of Warren Manning (1908–1913). Opened private practice in Boston, 1913. Considered the major link between Beaux-Arts and modern landscape design. Designed residential estates, cemeteries and cemetery plots, village greens, parks, and the grounds of churches, factories, and cultural institutions. Wrote numerous articles and books throughout his career.

TAYLOR, ALBERT DAVIS (1883–1951), landscape architect, author
Project: Megunticook Golf Course (pp. 115–117)
Home/Practice: Cambridge, Massachusetts (with Warren Manning); private offices in Cleveland, Ohio, and Florida. Superintendent of construction and general manager of office and field work for Manning. In his later private practice, provided training for numerous landscape architects. Wrote handbook for Civilian Conservation Corps (CCC, 1937); developed plans for Cleveland Heights, Ohio, and Tallahassee, Florida.

UNDERWOOD, LORING (1874–1930), landscape architect, planner, author
Project: Lincoln Street Project (pp. 204–205)
Home/Practice: Belmont (home) and Boston (office), Massachusetts. Early pioneer of lectures with colored glass lantern slides; lectured on old New England gardens and City Beautiful movement in many U.S. cities. Designed industrial village for Amoskeag Manufacturing Company, Manchester, New Hampshire (ca. 1911) and outdoor theater at Vassar College, Poughkeepsie, New York (1916).

WHEELWRIGHT, ROBERT (1884–1965), landscape architect, educator
Project: Spite House (pp. 145–148)
Home/Practice: Philadelphia; summer resident of North Haven, Maine. In practice with Markley Stevenson, 1926; firm name of Wheelwright and Stevenson. A founder and editor (1910–1920) of *Landscape Architecture* magazine. Founder of Department of Landscape Architecture at University of Pennsylvania, 1924; taught there until 1941. Designed private country estates; Federal housing project (1930s) in Wayne, Pennsylvania; and St. Laurent Cemetery on Omaha Beach, Normandy, France.

INDEX